Civic Storytelling

Jeff Wall, *The Storyteller*, 1986, transparency in lightbox, 229 x 437 cm. Courtesy of the artist.

Civic Storytelling

The Rise of Short Forms and the Agency of Literature

Florian Fuchs

ZONE BOOKS · NEW YORK

2023

© 2023 Florian Fuchs

ZONE BOOKS

633 Vanderbilt Street

Brooklyn, NY 11218

A different version of "Autonomy" was published in German in *Athenäum* 26
(2016), pp. 23–50, and an article discussing John Locke's commonplacing
has appeared in *Verkleinerung: Epistemologie und Literaturgeschichte kleiner
Formen*, eds. Maren Jäger, Ethel Matala de Mazza, and Joseph Vogl (Berlin: De
Gruyter, 2021), pp. 109–22. An extended variation of "Fabulatory Philosophy"
is included in *New German Critique* 145 (February 2022), pp. 163–83.

Printed in the United States of America.

Distributed by Princeton University Press,
Princeton, New Jersey, and Woodstock, United Kingdom

Library of Congress Cataloging-in-Publication Data
Names: Fuchs, Florian, 1984– author.
Title: Civic storytelling : the rise of short forms and the agency of literature /
    Florian Fuchs.
Description: New York : Zone Books, 2023. | Includes bibliographical
    references and index. | Summary: "This book recalibrates literature's
    political role for the twenty-first century by excavating the deep history
    of storytelling as a civic agency" — Provided by publisher.
Identifiers: LCCN 2022013270 (print) | LCCN 2022013271 (ebook) |
    ISBN 9781942130741 (hardcover) | ISBN 9781942130758 (ebook)
Subjects: LCSH: Fiction — Social aspects. | Fiction — History and criticism —
    Theory, etc. | Short story. | Storytelling. | Debates and debating
    in literature. | History, Modern, in literature. | Politics and literature.
Classification: LCC PN3344 .F83 2023 (print) | LCC PN3344 (ebook) |
    DDC 808.3/1 — dc23/eng/20220720
LC record available at https://lccn.loc.gov/2022013270
LC ebook record available at https://lccn.loc.gov/2022013271

Seen in this way, the storyteller must be counted among our teachers and sages.

—Walter Benjamin, "The Storyteller"

Contents

Two Ontologies of Prose Literature,

Short Form versus Novel

This study stems from a seemingly simple question: Why did short narrative forms such as the novella, fable, and fairy tale suddenly, yet widely emerge throughout Europe and the Americas in the decades around 1800? Attempts to answer this question have tended to take the form of simple chronology or sociohistorical speculation, assuming that these short forms were by-products of increasing literacy and of the arrival of reading culture. Such speculation points to the radical changes in reading culture of this period, during which authors experimented with genres, publishers and book traders diversified their products, reading practices broadened, and new pedagogical, religious, and journalistic uses for short pieces developed. The causes for the rise in short forms are myriad, goes the argument, and attempts to pin the emergence of the short form on a single causative factor are futile.

Sociohistorical answers, however, offer only metaliterary reasons for the rise of short forms and thus devalue literature's own role in shaping new genres and the communicative functions they embody. In fact, as we will see in the chapters of this book, there are fundamental and far-reaching causes for the rise of short narratives within the appearance of literature itself. In the language of literary studies, one could say that short forms partook of the deep phenomenological change that occurred between the fourteenth and seventeenth centuries in how textual fiction behaved between the reader and the world. During this era, what is called classical and medieval "poetry" — drama, lyric, and epic works written in verse and abiding by the poetic rulebooks from Aristotle's *Poetics* to Scaliger's *Poetices libri septem* — was increasingly challenged by a new mode of speech that we still call "literature" — fictional prose narratives without meter or verse and written in various lengths and genres.

This new regime of literature in modernity has thus been described — quite accurately — as the arrival of prose.[1] Its implications, vast in scope, were nothing less than the replacement of the spoken word by printed text and of the reciting of poetry by the silent reading of prose. In doing so, prose literature fundamentally disrupted and reconfigured the relationship between reader and world, initiating a new phenomenality of the behavior and appearance of prose genres in the world. The phenomenality was broad and broadly felt, affecting everything from the material apparatuses of reading and the technologies governing the circulation of readable forms to its imaginary, discursive, and social effects. To describe these changes, Michel Foucault, emphasizing that this new prose literature had altered the mode of social encounters in the world, chose to use the vague but accurate term of a new "ontology of literature."[2] Not only did printed prose narratives challenge, through the changes they wrought in reading culture and print technology, the very validity of recited epic, lyric, and dramatic poetry, they also generated modern forms of discourse — epistemology, affect, power, sexuality, family, science, and representation — that we would today locate in academia, journalism, and law.

Arguably, the first genuinely modern genre to implement the new mediality of prose and its fluid discursivity successfully across fictional and nonfictional areas was the novel. This explains why it is often seen as the epitome of modern literature, representing the clearest difference in form and content from all versed genres of poetry, making it into a powerful and measurable force behind the sociohistorical changes in reading culture. Keeping Foucault's concept of an ontology of modern literature in mind, however, the novel's success lies in the way it appears in the reader's world, in how it renders itself and its content as a virtual object, an imaginary realm, a parallel world. Describing it as a specific appearance, as a phenomenon, highlights the novel's unique quality: its ability to absorb its reader into the rich and detailed lives of one or more strangers because, as Hans Blumenberg has argued, it perfectly imitates the status of artificiality that reality itself has attained in modernity. According to Blumenberg's essay "The Concept of Reality and the Possibility of the Novel," the novel owes the condition for its own coming into being to the modern configuration of the lifeworld, of what since the seventeenth century and at least up to the digital age has been called "reality." Novels implement a version of reality by employing a narrative structure, for example that of biography, whose main achievement is to ensure a consistency among the distinct parts of a novel, that is, among its various figures, places, descriptions, chapters, and subplots. In modernity, "reality can no longer be considered an inherent quality of an object," writes Blumenberg, "but is the embodiment of a consistently applied *syntax of elements*. Reality presents itself now as ever before as a sort of text which takes on its particular form by obeying certain rules of internal consistency. Reality is for modernity a context."[7] Novels are extensions of modern reality, according to Blumenberg's argument because they render a probable string of events around main characters so that the resulting text appears to the readers as just another, additional context to their own reality.

For its complexity and adaptability, the novel has been treated as the most important genre of modern prose fiction. Yet the theory of the modern novel took many centuries of slow development, arguably until György Lukács wrote the first generally accepted attempt at such a theory in 1916. Given the lagging development of the theory of the novel, where did the theories of other, shorter prose genres stand since the inception of modern prose? Did they also take more than four centuries to come to fruition? Were theories like Lukács's or arguments like Blumenberg's made for short narrative forms? How do short narrative forms behave in the world? What is the particular ontology of short narrative forms?

In contrast with the novel, there is no theory of short narrative forms that aims at a basic theory and an understanding of their ontology, even though the many genres of short narrative prose fiction have been thoroughly analyzed. One important reason short narrative forms have not been studied for their fundamental context and appearance is that they include a whole range of genres, from fable to fairy tale, from proverb to novella, from epiphany even to multimedia narratives, spanning modernity from the early modern revival of the classical fable in the seventeenth century to postliterary genres composed of prose text and images. Single genres have usually been covered in separate studies or articles; this study instead covers a nonexhaustive, but exemplary set of six short genres: fable, novella, proverb, fairy tale, epiphany, and postliterary story, selected because these range from the beginning to the end of what could be called short narrative prose's monopoly on short fiction. This monopoly is determined by the currency of prose, beginning after the decline of versification in the seventeenth century and lasting up to the current decline of textuality in the twenty-first.

One can begin to understand the phenomenality of the short form by tracking where and how it diverges from the novel. The short form's few pages are insufficient to immerse a reader in a detailed, absorbing life that a protagonist inhabits; the absorption into the richness of a new, unknown world, which the novel's hundreds or thousands of pages can induce sentence by sentence, is impossible for the short form. From this mere quantitative difference results the alternative economy of imagination in which the short form operates. Where the novel aims to simulate a fictional new world for the reader, such as the widely read adventure novels of early modernity successfully did, the short form must limit itself to drawing on settings and situations that already exist in the reader's world. Where the novel creates a parallel reality — whether life in a modern suburb or on a faraway planet in a distant future — the short form creates a feedback loop, playing back to a reader bits of a familiar life, albeit in a transformed, surprising state. Because of their brevity, short forms can usually be read in a single sitting; this allows their phenomenality to be embedded as a single continuous experience within the reader's world.

Put simply, while novels *extract* readers *from* their current reality, short forms *occur to* readers and *enter into* their ongoing everyday reality. Whereas the novel's ontology as a fictional artwork is based on ensuring the separation of lived and imagined realities, the short form's ontology is designed to confuse any such separability of realities. Where a novel motivates its actions and events through the psychological, causal, and atmospheric impulses of the protagonists within the context of the protagonist's fictional life, the short form proposes its events and occurrences in such a way that readers must contextualize them with motivations found in their own lived reality. Short narrative forms are based on the ability to create a fictional replica of reality while at the same time tearing through those realities we thought we lived in — a poetological process that the visual storytelling artist Hito Steyerl has pointedly called "ripping reality."[4]

Rhetorical Speech versus Topical Speech

Such fundamental but schematic considerations of the short form's ontology partly justify the short form's position as the novel's counterpart during the rise of narrative prose genres in early modernity. However, while this schematic perspective might help explain the Foucauldian interest of understanding modern literature as an ontology and a prose phenomenality, it does not explain why the short form and its paradigmatic modern genres such as the novella and the fable took so much longer than the novel to emerge. Again, sociohistorical arguments seem to offer a first explanation here, especially the fact that the spread of journalistic media such as broadsheets, newspapers, and other periodicals since the sixteenth century popularized shorter types of texts that reported on political, religious, criminal, medical, supernatural, and other extraordinary occurrences. Yet such quantitative circumstances help explain only the spread and acceptance of short forms; they don't fully account for their active part in this rise, which is due to their inherently literary quality. To understand the communicative function that short forms took on and to decipher their rapid ascent in importance requires explanation of another, different development: the updating of the essential role of literature within the classical civic discourse of storytelling into new forms of civic discourse in modernity.

A first clue to the rise of short forms can be taken from a crucial intuition by Hannah Arendt. In her studies of the public sphere, she set in opposition two fundamental types of speech: rhetorical speech, which demands and ensures political authority; and topical speech, which is the discourse practice of participants in a political argument or conversation. In siding with Arendt and her insistence on the political necessity of topical forms of speech as opposed to rhetorical speech, this study moves beyond Arendt's project by not simply assuming a modern history of the decline of topical speech and its political function. On the contrary, I argue that after the dissolution of the *ars topica* in the eighteenth century, various forms of literary speech took up the discursive role of topical speech that Aristotle had already identified. I show that during modernity, this topical function has been realized by various types of short forms. Instead of offering a history of the decline of the *ars topica*, as Arendt described it, this book proposes a genealogy of various parallel lines of literary short forms—from the eighteenth-century fable to the twentieth-century epiphany and the twenty-first-century postliterary story—that attempted, on both "high" and "low" levels of culture, to exercise again the social function of topical speech.

Aristotle distinguished rhetorical speech, the monologue of the one before the many, from topical speech, the polylogue of the many with each other. Where rhetoric's authority demands long arcs and sufficient space for intricate and detailed accounts, topical speech's efficacy demands pointed brevity and pragmatism so that interlocutors can respond to each other with short accounts and personal remarks. This topical form of speech was the original function of what was known as *ars topica*, the skill of arguing dynamically and in brief among citizens of the Greek polis. As Arendt noted, only the discourse of rhetoric remained hegemonic throughout antiquity, the medieval period, and modernity. Because the *ars topica* was increasingly used for legal and formal disputations, for example by Cicero and Quintilian, it eventually fell from its position coequal with rhetoric and slowly waned. Through the Middle Ages and the Renaissance, it devolved to little more than a toolbox of topoi in humanistic systems of knowledge and decorum, offering lists of fixed phrases, clichés, and arguments for occasional discourse of the learned; its original function as a socially pragmatic form of speaking vanished. It took the innovations of prose style — unversed speech, the combination of orality and literacy, interest in everyday characters, and narrative form — to reinvent a genre of short, popular, pragmatic, and social storytelling around 1800, a development that reactivated the topical function, even if it no longer carried the label of *ars topica*.

In the span of only a few decades, the fable, the novella, the fairy tale, the literary proverb, and similar small forms emerged in the literary landscape of the late eighteenth century, evoking issues of civic life in a horizontal mode that went against rhetorical verticality. The trend toward these quotidian narratives is most visible in the long nineteenth-century history of the novella, from Johann Wolfgang von Goethe's *Conversations of German Refugees* (*Unterhaltungen deutscher Ausgewanderten*, 1795) to Thomas Mann's *Death in Venice* (1912). Readable in one sitting of a few hours, the novella extended the limits of the anecdote genre but retained the popular and prosaic style of the folk story. Novellas became the paradigm of revived topical speech, drawing readers into contemporary issues of civic life such as war, racism, law, and divine justice.

But other less prominent short literary forms, such as the prose fable, the literary proverb, and the fairy tale also used topical speech for other quotidian functions, such as argumentation or the change of perception. By these and other forms, the afterlife of the *ars topica* was continued into the twentieth century, where its particular use of literature was seen increasingly as a tool to reflect on the status of literature as a medium. Whether it is through the short-form experiments by modernist writers such as James Joyce and Daniil Kharms, which resulted in clean-cut versions of pragmatic micronarratives, or through actual theories of short-form narrations such as those of Russian formalism or the New Criticism, the short form was used as topical discursive argument, particularly with respect to the role of literature in society.

After the decline of the *ars topica*, beginning around 1700, an epistemological shift occurred that followed the Cartesian model of a subject-centered perception of the world. This shift changed the status and function of literature. Short forms reclaimed for prose what only lyric and drama had been thought capable of in the old poetics: they speak directly to what is present, to the here and now of the reader. John Locke's epistemological writings are among those demonstrating this shift from the waning humanist *ars topica* to the new topical speech. While in antiquity, the *locus communis*, or commonplace, had been another term for "topos," Locke turned this concept inside out, discouraging students from learning merely "topical" knowledge and pressing them—and ultimately forcing philosophers and scholars, as well—to write their own short, commonplace, microstories that drew for relevance on their own immediate experience. Locke's shift indicates the first of a set of theoretical transformations that continued through Giambattista Vico's *New Science* and up to the first aesthetic theory, by Alexander Gottlieb Baumgarten in 1750, which gradually created the conditions for the afterlife of the *ars topica* in short literary forms. Only with the return of this mode of addressing the present—spatially, historically, and socially—that writers such as Guy de Maupassant, Edgar Allan Poe, and Nikolai Gogol helped establish could Theodor Storm, one of Germany's most enduringly popular novella writers, point in 1851 to the powerful effect that novellas had on their readers by calling the novella "the sister of drama."

In a first step, *Civic Storytelling* traces the inception and disappearance of the *ars topica* — from Aristotle to Baumgarten — to describe what I call the "topical function" of speech. I claim that the topical function survived the end of the *ars topica* because it comprises both the thematic, practical ability of speech to address the here and now of the speaker and the immediate eliciting of responses and reactions from potential interlocutors. The old poetics, rhetoric, and the novel simply could not speak in brief to the living, present moment. For that, Enlightenment writers such as Gotthold Ephraim Lessing were compelled to turn to the Aesopic fable as a tool of literary pragmatism. While the fable's revival failed, and the genre remained limited to the Aesopic canon, this experiment demonstrated the eighteenth-century desire for a new form of storytelling whose orientation was to the immediate. Such use of the fable resembled the classical fable, which had once been recited not as an illustration of an attached moral, but in lieu of an argument.

From the German novella around 1800 to the Joycean epiphany, the topical function established a new pragmatic version of prose literature in the world. The novel famously makes the reader enter another world, thus developing the reader's judgment, and the anecdote helps the reader see the world from the point of view of the other and thus liberates the reader from his or her natural world. In contrast, the short form, as defined here, accomplishes something that has often been ignored as an important and even more constitutive quality of a speaker's and an audience's daily discourse: the ability to concentrate on their own world and situation. Short forms draw us into their force field by demanding that we respond and react to what they signal and that we then cope with real-world issues on their behalf. Short topical forms generally demand no change of everyday perspective; they address us not as idealized readers, but as everyday participants living everyday lives. To this day, short forms, exemplified even by their multimedia incarnations, continue to perform a topical function and to behave like autonomous actors. Reading them renders the world inescapably present.

The formation of short narrative forms in modernity as a result of the disappearance of the ancient *ars topica* is the focus of Chapter 1, "The *Ars Topica*, Its Disappearance, and Its Afterlife." The original Aristotelian *ars topica* comprised procedures that solved intellectual and quotidian problems through preexisting short stratagems of language. This "art" of using topoi shaped the skill of employing language within pragmatic contexts, but the topical function of short forms of speech did not cease to exist when the overall *ars topica* expired. Through the epistemological changes in the seventeenth century, what I call the topical function of speech became liberated from mere rhetorical and dialectical uses and was acquired by the newly arising form of discourse that we know today as literature.

Among the works of scholars such as Francis Bacon, Ortolf Fuchsberger, Peter Ramus, Locke, Vico, and Baumgarten, Locke's writings contain the clearest indicators of this epistemological shift. Locke cautioned against collecting preexisting topoi from books — which, he asserts, makes a scholar "a topical man" — and advocated instead writing topoi from personal observation for future reuse in the form "commonplace books." Locke, then, did not, as some might suggest, end the art of using short forms of writing like topoi; he only changed the type of knowledge the *ars topica* administered and abandoned its surface visibility. Vico and Baumgarten, in fact, tried to revive the *ars topica* by designing a *topica sensibile* and a *topica aesthetica*, respectively, but in the first half of the eighteenth century, subjective notation and writing practices — literary discourse — had already taken over the topical function.

The fable was the first form that, during the late eighteenth century, was widely seen to have a topical function, despite belonging to the literary realm. That development is the topic of Chapter 2, "After the *Ars Topica*: The Failed Return of the Fable in Modernity." While the exemplary nature of fables always remained a classical form of discourse, especially since Jean de La Fontaine's revival, and thus could never actually fulfill this modern function, I show in two exemplary readings of Friedrich Hölderlin and Heinrich von Kleist that attempts to use the fable in such a modern way were a first indication that the existing set of short narratives was insufficient to master the task of solving topical problems of knowledge, philosophy, and life. Lessing suggested in the 1750s that the Aesopic fables should be read at face value, namely, as vivid accounts of realistic problems, not as didactic or allegorical illustrations of moralistic arguments. Shortly after 1800, Hölderlin and Kleist then actively experimented with the fable genre and discovered its topical potential as a mode of speech that could immediately speak to their own present. I show that by stripping the fable of its didactic framing, Hölderlin and Kleist led it back to its pre-Aristotelian concept of *ainos*—a story told in a specific instance for practical use. By demanding that modern poetic speech must be "praising what is present" (*das Gegenwärtige lobend*), as he writes in a programmatic Pindar translation, Hölderlin echoed the fable's original *ainos* quality. Similarly, Kleist's rhetorico-poetical treatise "On the Gradual Production of Thoughts while Speaking" ("Über die allmählige Verfertigung der Gedanken beim Reden") contains a fable at its heart, which demonstrates the topical immediacy of fabulatoric speech that all future short narrative forms should manifest.

While Lessing, Hölderlin, and Kleist use the fable as an experimental site to work out in theory and practice how short forms can inherit the *ars topica*, I end the fable chapter with a postmodern rearview on these experiments. Looking back on the struggles of modern forms of discourse, in the 1980s, the philosopher Blumenberg conceived of the fable as a symptomatically overlooked modern form of storytelling that is both philosophical and poetical. Blumenberg confirmed in his explicit theory what is implicitly anticipated in the works of Hölderlin and Kleist.

Chapter 3, "Form: The Novella and the Agency of Short Narrative Forms," presents the first of three case studies of modern genres to show how short narrative forms began to make use of the topical function. The novella, literary proverb, and fairy tale were established as fixed literary forms during the nineteenth century, and each focused on a different quality of the *ars topica*. My close readings analyze how short narrative works and their specific genre semantics inherited the topical function through specific, applicable concepts in the reader's world.

Novellas have a specific form that renders the world and the protagonists irrelevant, focusing instead only on one particular incident. From Giovanni Boccaccio's *Decameron* to Miguel de Cervantes's *Exemplary Novellas* (*Novelas ejemplares*), the tradition consisted primarily of isolated books before writers such as Gogol, Herman Melville, Maupassant, and Stefan Zweig made wide and often pointed use of the genre beginning in the nineteenth century. Looking back at this century, as Lukács had already done, André Jolles strikingly defined this form in 1921, arguing that in a novella, "it all comes down to what happens; the psychology and the characters of those acting and suffering do not interest us in themselves, but only inasmuch as what happens is caused by them." Through a theory of the novella and a close reading of Storm's novella *The Rider on the White Horse* (*Der Schimmelreiter*, 1888) — a famous and indeed paradigmatic instance of the nineteenth-century novella tradition — I show how the novella form is powerful enough to incorporate even the content of a novel, effectively forcing its author to organize narratively not a single episode, but his protagonist's whole life around one incident. I continue this formal study of the novella by also assessing its effects on a theoretical level, tracing how the novella form is partly responsible for the conception of an early narratology around 1800 by Friedrich Schlegel, which decisively shaped modern literary theory. To illustrate the influence that novellas also have in paraliterary versions, I analyze Foucault's use of the novella form as an epistemological backdrop in his description of the *lettre de cachet*, one of the novella's predecessors, which actively shaped criminal prosecutions around 1700. In such *lettres*, Parisian citizens narrated to the police single incidents about other individuals to denounce them as incorrigible criminals, prefiguring both the form of the novella and its practical agency. Like topoi, novellas organize reality by providing frames of reference for their readers that can cause readers to act or behave in a certain way in the public sphere.

Chapter 4, "Argumentation: The Proverb as Micronarrative Agent," presents the second case study: the afterlife of the topical argument in the nineteenth-century literary proverb. Contrary to the dismissal of the people's proverb, which I briefly trace from Erasmus to Immanuel Kant, who called proverbs the "language of the rabble," I show that Gustave Flaubert rediscovered the proverb as the people's poetry by turning it into a minute literary genre. He began by writing a faux dictionary of proverbs and commonplaces, the *Dictionary of Accepted Ideas* (*Le dictionnaire des idées reçues*, c. 1850), which consists of a glossary of the banal and fictive opinions held by the public. Besides arguing that Flaubert thus created a literalized continuation of a topical Renaissance florilegium, I also show that this return of the proverb was Flaubert's test drive for his unfinished *Bouvard et Pécuchet*, a grotesque novel about two copy clerks who decide to live by literalizing topical forms and topical systems of knowledge. From this general return of the proverb and of topical knowledge as an initiator of fictional narration, I move to Gottfried Keller's discovery of the proverb as a prosaic, realistic speech of the people, intended to elevate it back to the respectable status it had lost during the baroque period. Half the novellas of his ten-novella cycle *The People of Seldwyla* (*Die Leute von Seldwyla*, 1856 and 1873/74) use proverbs to encapsulate the minimal plots that each story unfolds. My reading of the novella *Clothes Make the Man* (*Kleider machen Leute*, 1873/74) traces how this structure not only provides the novella with a meaningful format on the extradiegetic level, but also causes the novella to demonstrate on the intradiegetic level of its protagonists' actions how proverbs can again become pragmatic arguments in daily life. Where Flaubert elevated proverbs to the socially relevant realm by taking them literally for parodic purposes, Keller's novellas continue further by deeply investigating not only the topical structure of nineteenth-century everyday life, but also its receptivity to small narrative forms.

The last literary case study, Chapter 5, "Perception: The Fairy Tale as Topical Archive," focuses on the discovery of the fairy tale as literary short narrative with the qualities to change or augment the perception of reality. After its being treated as a folkloristic tale or a magical story from Charles Perrault's seventeenth century to the Grimm brothers' nineteenth, I argue that the belated theoretical discovery of the fairy tale happened only in the 1920s, when literary theorists were analyzing literature through a study of its formal structure. Since Vladimir Propp's *Morphology of the Folktale* (1928), the original and most famous formalist fairy tale theory, is already so widely discussed, only part of the chapter is dedicated to him. Instead, I focus on Walter Benjamin's nearly forgotten theory of the fairy tale, which he developed in combination with a theory of the legend or *Sage*.

Benjamin's theory holds that each fairy tale centers on or encrypts a particular concept, idea, or practice, which it discloses only through its narrative. By reconstructing Benjamin's readings, I show how he extracted the concept of "disappearing" (*Verschwinden*) from Goethe's "The New Melusine" and the concept of "forgetting" (*Vergessen*) from Ludwig Tieck's "The Fair-Haired Eckbert" — both of which are paradigmatic examples of literary fairy tales, or *Kunst-märchen*, in the German tradition — and how these and other readings later led him to work on an uncompleted book on fairy tales, the *Märchenbuch* project. In it, I argue, Benjamin wanted to collect the fairy tales that over the centuries had kept humanity's crucial topoi safe, a function of the fairy tale he described by arguing that "the fairy tale tells us of the earliest arrangements that mankind made to shake off the nightmare which the myth had placed upon its chest."[5] In comparison with the novella and the proverb, I conclude that the fairy tale has universal topical force because, like an archive of the *Homo narrans* — humans as a storytelling species — fairy tales are applicable to different realities at different times as a reminder of the central notions of everyday human life.

While these three case studies establish the topical quality of short narrative forms by close readings and by implication, a

culminating Chapter 6, "Epiphanies, Enacted Stories, and the Praxeology of Short Forms," looks at two sites in the twentieth century
where the inheritance of the *ars topica* in short narrative forms fully
resurfaced in literary discourse. The first is James Joyce's 1903 invention of a new genre of short narratives that he calls "epiphanies,"
unpublished, hyperrealist depictions of scenes from everyday life. I
argue that the sudden coming into existence of the epiphanies shows
that by 1900, short narrative forms had fully inherited the qualities
of a topical discourse. Since the epiphanies contain all three features
of my case studies—a clear form, the posing of arguments, and the
ability to change perception—I conclude that Joyce could invent the
epiphany ex nihilo only because the literary discourse of his time had
fully inherited and adapted the former *ars topica*.

In the second half of this chapter, I analyze how Arendt implicitly confirms this state of literary discourse on a philosophical level
by calling for a form of public storytelling that she terms "enacted
stories." Arendt argues that only this new type of storytelling can successfully acquire the pragmatic capacity for truly political public discourse because it fully accounts for the present and the presence of the
speaker. This argument leads Arendt back to the birth of the *ars topica*
between Socrates and Aristotle. Arendt's critique of the Aristotelian
distinction between dialectic and rhetoric and her favoring of Socratic
discourse among peers is in effect a plea to acknowledge the topical
function that short narrative forms can have in the twentieth century.
I conclude by framing the results of the study into a praxeological theory of literary forms that considers short narrative forms as "epistemic
things" in the sense of conceptually indeterminate representations
that are used in specific practices, as the historian of science Hans-Jörg
Rheinberger has defined the term. I argue that short narrative forms
should be considered as having their own agency because the literary
discourse up to the twentieth century has established them as tools of
fiction that emerge in quotidian practices between reader and world.

In a coda, "Civic Storytelling and the Postliterary Image Life,"
I offer contemporary examples for the ongoing iteration of the *ars*

topica, finally bringing the historical argument into the context of nonliterary narrative media. I show how Arendt's concept of the "enacted story" also lends itself to nontextual media in which multimedia storytelling combines image, sound, text, animation, and video. Here I examine media artist Steyerl's video stories, for example, her 2013 *How Not to Be Seen*, to show that these forms of storytelling, too, open the "space of appearance" that Arendt demanded from "enacted stories." Steyerl's works construct the narrative emergence of an integrative speaker, a concrete or abstract "I" that tells its story while she explicitly theorizes the arrival of a new form of storytelling — "stranger than fiction" and, at the same time, political in Arendt's sense.

Steyerl allows her postliterary stories to combine speech and action so that they achieve the renegotiation of what becomes public and of civic interest in the current era of online mass media. I also show that a similar effect is achieved by the collective storytelling projects appearing globally, which are focused on rendering, from a bottom-up perspective, realities affected by the current climate crisis. This climate storytelling is interested less in empirical data than in the agency of partly fictional narratives about climate realities told not just in text, but also in photos, videos, and other multimedia formats. By comparing different such projects, I offer a sister figure to the increasingly respected citizen scientist: the return of citizen storyteller, who recalls the civic practices last captured by Locke's seventeenth-century commonplace writing and excavated by Benjamin's 1920s fairy-tale theory for their return as folk practices necessary to democratic societies in the twenty-first century. With a list of other examples, I conclude that these new contemporary short forms reaffirm the function of topical storytelling against rhetoric's monologic hegemony. Civic storytellers today are increasingly powerful because they open and reestablish spaces of appearance among the fragmented, imagined, and neotribalistic communities of the globally connected era.

CHAPTER ONE

The *Ars Topica*, Its Disappearance,

and Its Afterlife

A surprising conjunction in the cosmos of arts and letters happened in March 2011 when the literary magazine *Cabinet* organized an event titled "Clipping, Copying, and Thinking." The historian Ann M. Blair and the poet Kenneth Goldsmith were invited to talk about the ways writers have tended to organize pieces of notation for their work. In the first part of the event, Blair, one of the foremost scholars of early modern practices of commonplacing, note taking, and knowledge organization, and Goldsmith, an author widely known for his poetics of recycling and methods of "uncreative writing," spoke separately about their recent books. Afterward, they were meant to weigh in on each other's projects and discuss what they had in common. Yet only after the moderator's strenuous attempts did they hesitantly begin to point out possible overlaps, remaining almost consciously blind to such affinities.[1]

Two critical observations can be grasped from this mutual estrangement between the historical theoretician of bits of writing and the contemporary practitioner of written bits. The first is that sometime between 1400 and 2011, literature appropriated from the humanists and the empirical sciences the practice of composing writing in discrete — that is, self-contained and separable — forms. The other observation is that today, this appropriation of practices is largely forgotten, leaving a historian of science and a data-science-influenced writer out of touch about the fact that their work is indebted to one and the same tradition. In retrospect, the fact that neither Blair nor Goldsmith seemed to condone what *Cabinet* had hoped to ignite at the event becomes even firmer proof of the deep relation of forms of writing between post-1750 literature and pre-1750 sciences.

To the event's audience, the synopsis of Blair's thought and Goldsmith's practice specifically suggested that there is indeed a lost lineage that could accommodate the transfer between the practices of knowledge collection and the art of writing literature. Taking the viewpoint of such an observer, this study will argue that the common ground on which both are concerned is the existence of the ancient *ars topica*, a process of thought that since Aristotle aimed to determine the function of language in discourse by lending separate pieces of language an agency beyond their own self-contained meaning. On the one hand, topoi were generally recognized in certain reoccurring motifs or formulations that acted as anchors in reception histories or could seat arguments in discourses. The *ars topica*, on the other hand — also called "topics" in English, *Topik* in German, and *topique* in French — was the lineage of reflections that arose from the use of topoi and began to extend its thought to other fixed forms of notation.[2] If topoi are understood not only as reoccurring motifs, but also in the broader sense as discrete forms of narrative writing, then the *ars topica* is a theoretical discussion that reflects the autonomous agency of these units and thus indicates at the same time, in a meta sense, how they have shaped the form of discourses as such.

Although the *ars topica* indeed still exists as an undercurrent of literary form, as this study argues, it has moved from a visible lineage of thought regarding knowledge organization since antiquity to an invisible backdrop affecting the fictional narrative realm of modernity and beyond. Such a switch means that the *ars topica* morphed from data technology to media subdiscourse, from the sciences to the arts, from a well-known activity located in quotidian work routines of the learned to a hidden condition of literary form for the moderns that melds together life and literature. While the *ars topica* that Blair

26

described conjured up and organized knowledge as well as thought, its disappearance allowed writers such as Goldsmith to conjure up, organize, and recompose literature and everyday narratives as autonomous stories. The main focus of this study will be the intersection of the two, where *ars topica* disappeared and literary prose form appeared: the afterlife of *ars topica* in the short narrative form.

This chapter traces the historical changes that resulted in the disappearance of the *ars topica* in the eighteenth century. While many studies discuss particular topoi, motifs, or commonplaces and where they appeared and became theorized across this period, no study so far has asked what function the *ars topica* played in the course of history and what happened to its capability once it was discarded. As the final part of this chapter will show, the resulting autonomous narratives are like topoi of the everyday intending to act against itself because the short form can distinguish one day from another by inserting itself, interrupting the sameness of life in the age of the quotidian.

Central to this development is the shift in the basis for *ars topica* from knowledge to narrative forms, plots, and structures, thriving in the relation between literature and life. A few literary scholars have hinted in this direction, though primarily in the context of continuities of particular topoi or their application. Ernst Robert Curtius's *European Literature and the Latin Middle Ages* (1948) is the most extensive of these works, an impressive neohumanistic study of numerous topoi ranging across the Western European vernacular literatures and their rootedness in the Latin tradition. But Curtius was a collector, and his work is itself a symptom of the afterlife of *ars topica*, rather than an explanation of its own indebtedness to early twentieth-century topical thought.[3] Rather than giving reasons for this return of topical practices in early twentieth-century humanities, as suggested by Aby Warburg's transhistorical pathos formulas in art history and Carl Jung's archetypes in psychoanalysis, Curtius saw his work as an emblematic defense of the common European project in a time of crisis.[4] His elitist methods and his lack of definitions have drawn much criticism from literary scholars since they were written, prompting the contemptuous use of the term "topical research" (*Toposforschung*) that marked how distanced from the actual literature his surveying method remained, contrary to the vivid potential of the *Topik*.[5]

Despite a modest comeback of the *ars topica* in linguistic, discursive, and communication studies since the 1960s, most prominently fueled by *The New Rhetoric* of Chaïm Perelman, its recognition as a motor of literature has been minimal.[6] Even other studies more aware of the *ars topica* have trouble tracing its functions after its disappearance. Gerhart von Graevenitz has argued, for example, that mythology has been a topically organized discursive system from Vico's eighteenth-century *New Science* to Claude Levi-Strauss's twentieth-century studies on mythemes, all of which employ the gods as topical figures that can very flexibly be used to match the discursive inventory and explanatory needs of a particular time.[7] The argument also has been made that the eighteenth-century and nineteenth-century novel consists of a "topical inventory" of its respective settings and therefore forms an immediate enmeshing of life and literature, which remotely affirms the closer analysis attempted here because the rise of the novel coincides with the disappearance of the *ars topica*.[8] Both attempts at least treat the *ars topica* as the universal mode of collecting and sorting knowledge about the world, which it had become in the early seventeenth century, as Wilhelm Schmidt-Biggemann showed in his 1983 study *Topica Universalis*, which portrays the topical organization of Renaissance and early modern natural sciences.[9]

In the most interesting attempt so far to understand the ongoing implications of the historical *ars topica*, the medievalist Peter von Moos has moved the concept of topos far away from Curtius's interest and understands a topos as a functional form when he traces how particular historical stories became exemplary for literary narration in the later Middle Ages, especially in their role as exempla.[10] While von Moos focuses largely on his historical area of expertise, his actual argument prefigures a problem in modernity, namely, extending the *ars topica* to a "procedure [*Verfahren*] for the communicative overcoming of problems and aporias through opinion-based knowledge," as

Walter Haug has summarized it.[11] In von Moos's study, history not only consists of topoi, but actually becomes an *ars topica* of narrativity because the late medieval authors used their topical thinking and writing practices to treat history as a second-degree language, applying for the first time the philosophical and purely dialectical principles of Aristotle's work *Topics* to the realm of narration. While this might imply that a straightforward analogy can be made between the topical rhetoric and the intertextual structure of texts, as Frauke Berndt has briefly outlined, von Moos's study points ahead to the more crucial historical alignment of *ars topica* between 1700 and 1900 that this chapter will develop as the groundwork for the case studies that follow it.[12]

First, however, an overview of the larger historical movement up to the disappearance of the *ars topica* in eighteenth century will help lay out the discursive functionality of the *ars topica* while it was still visible and will hence determine how its afterlife could possibly be located in literary narrative forms.[13] It will become clear how the *ars topica*, through dealing with historical quotations and empirical notations, abolished itself, only to return in its afterlife as the *ars topica* of narrative forms, that is, as carrier of the unprecedented.

The Ars Topica*: Method, Form, Storehouse*

A general dictionary of English defines a topic as "a matter dealt with in a text, discourse, or conversation; a subject" and provides the following example: "*sleep deprivation became a frequent topic of conversation.*"[14] The question, "What's the topic of conversation?," could thus be rephrased as "What is being said?" or "What is to be spoken of here?" Or more elaborately, "What do I need to know so that I can join the conversation?" A typical response, "Our topic right now is sleep deprivation" for example, confirms a key point: a topic is not a static or fixed thing but rather a momentary state in a dynamic and shifting process — the living conversation. Going back to the dictionary, which tells us that the word "topic" derives from the Greek *topos*, meaning "place" or "location," one could once more rephrase the question according to its Greek etymology with spatial metaphors.

29

"What's the topic of conversation?" now becomes "Where do you stand?" "What's your position?" "Which point are you getting at?" In this sense, a topic is a place on which a subject matter is in flux, unsettled—a structural spot that a discussion is running through and that therefore allows for the observation of the movement of words, thoughts, opinions, agreements, and so forth.

Pushing the definition this far somewhat contradicts the current, general meaning of "topic," which is usually seen as the fixed and settled content of a book or a meeting, for example, as in "Our topic today will be the city's emergency plans." Given this apparent distance between the classical Greek and the latest notion behind the word, there is good reason for going back to the Greek metaphorical meaning of the concept of a topic. Aristotle, who is considered responsible for initially metaphorizing topos as a "point of discourse," coupled physical location and subject matter in a semantic calculation.[15] Under the same name, *Topics* (*ta topiká*), he wrote a treatise that provided instructions for positioning arguments at specific "locations"—here, the "topoi" of a conversation—and added his thoughts about the various effects that occupation of such discursive locations may have. This work later became one of the six parts of the *Organon*, Aristotle's work dealing with logic and logical reasoning. More than the rather formalistic logic in the modern, post-Cartesian sense, the *Topics* were designed for daily use in the Greek polis, helping to locate probable arguments and identify falsely reasoned syllogisms. As is still concealed in the meaning of today's concept of the topic, the topoi that Aristotle listed in his work are not subjects to be discussed, but rather places and locations from which an unfolding discourse can reasonably be questioned and furthered or through which it can be led and constrained.

"Topics," or *ars topica*, is therefore not the name of a collection of topoi, but rather the name of the art, or the method, of reflecting about a conversation or any other kind of discourse best imagined in a spatial, maplike manner to influence it at its various waypoints. Using the *ars topica* in Aristotle's sense therefore implies that one agrees with two preconditions: that conversations run through such way-points or locations and that each of these potential waypoints will relate to a knowable set of such waypoints or topoi. Thus, according to Aristotle's *Topics*, discussions and discourses are dynamic networks of units of speech paralleled by equal networks of thought. Aristotle's focus on "places" suggests not only that thinking of a discussion as a network in space helps in memorizing what to say at which position, a mnemotechnical side of the *ars topica* that continued throughout its history, but more importantly that the force of arguments rests in the singular notions and nodes of conversation.[16] The *ars topica*, in other words, makes first of all a claim about all conversations, dialogues, and disputations as such, namely, that separate items of speech, if presented in the right sequence and form, can have a decisive influence on any discourse. Not only, then, does the existence of topoi hinge on the *ars topica*, but the function of the *ars topica* itself also determines the state of a topos, of topoi collections, and of topical material.

Looking at the relation of *ars topica* and topoi since Aristotle will therefore explain how what was known as *ars topica* became a strong method of thinking about discourses, especially in the way they function through formalized elements. As this chapter will show, the *ars topica* was a habit of thought that remained even after the *ars topica* was dismissed in the eighteenth century for exerting too much formalizing power on discourses and allowing too little subjectivism in discourses. Yet there, *ars topica* had an afterlife, a continuity of imagining dialogues, conversations, and discourses as functioning through formalized elements. Formalized short narrative genres would take up this discursive habit, allowing for the *ars topica* to develop its afterlife within literature beginning in the eighteenth century.

What to Say

A tradition developed from Aristotle's work *Topics* that aimed to understand discussions and conversations as networks whose discursive knots and points of deviation could be studied and followed by conceptualizing them as topoi. The topoi that Aristotle lists are hence the most common forms of discursive reasoning and mis-reasoning: "Substitute more familiar with less familiar terms" (*Topics* 2.4); "Nothing which can be predicated of a thing must involve contrary predicates" (2.7); "What is desirable for its own sake is preferable" (3.1); "Does change of a term involve change of a genus?" (6.11); "Definition is of all things the most easy to destroy, the most difficult to confirm" (7.5). Aristotle's focus lay not so much on providing any disputant with a ready-at-hand collection of subject matter, contrary to the very common idea today of what the purpose of an *ars topica* is, but in offering means to train them to identify the specific forms of informal, discursive reasoning and misreasoning in any discussion so they could follow it, enter it, and actively alter its course. To accommodate this demand, the *Topics* conceives of discussions as dynamic and requires flexibility from discussants before they can make the best use of the topoi. In other words, the goal of Aristotle's treatise is to prepare readers to enter into and perform in the contingent dynamics of every new communicative situation by suggesting that it is necessary to train the ability to reduplicate in the mind the form of the dynamics of any discussion. Before one can partake in a discourse, one needs to be able to conceive of it as a network of points; only then can these be filled with the argumentative content or subject matter. The fundamentally new exercise performed by Aristotle's *Topics* that allows the *ars topica* to grow into a method is that the network of topoi of an individual's mind must be used to train them to understand any collective communication as a fluid network of topoi.[17]

Besides initiating a crucial lineage for the philosophy of discourses, the reception of Aristotle's *Topics* — reaching, as followed below from Cicero's and Quintilian's legal applications to Vico's and Baumgarten's sensualist modifications — is proof of the flexibility of the Aristotelian method itself. For every purpose and within each intellectual atmosphere, the *ars topica* can suppose less or more dynamism for the respective discursive situations for which it tries to give instructions. For this reason, in his notes for the seminar

"Recherches sur la rhétorique" (1964–66) at the École Pratique des Hautes Études, Roland Barthes recalled the relevance of formalist rhetoric and dialectics for understanding mass-communication societies, and he more accurately observed how Aristotle's *Topics* has been understood over its history.

Barthes differentiated three functions of the *ars topica*: "1. a method; 2. a grid of empty forms; 3. a storehouse of filled forms."[18] Besides pointing out the distinct function of the *ars topica* already present in Aristotle — before *ars topica* or topos became solidified technical terms in the history of ideas — Barthes's interest in reactivating rhetorical and topical elements to understand mediatized societies also led him to identify the dynamism of relations among forms as the most important factor of discursivity. The *ars topica* especially, both in its dialectical and its rhetorical function, has remained over time a system of movable, variable forms that activate discourses and their participants. Aristotle's *Topics*, claimed Barthes, was responsible for discovering answers to the fundamental question behind acts of speaking, conversation, and discourse itself, positing a systemic procedure for answering the question fundamental to all speech: "What to say?" (*Quoi dire?*)[19]

The *ars topica* addresses this lack of knowing what to speak about through a systematic procedure of running the subject matter one intends to deal with through a collection of topoi as Aristotle understood them. As Barthes explains, the *Topics* "was a collection of commonplaces of dialectic, i.e., of the syllogism based on probability," that is, a mere list, before Aristotle turned it into a technique. At the beginning of the treatise, Aristotle defined his *Topics* as "a method . . . by which we shall be able to reason from generally accepted opinions about any problem set before us and shall ourselves, when sustaining an argument, avoid saying anything self-contradictory."[20] In this conception as method, the *Topics* remained solely teleological, aimed at finding suitable arguments and counter-arguments helpful for dialectical reasoning. In his *Rhetoric*, Aristotle would later extend this method to the *heuresis* or *inventio* of oratory, the first, preparatory part of giving a speech, strengthening the linguistic aspect over the logical one.

Less teleological is Barthes's second characterization of the *ars topica* as "a grid of empty forms," which is the version most resembling a systems theory of discourse, namely, a number of questions (a grid) over which any subject may be placed in order to discuss it. Barthes provides a canonical list of these questions taught since antiquity, also called "circumstances" — *quis, quid, ubi, quibus auxiliis, cur, quomodo, quando* (who, what, where, with what, why, how, when).[21] He parallels this list with Bernard Lamy's seventeenth-century list of attributive features to be laid out from the subject at hand: genre, difference, definition, enumeration of parts, etymology, conjugations, comparison, repugnance, effects, and causes. To illustrate how the application of such a grid of topics is a tool to unfold a discourse on any subject, Barthes then sketches the following topical beginning of a discourse on literature:

> Let us suppose that we must produce a discourse on literature: we "dry up" (with good reason), but fortunately we possess Lamy's Topics: we can then, at least, ask ourselves questions and try to answer them: to what "genre" will we attach literature? art? discourse? cultural production? If it is an "art," how does it differ from the other arts? How many parts are we to assign to it, and which ones? What does the etymology of the word suggest us? Its relation to morphological neighbors (*literary, literal, letters,* etc.)? With what does literature sustain a relation of repugnance? Money? Truth? etc.[22]

Not necessarily truthful or methodological but discursive in their manner, these "attributive topics" are formal places containing no content through which a discourse on a subject can be led, eliciting insightful features of the respective material and allowing this discourse to be immediately comprehensible to anyone familiar with the topical grid. Barthes defines this second kind of *ars topica* as "a form which articulates contents and thereby produces fragments of meaning, intelligible units." Here, the *ars topica* helps ideas, thoughts, and subjects to unfold their full semantic potential, which is why

Barthes also named this second version of *ars topica* "the midwife of the *latent*." It is concerned not with what is to be said here and now in a particular speech or disputation, but much more importantly and universally, this *ars topica* is a system concerned with the sayable as such, with the potentiality of the discursive human mind: What can possibly ever be said about this, be it now, tomorrow, or whenever? On the one hand, this second definition describes the most extensive version by far of the *ars topica*. Yet on the other hand, this version of the *ars topica* has left its teleological trajectory, which causes the whole rhetorical technique to become increasingly obsolete, especially if applied again and again to the same questions.

Following this historical trajectory that the *ars topica* took, Barthes therefore closes with a third definition of the *ars topica*: "a storehouse of filled forms." This storehouse consists of solidified answers that were repeated in discourses and conversations, that is, of stereotypes, hearsay, or "commonplaces," a term coined not in relation to the *ars topica* but for its use in rhetorical *elocutio* by Aristotle (*topoi konoi*) and Cicero (*loci communes*).[23] Anybody partaking in discourses about the world, life, politics, or more particular subjects such as geographical places, people, and objects will sooner or later arrive at a set of common answers if the same "grid" of the *ars topica* is used over and over. As will be shown later in this chapter, this development from a discourse to a storehouse could most clearly be observed in humanistic collections of commentaries on mostly classical writers, for example in the *Adagia* collection of Erasmus. It would reach less elitist circulation with the rise of the printed commonplace books in vernacular languages after the sixteenth and seventeenth centuries. At this point in its lineage, the success of Cartesianism's radical disfavoring of existing knowledge completed the decline of the *ars topica* as a method of finding arguments through a grid.

Form through Content: The Topical Function
Barthes's three versions of *ars topica* — from inventive method, to potentialist discourse, to fixed responses — very accurately

differentiate the major phases in the history of the *ars topica*. Its solidification into a storehouse practice in the third step shows why the *ars topica* became obsolete while discursivity and communication increased through printing techniques, vernacularization, and rising literacy. These developments were hostile to repeating received ideas and instead emphasized, first and foremost, finding and including novelties, quickly eliminating any stale answers from the topical storehouse. The true potential of the *ars topica* was thus fully developed solely in the second version in which, according to Barthes, the *ars topica* became "a network of forms" because it can create, as he writes, "a quasi-cybernetic process" from its formalistic depository.[24] This characterization of the potential of the *ars topica*, which is independent from any particular work, function, or time period, extracts the core function of the *ars topica*. Even after having solidified as a storehouse, the original dynamism of the topical system is still contained in commonplace topoi such as the *locus amoenus* (pleasance; "a beautiful, shaded natural site," writes Curtius), which, as Barthes noted, can "be mobilized [and] transported" precisely because they appear to be "detachable pieces."[25] The most important takeaway from Barthes's synopsis is that topoi stemming from discourse systems continuously carry the discursive power they had within the system. While Barthes's observations are among the few that point to the existence of topical discursive forces that continued after the decline of the *ars topica*, the true effects of what this study calls "the afterlife of *ars topica*" requires much more explanation.

A topos has its own agency because it has been charged with a discursive force by the topical system that formed and circulated it. As a node in a system of discourse, a topos is both content and form in a rare unity. Topoi tell or retell a story, at the same time bringing forth this story because of its formal impact, its topical embeddedness, one might say. While the instance of a well-known literary topos such as the *locus amoenus*, on which Curtius hinges a complete chapter of his 1948 study, tells internally of a beautiful landscape; it also signals externally that it is not new, only reappearing, that this "pleasant place" has not only a fixed content but, more importantly, a structural function proven to be effective beyond itself. This external function stems from the tension between each synchronous contextualization, on the one hand, and the diachronic charge, on the other. The positioning of the topos in each work and in their reception compose its "topical embeddedness," charge it with the systemic force of the *ars topica* and thus determine its autonomous agency.

This functional aspect of the *ars topica* will become more clear in the following part of this chapter, which traces crucial reception points of the *ars topica* from Aristotle to Baumgarten's eighteenth century, where its history comes to an end, or rather, where it transforms into a motor of literary form. This "functional history" will bring forth the various aspects in which the *ars topica* theoretically pointed out and retained a specific discursive agency and autonomy for the topoi it organizes. After having presented this historical lineage of the effect of this "topical function" of small narratives, the third and final part of this introductory chapter looks ahead to where the afterlife of the *ars topica* can be found, including the work of writers and scholars who have made first attempts to work out in theory, mostly under a different name, what this afterlife looks like. It sums up the results of this initial survey of the *ars topica* to establish the basis for the accounts that follow, specific cases in which brief narrative forms behave topically.

The Eclipse of Formal Agency

Aristotle's *Topics* can be viewed as an attempt to universalize previous dialectic traditions, most prominently that of Socrates. Whereas the Socratic dialogue always remains hierarchical (Socrates asks his partner a number of questions whose answers he partly rejects each time to allow furthering his inquiry) Aristotle's project of the *Topics* tried to open up dialectics by providing a collection of argumentative schemata and the instruction for how to use them. Whereas for Socrates, dialectics and philosophy were necessarily connected, Aristotle separated the philosophical inquiry of truth from the dialectical process in which knowledge of truth might be reached, as he states in a brief but clear differentiation in his *Metaphysics*: "Dialectic treats as an exercise what philosophy tries to understand."[26] Keeping in mind the quoted first sentence of the *Topics* that calls it a "method," his project can be rephrased as a training program for conversational behavior that can become useful in three different fields: "exercises [*gymnasia*], encounters [*enteuxis*] and the philosophic sciences."[27] The *Topics* introduce the basic concepts of dialectics in book 1 and list different topoi during the major part of the treatise (books 2 to 7), before turning to secondary, strategic considerations for disputations in the last book. This structure is rich in topical examples and underlines the attempt to present a universal toolbox for discursive inquiry.

The second purpose, "encounters" (*enteuxis*), especially can be read this way because it refers not only to conversations within the academy, but equally to those held outside it. Robin Smith convincingly explains Aristotle's word "encounters" (*enteuxis*) with a phrase from the *Rhetoric* that mentions "encounters with the public" (*he pros tous pollous enteuxis*), rendering the *Topics* as a handbook conceived for discussions among all members of the polis.[28] Aristotle gets at this aspect when he writes that the *Topics* "is useful in relation to encounters because, once we have reckoned up the opinions of the public, we shall speak to them, not from their own beliefs, but changing their minds about anything they may seem to us not to have stated well."[29] It is not the scene of a rhetorical speech before the public that Aristotle conjures up here. Instead, he opposes topical discussion to oratory to emphasize that the *Topics* had in mind a one-to-one discussion between a philosopher or expert and one or a few members of the public, a fact on which Arendt would later base her plea for a new form of political discourse, as will be examined in Chapter 6.

Unlike a long monological speech, the topical discussion unfolds in separate steps of dialogue or polylogue, in questions and answers, as the expert begins her discussion from the opinions already held by the public, which she is supposed gradually to draw near her own views. This is an especially typical and perhaps the most realistic situation for the use of the *ars topica*, since the topical dialectics are first of all aimed to discuss "acceptable premises" (*endoxa*) according to its first programmatic sentence cited earlier. What is discussed topically is thus not based on absolute truths, nor on deductions of principles, but on the altering of relative opinions that are being "deduced from what is acceptable."[30] Someone hence always already holds these *endoxa*. They are enwrapped and even defined by the discursive agency that those speakers have repeatedly given to them over time, gradually charging them with discursive effectiveness.

This quality can be called "embodied effectiveness" because it is the de facto agency of an *endoxon* to have been uttered before in lived discourse. This is its preexisting condition. Aristotle rightly suggested that *endoxa* be altered only by becoming arguments anew that acquire their persuasion not merely through logic, but by taking up and redirecting in person the already active opinion of someone else. In that sense, *endoxa* are embodiments of public opinions. While *endoxa* are only one type of content occupying topoi in a discourse, their condition of "embodied effectiveness" provides the model for the active, vivid quality at the basis of the Aristotelian concept of the topos. All topoi are potentialities for acting with such embodied effectiveness. The same idea of topoi as discursive embodiments can be arrived at from the fact that many topoi Aristotle listed contain deductions based on relative hypotheses that have already occurred as utterances during prior discourse. Thus the literal meaning of the Aristotelian concept of syllogism as "to summarize, to add up."

The relationality of a syllogism not only takes into account former arguments, but also incorporates the lived quality of earlier utterances. Take for example the following topos that Aristotle unfolds by taking the reader through their own procession of thoughts, echoing the mode of the Socratic method:

> You must also see whether conditions are alike in the case of a single thing and a number of things; for there is sometimes a discrepancy. For example, if to "know" a thing is to "think of" a thing, then to "know many things" is to

"think of many things." But this is not so; for it is possible to know many things and not be thinking of them. If, therefore, the second statement is not true, then the first, which dealt with a single thing, namely, "to know a thing" is "to think of a thing" is not true either.[31]

From Cicero to the Scholastics

In its holistic approach to discourses as live procedures, Aristotle's *Topics* stood out not only against its predecessor's instructions in argumentation by taking a universalist, all-encompassing approach, but also against its successors. Cicero's reception reduced the *Topics* again to a narrow utility. All "loci" that Cicero's *Topica* listed are introduced according to their practicability for legal arguments or legal heuristics and, more specifically, to help find arguments for a particular case in court. Cicero's *ars topica*, in other words, was meant to aid preparation for legal disputations that are by definition combative and hence teleological. Its purpose, Cicero writes, is "a system for . . . inventing arguments [*disciplinam inveniendorum argumentorum*] so that we might come upon them by a rational system without wandering about."[32] While the function of invention was already present in Aristotle's *ars topica*, Cicero's legal *ars topica* completely replaced the open, universally applicable ambition that had been Aristotle's motivation for writing the *Topics* in the first place. Opening the awareness of the dynamic network of a discourse situation was no longer the purpose of the *ars topica*, since the teleology with which court disputations needed to proceed is much more comparable to a rhetorical effort than to the vivid, eventlike character of a discussion among citizens in the polis. For Cicero, the formal regulation of public controversies by the Roman legal system had for a large part replaced the formalistic interest of Aristotle to understand, describe, and teach holistically the ontology of discussions among individuals. For that reason, Cicero could quite simply define his endeavor by saying that "we may define a topic as the seat of an argument [*locum esse argumenti sedem*], and an argument as a course of reasoning which firmly establishes a matter about which there is

some doubt."[33] His definition was the first of many reductionist mis-
understandings of the Aristotelian origin of the *ars topica*.

One reason Cicero eliminated the fundamental aspect of discourse analysis from his *Topica* was that he conceived of it only against
the fixed background of the Roman legal system.[34] For the reception
of Cicero outside the legal field, however, this meant that his *ars topica* no longer contained a groundwork or theory regarding the original purpose of the *ars topica*. When Boethius, who most likely knew
Aristotle's *Topics* in a very different form from the more original
version we have today, wrote his philosophical *De topicis differentiis*,
he therefore needed to fill the lack of a foundational theory of the *ars
topica* in Cicero with his own groundwork, replacing the legal with a
metaphysical teleology.[35] As the title states, his general approach was
based on further distinguishing the various topoi from one another,
on which Boethius spent the major part of his work, referring his
readers to Cicero and Aristotle for the details of the actual topoi
themselves.[36] While his predecessors found their topoi through differentiation, he explained, they had not exceeded all possibilities,
which is why further differentiation of topoi not only would multiply
the number of topoi, but also would provide a systemic foundation
for the *ars topica* itself: "We must take care to pursue . . . the way in
which the rhetorical Topics differ among themselves and from the
dialectical Topics, so that when all the Topics have been completely
and fully considered and their differences and similarities have been
thoroughly examined, an abundance of arguments will be provided
and there can be a clear distinguishing among the Topics."[37]

This need for a differentiation between topoi placed Boethius's
ars topica closer to problems of Scholastic logic and further from
the dialectical training useful in a public sphere where Aristotle's
project had originated. Boethius thus effectively further separated
the practice and the logic of philosophy. Whereas Aristotle's *ars
topica* contained a method for discourse, because they were meant
for practitioners and directed externally, Boethius's work is internally directed, toward scholars, conjuring up an *ars topica* only in the

second degree and effectively replacing the practical use of the *ars topica* with a mere discussion about its uses and abuses. In the temporary absence of the original Aristotelian work, the whole medieval situation of the *ars topica* was left with Boethius's limited definition, as Christoph Kann has summarized:

> Generally, the medieval topics or dialectics can be determined to represent a differentiated doctrine of argumentation that . . . was significantly shaped by Boethius and, according to its original aspiration, distinguished itself from the demonstrative syllogistics as a doctrine of probabilistic reasoning. Yet, after a flattening of this opposition in the fourteenth century, it integrated into a general doctrine of inference and hence largely disappeared as a distinct doctrine within logic.[38]

This medieval end of the logical *ars topica* confirmed the antagonistic opposition between logic and *ars topica* to which Aristotle had pointed.

His observation was equally confirmed, only on the level of pedagogy, by the return of topical thought in the fifteenth century through developments in didactics and the arrival of printed books. Printed schoolbooks that instructed students in rhetoric, dialectic, and logic through topical methods gained influence in the newly emerging fifteenth-century and sixteenth-century educated public spheres that resulted from the spreading of universities in Europe and the parallel proliferation of print technology. This return of the *ars topica* through the growth of education also helped rediscover the pragmatic function of topical thought as a cognitive method for joining any form of discourse, be it quotidian or scholarly. Walter J. Ong has shown in *Ramus: Method, and the Decay of Dialogue* (1958) that the simplified dialectic taught by those schoolbooks was prepared for by the simplification of Scholastic topics and logic, foremost by the work of Petrus Hispanus. His thirteenth-century *Summulae logicales*, also called *Tractatus*, contains a book "Of Places" ("De locis"), which rendered the Boethian *ars topica* while simplifying the function of a topos so much that it paradoxically suggested a return from the complex Scholastic logic to spoken discussion. A topos "confirms" an argument, writes Petrus, and is hence "the basis of an argument," while "an argument is a reason grounding conviction in debatable manner [*ratio rei dubiae faciens fidem*]."[39]

In argumentation organized by an *ars topica*, truth is not at stake; "conviction" (*fides*) is all that it can achieve. This approximates the function of *ars topica* to the dialectical situation, taking into account the "embodied effectiveness" present in Aristotle: to convince listeners based on a situational, environmental setting. "Here," comments Ong on Petrus's definition, "reason . . . is supported not on the pillars of science, but on the topics or arguments of a merely probable dialectic of rhetoric."[40] In short, Petrus's intent to write a logical tractate that could be taught to teenage students forced him to simplify topical reasoning for the first time since Aristotle.

In the end, this attempt to revive the *ars topica* failed to take off. However, teaching logic in schools meant a return of the pedagogical element in topical reasoning, which had been part of its origin. As can be grasped already from Aristotle's example of a topos cited earlier, explaining topoi in written language proved unfit for employing or even remembering them. This stems from the limits of the linguistic notation of logic, which would be solved only by new systems of symbolic representation for logic developed by George Boole, Charles Sanders Peirce, and Gottlob Frege in the nineteenth century.

Didactic and Compilational Ars Topica

In the face of these overcomplicated medieval topics, Rudolph Agricola's dialectical treatise *De inventiona dialectica libri tres* (written in 1482, first printed in 1515) continued the simplification of logic, focusing more heavily than Petrus Hispanus on how to create *fides*, conviction, in the opponent. In order to achieve this, Agricola combined aspects of logic, dialectic, and rhetoric into a new art of discursively aware speech, and these pragmatic intentions proved successful. In 1535, for instance, the University of Cambridge made his dialectical work a mandatory reading for students of all subjects.[41]

At that time, Petrus Ramus furthered Agricola's achievements by writing his own schoolbooks for Parisian grammar schools that were quickly translated, printed, and spread throughout Europe. The print medium furthered the didactic interest because it allowed for the development of instructions in topical logic through diagrams that transported dialectical reasoning into the visual realm. The earliest print visualizations of a discursive *ars topica* were designed by the Ramists (Figures 1 and 2), who took the spatial metaphor of *ars topica* literally to use diagrammatic relations to represent discursive relations.[42]

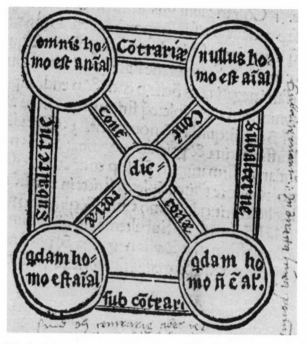

Figure 1. Didactic diagram showing topical logic (on categorical propositions): "Every man is an animal" (*Omnis homo est animal*), "Some man is an animal" (*quidam homo est animal*), etc. From Thomas Murner, *Logica memorativa Chartiludiu logice, sive totius dialectice memoria; & novus Petri hyspani textus emendatus* (Strasbourg: Gruninger, 1509), Tractatus primus, Applicatio quarta. This diagram is from a schoolbook containing "playing cards" that depict a logical problem according to specific symbols.

Figure 2. Logic as figurative diagram (*typus logice*), depicting philosophy hunting the rabbit Problema out of the area of Unsolvables (*Insolubilia*) with her dogs Veritas and Falsitas, her bow Questio, her sword Syllogismus, and most importantly, by help of her voice through a megaphone (*Sonus vox*) that is held up by her arm Argumenta. Frontispiece to Book 2, "De principiis logice," in Gregor Reisch, *Margarita Philosophica, totius Philosophiae Rationalis, Naturalis & Moralis principia dialogice* (Freiburg: Schott, 1503).

Placing words and symbols as topical arguments on a two-dimensional page doubled the efforts to simplify logic, associating the *ars topica* with the training of memory, which could be called its paradigmatic application. Didacticism and media technology, forces external to philosophy, thus caused a return of topical reasoning to its original Aristotelian state, grounding it in life-related practice, education, and discussion.

These dramatic changes also meant a return of the *ars topica* to the public sphere, as can be shown in the work of another early sixteenth-century dialectician, Fuchsberger, who worked parallel to Ramus and, like him, had been influenced by Agricola and the possibilities brought by print. His *Dialectica* from 1533, which was the first in vernacular German directed at the literate citizen, begins by underlining that it is aimed at quotidian use.[43] For Fuchsberger, the "dialectical difference from rhetoric" is that dialectic is the art "that presents in brief speech [*mit kurtzen worten*] the pure action, which afterward is brought forth by rhetoric with many attachments of graceful speech."[44] The "Topik," which he translates as "finding of common places and citations" (*erfindung gemeiner Stett und anzüg*), proves to be central for this purpose because it is a specifically functional practice. Topical dialectic "does not teach one to find what one must say or write, but how what was previously thought and invented must be formed [*gefoermbt*] and with what order of words it should be described and discussed."[45]

As an example for where topoi are at work, that is, where the knowledge of *ars topica* might be useful, Fuchsberger presents among others a report of a discussion he witnessed in public. He once had observed "two farmers discussing by the linden tree after the sermon" whether it was right for people to stay away from church if the pastor had preached in a querulous (*verdrossen*) manner. Fuchsberger's example is meant to show that even though these peasants had never learned anything about dialectics, they were still performing dialectical discussion and reasoning by using propositions (*fürschlag*) and syllogisms (*schlußred*):

From this dialogue of peasants [one can actually see that] this art is so much related to nature that it is nothing else than nature. For these peasants had never learned an art, but still give an example of it. The first seeks and finds causes that he wants to cite to substantiate his proposition. But the other puts the same found quotations into an argumentative form or syllogism, which could be resolved or made more evident by saying: All things that draw the hearts of humans away from God are to be avoided: querulous sermons do such a thing, for this reason they should be avoided.[46]

If the *ars topica* is the natural way of discussion, as Fuchsberger reasoned, topoi are active during any kind of discourse; not topoi in the material sense, such as the topos "A man is a wolf to another man" (*Homo homini lupus*), but topoi in the sense of dialectical stratagems such as the one active in the exchange between the peasants: "All things that draw the hearts of humans away from god are to be avoided." Speech or even texts can become formed (*gefoermbt*), given that they include inner dialectic schemata. This form might not be immediately perceivable on the outside, but it can be analyzed if the text or speech is perceived as having been driven by a dialectical intention.

Peter Mack has confirmed this in his study *Renaissance Argument*, which counts among the sixteenth-century "impact of Agricola's general ideas" not only that Agricola's work had influenced the use of everyday vernacular languages for dialectical disputations and treatises on dialectic. Even further, in a much deeper change in the use of languages, topoi were no longer considered purely methodical means of coming up with arguments. Now a topos was seen as reflecting actual relations between things in the world. Instead of helping to discuss abstract philosophical problems, the *ars topica* acquired an immanent quality that reflected links between real objects, just as the 1503 visualization from logic as a hunting scene suggests (see Figure 2). "The topics are reminders of where to look for arguments," writes Mack. "Their force comes from the fact that they describe common types of connection which exist between things in the world."[47] However difficult it may be to prove Mack's thesis in detail, it underlines the effect and the direction of post-Agricolaen topics on discursivity in general.

Seconding Mack's focus on dialectics regarding notational practices, Ann Moss has further argued that the productive, compositional side of Agricola's topics can already in fact be found in his didactic treatise *De formando studio*, written as part of a letter in 1484 shortly after completing *De inventione dialectica*.[48] In the letter, Agricola demanded three skills from a serious student or scholar: "He has to clearly and unambiguously grasp what he is learning, firmly retain what he has grasped, then have the ability to also create and produce from that something of his own."[49] Here it can be observed, according to Moss, how dialectics — the ability to discover, map out, and produce arguments — came together with practices of reading, note taking, memorizing, and composition. Agricola linked for the first time the dialectic, mental, and notational aspects of intellectual activity when he argued that dialectics and erudition are not enough when trying to come up with a convincing sermon or speech. Knowledge must be structured through dialectics, while dialectics in turn needs knowledge to have something to argue about, and this can be achieved through writing down topoi as separate argumentative forms or places.[50] The ontological potential of things — to present the dialectical mind with the topical connections of the world — was seen to have its counterpart in the practice of writing personal notes, commonplaces, and observations. Suggesting a unity between the scholarly mind and activities of the scholar, Agricola implied that topical thinking and topical notation are the two conditions of the function of *ars topica*. If the scholar understands his life to be a combination of the two, he can turn the mental condition of topical connections in the world into a written condition by writing this *ars topica* down. *Ars topica* as a mental system begins to have its equivalent in the written *ars topica* in a form of a personal book of commonplaces.[51]

Erasmus's *Adages* (*Adagia*), which reached over four thousand entries in its final 1536 edition, is perhaps the most famous of such collections of topical material. It consists of quotations from ancient and

48

later authors, philosophical questions, literary sententiae, proverbs, political expressions, short essays, a few autobiographical entries, and anecdotes, all of them furnished with Erasmus's own comments that he expanded further in every edition. Less and more explicitly personalized versions of such collections exist, presented as the summary of one author's complete erudite mind, or rather, as an aid for the minds of others, specifically ordered and indexed to be easily accessible. In either case, such books of commonplaces claimed to be universal collections, containing, like a scholar's mind, potentially all knowledge available in the world.[52] Their authors posed as polymaths, outstanding examples of human erudition who set the standard for knowledge and argumentation, leaving their books as monograph encyclopedias before such projects became collaborative efforts in the early eighteenth century.

In the course of the sixteenth century, however, this genre changed, and the mere authority of the collector of notes was no longer sufficient reason to make his collection respected, reliable, and relevant for others to use. As Blair has shown, the decline of the florilegium, or collection of *loci communes,* began with its own success in the print age and the general proliferation of printed knowledge books, which often dispersed reliable with unreliable information, factual with fictive accounts, the cryptic with the dull.[53] In 1605, Bacon, whose 1620 *Novum Organum* aimed to replace the Aristotelian *Organon* and its *Topics,* wrote in his *Advancement of Learning* that the humanist commonplace books fail to record the world. Instead, they are "referring to vulgar matters, and Pedanticall Diuisions without all life, or respect to Action."[54] The 1624 edition extended this criticism, with Bacon now calling for the replacement of the old *topica universalis* of the Erasmian commonplace book with a *topica particularis* that reflected the individual's own particular arguments, conclusions, and observations.[55] When investigating a problem, for example, the nature of gravity, the use of *topica particularis* is much more appropriate, he argued, because just as "men vary their *Particular Topiques* so, as after further Progression made by *Inquiry*, they doe substitute one, and after that another *Topiques*, if ever they desire to reach the top of Sciences." While this foreshadows the "new" *ars topica* of the eighteenth century, and with it also a new commonplacing, which the next part of this chapter will explore, Bacon still ended his proposal by mentioning his indebtedness to the Scholastic *quaestio disputata* method of investigating an issue, as opposed to the mere observation of "things."[56]

The use of these collections of traditional material finally came to an end with the success of Cartesianism in the early seventeenth century, which argued that the only knowledge to be trusted is what one has gained clearly and distinctively with one's own intellect. Influenced by this tradition, the French rhetorician and logician Bernard Lamy in 1684 was still repeating the Baconian warning that commonplace books are chaotic, confusing collections whose study hinders the clear and distinct ideas in the mind of the scholar:

> For anyone who wants to treat a certain topic, it is tremendously dangerous to orient oneself by commonplaces over and over, because many different things and the great number of diverse impressions confuse and obscure the mind, and hence even more its owner, because he is no longer free to turn attentively toward the truth; instead of acquiring a clear picture, he lets himself be blinded by beautiful subject titles, like those in [Theodor Zwinger's] *Theatrum Humanae Vitae*, [Joseph Lang's] *Polyanthea*, or in *Le Parterre des Orateurs*.[57]

What was at stake in the middle of the seventeenth century was therefore not the validity of the ars topica or dialectics as methods for shaping social argumentation, speech, and writing but rather the validity of the material that could possibly be structured and discussed through them. From the Cartesian point of view, this means that causes, effects, classifications, relations, and other topical categories were to be taken or found through observation of the world itself, together with the material one argued about. Here, the mind's role as agent of *ars topica* was further reduced, and the ordering of things found in the world suggested its own structuring of narratives. Experience, observation, and perception were coming to replace argumentation. This, in turn, furthered the relocation of the *ars topica* from a strategic mental practice to an agency, that is, a network of stratagems arising from written collections of topoi, a network that possesses its own operational influence.

Commonplacing and the Matter Itself

Following this change toward a notational condition of *ars topica*, by the end of the seventeenth century, two threads of development would align during a second crucial phase in the transformation of the *ars topica*. This change concerned the epistemological status of the *ars topica*, and one of its paradigmatic examples is found in the philosophical work and working methods of the empiricist philosopher Locke. Locke faced an evolved *ars topica* whose expressive modes had shifted in two important ways: topoi were now seen less as formal argumentation schemata and more as didactic instructions, quotations, or proverbs collected for personal, private use, and knowledge was considered less what could be found in books through reading and more what presented itself through observation, sensate experience, and intuition. *Ars topica*, having become officially disregarded as a purely rhetorical technology, had instead acquired the role of the collection of personal writings, ready for subjective use in the everyday. In its new guise for Locke, *ars topica* thus epistemologically foreshadowed subjective, if not realist narration.

While the tradition of printed commonplace books since Erasmus had come under scrutiny for promoting the impossibility of a universalist, total knowledge and for its distracting effects on the reader, it was succeeded by a new custom: to write a book of one's *own* "places" that paradoxically kept the name "commonplace book," despite not reflecting at all common knowledge. Locke had begun "commonplacing," as it was called, at the age of twenty in 1652 and continued to write commonplace books until his death in 1704.[58] The habit, even though he didn't follow it consistently, provided a lifelong foundation for his education, his thought, and his philosophical works.[59] The most open proof of this is a 1686 essay originally published in French, translated in 1706 as "A New Method of Making Common-Place-Books," in which Locke briefly laid out his method of copying, indexing, and referencing notes and thoughts in such a commonplace book, including even the correct table layout for the chart that the keeper of the commonplace book was supposed to use as an entry form when indexing.[60] The essay's influence can be traced to numerous scholars throughout the eighteenth century and was especially praised for offering an undogmatic way of indexing because its charts proposed a manner of notation and registering that each individual could adapt to their own preferences, needs, and perceptions. Thus, for example, the recommendation of the logician and theologian Isaac Watts, who wrote in his 1726 *Logick; Or, The Right Use of Reason*: "I think Mr. *Locke*'s Method of *Adversaria* or *common Places* . . . is the best" because it proposes "no learned Method at all" and allows "setting down Things as they occur."[61]

No longer were quotations, proverbs, or lines of thought from respected philosophers to be placed in commonplace books; "things as they occur" now corresponded to the categories of commonplaces. Locke's "New Method" required that the true commonplacer who "would put any Thing in [their] Common-Place-Book" sorted those "things" into corresponding table "heads" that reflected the commonplacer's individual system of *ars topica* that therefore should be in their own words.[62] The "place" of the commonplace had become a subjective *ars topica* whose quality consisted in recording "things as they occur" in writing and structuring them by headings that are personal "essential words" and no longer the Aristotelian topical headings such as relations, *accidens*, or genre.

For Locke, keeping a commonplace book was a practice for observation, studying, and writing that corresponded to his philosophy of empiricism. The sides had changed since Agricola's linking of knowledge and notation, and the notational now directed the mental. In the way Locke's commonplacing was based on subjective perceptions, understanding, and knowledge, it was fundamentally opposed to the Aristotelian notion of learning and studying based on traditional laws, concepts, and authors. Commonplacing, in other words, was for Locke a programmatically anti-Scholastic and antihumanist practice. The decisive shift between the humanist florilegia and the early modern commonplace book thus lay in turning a traditionalist collection of notes almost exclusively derived from books into a personal, subjective collection of everything on one's mind, especially personal judgments, observations, and intuitions. The crucial point for the functionalist history of *ars topica*, however, was that the actual practice of note taking itself did not change much from the humanist to the circa-1700 collector. Systems of indexes, headings, charts, and various methods of copying between books remained the same and were in both versions paired with special awareness of their mnemotechnical purposes. One could briefly formulate this shift by saying that the old *ars topica* administered *accepted* knowledge, while the new *ars topica* organized *new* knowledge. Yet the difference is relatively small and leads to the most interesting aspect of this shift. The notation methods between old *ars topica* and new *ars topica* remained constant because both Erasmus's *adagia* and Locke's *adversaria* remained structured like a list of topoi ready for further use.

Accordingly, Locke not only praised the use of commonplaces, but also positioned himself in respect to the *Topics* and syllogistic logic. While already relying heavily on his *adversaria* commonplace books, in 1677, he wrote in his journal a draft for an essay later entitled "Of Study,"[63] which is a hybrid between a sketch of his epistemology and an instructive treatise in the tradition of Agricola's and Erasmus's *ratio studii*.[64] After giving directions about the physical condition of the scholar, Locke turns to mental conduct. In the second paragraph, he cautions that reading a great number of authors "very intently and diligently [and minding] the arguments pro and con they use . . . may make a man a ready talker and disputant, but not an able man."[65] This form of reading, of memorizing various forms of argument, represents for Locke the humanist *ars topica*, which turns its student not into a thinker, but merely a "topical man."[66] Even though such topical men might be equipped with a "great stock of borrowed and collected arguments," he continues, they are still unable to judge these arguments, that is, unable to "choose the right side, or to defend it well."[67]

A few years later, Locke laid out his full empiricist philosophy in his *Essay on Human Understanding* (1690), in which he furthered his earlier remarks on the *ars topica* by adding a dismissal of syllogisms, explicitly referring to Aristotle. "If we will observe the actings of our own minds," Locke argues, "we shall find, that we reason best and clearest, when we only observe the connexion of the proof without reducing our thoughts to any rule of syllogism."[68] Human reason does not function at all like syllogistic logic and hence should not adapt to it, but, on the contrary, logic should adapt to the nature of the human mind. To show how "perplexed" the mind is left by syllogisms, Locke referred to the three statements of a classic didactic syllogism already shown above in Murner's visual simplification (see Figure 1) — every animal is alive; man is alive; therefore man is an animal — and translated them back into the sequence of notions they present to the mind (animal, alive, man, animal). This allowed him to compare it with the thought sequence one would encounter when observing the same reasoning in the world:

> I ask whether the mind does not more readily and plainly see that connexion, in the simple and proper position of the connecting idea in the middle; thus,
> *homo — animal — vivens*,
> than in this perplexed one,
> *animal — vivens — homo — animal.*
> Which is the position these ideas have in a syllogism, to show the connexion between homo and vivens by the intervention of animal.[69]

His proposed change is based on the sequence of reasoning found in everyday observations, most strikingly those of common people. "Tell a country gentlewoman, that the wind is south-west, and the weather louring [sic], and like to rain," he explains, "and she will easily understand, 'tis not safe for her to go abroad thin clad, in such a day, after a fever: she clearly sees the probable connexion of all these, viz. south-west wind, and clouds, rain, wetting, taking cold, relapse, and danger of death, without tying them together in those artificial and cumbersome fetters of several syllogisms."[70]

What a syllogism or any reasoning must adhere to is the "natural order of the connecting ideas," because according to Locke, the mind reasons by forming a "chain of ideas thus visibly linked together in train." As in an anecdotal narration, ideas, observations, and thoughts contextualize each other for Locke, making "each intermediate idea agreeing on each side with those two it is immediately placed between."[71] It becomes clear that Locke's favored method was indeed topical *après la lettre*, the first of a "new" *ars topica*, because it bore the marks of the commonplacer who collects items of thought, just as the world presents itself in individual items. Writing, as well as thinking and — in the example of the country gentlewoman — even living function according to a narrative logic that puts the commonplaces, or rather subjective topoi, into a sequence that fits them into the nature of mind and world.

Locke's method of commonplacing and his philosophy of understanding were therefore based on the same principle of registering things, that is, particulars as they appear in the mind, in order to allow for the best form of reasoning, memorization, and re-creation of the issue for oneself.[72] Not only do the paragraphs of his *Essay* argue in that manner of a "natural order," the *Essay*'s chapter structure itself is in some part a listing of singular issues — "Of Infinity," "Of Enthusiasm," "Of the Imperfection of Words," "Of Reason" — often written like stand-alone treatises. Locke's *Essay* has been compared to Michel de Montaigne's *Essais*, not only because of its title and its inclusion of self-contained studies, but also because of its lose organization, which allowed Locke continually to insert new essays in later editions.[73] Keeping the work alive in this way shows that Locke saw it not as a projection of a thought system, but like Montaigne, as product of ongoing written thinking. While his "New Method of Making Common-Place Books" instructed how to collect and order subjective notes, his *Essay on Human Understanding* traced what kind of philosophy corresponded to such a mind shaped by exercising itself through commonplacing. In another parallel to writers such as Montaigne, both works carry an autobiographical undertone, which is confirmed by the fact that early notes and drafts of the *Essay* are scattered all over Locke's commonplace books.[74] Only a relatively small step lay between the final book and the notes that preceded it, rendering the *Essay*, and thus potentially all monographs after 1700, as their author's commonplace books in the disguise of linear prose.

Although Locke's works were undoubtedly influential, with the references and reprints of his "New Method" and his *Essay* reaching throughout the eighteenth into the nineteenth century, the shifts identified here were not, of course, caused by any one individual. Rather, Locke is a symptomatic figure whose works reflect how *ars topica* and humanistic commonplace books were finally dismissed in the seventeenth century and turned into data collections of the self that now split themselves up into discrete narrative entries. How little this shift from common to personal, from universal to particular, was fully understood is indicated by the fact that these new books of notation were still called *common*place books, even though what they recorded was highly subjective and not common at all or specifically directed at common discourse.[75] Given the seventeenth-century rejection of Aristotelian philosophy and science, *ars topica* and the practice of topical thought could be maintained only under the cover of new names, such as the misused "commonplace" in English, before its meaning changed to "cliché" and "platitude," while the topical habit had to take on different veils.[76] In its state *après la lettre*, the crucial shift in *ars topica*, focusing on writing and notation, influenced the media technologies of scientific research, experimentation, and observation and replaced the universal formulation with the subjective narration of arguments. As Locke argued in his *Essay*, logical, syllogistic, or topical argumentation from now on could be replaced by a narrative argumentation based on natural perception. As Fuchsberger argued in his *Dialectica* by recounting the scene of the two peasants knowing "naturally" to use Aristotelian dialectics and as Locke insisted when recounting the country woman's reasoning about the weather, neither universal dialectics nor topical erudition were required at all. While Fuchsberger did away with a need for learning a scholarly method, Locke goes further by also declaring erudite knowledge obsolete; the country woman's subjective perception supplies her very own *ars topica* of her very own world.

During the early eighteenth century, other even clearer positions appeared that marked the end of the *ars topica* while transporting the practices of thought and forms of note taking into other areas. One such position was provided by Johann Christoph Gottsched in his *Complete Rhetoric (Ausführliche Redekunst*, 1735), one of the principal rhetorical treatises of the eighteenth century. Gottsched instructed his readers that no one should continue to use the old topical categories for reasoning and instead should focus on expertise of the matter itself:

> I will draw on another method through which the issue can be made very short. For, what made the teachings of the ancients so extensive were the so-called *Loca*, or classes, or subjects of reasons, to which they referred their students if they wanted to find good evidence [*Beweise*]. Their number was terribly high.... According to today's ways of speaking, however ... we can easily get by without the topics of the ancients [*ohne die Topik der Alten*]. ... We no longer have similar speech, and neither in our eulogies [*Lobreden*], nor discourses [*Lehrreden*], nor compliments can such topical subjects help anything. Thus, we have to take a different path if we want to give rules of argumentation.[77]

What Locke had requested for the sciences, Gottsched now argued for rhetoric, that speakers should develop their arguments "from the thing itself" (*aus der Sache selbst*), instead of deriving them from a method of *ars topica*. "Because the speaker must have the things themselves well within him that he wants to speak of.... Here, thus, anyone can see that one can very easily find arguments without all topical subjects of invention."[78] The matter itself now offered the insights for the individual person that were necessary to understand any subject at hand and to speak or write about it. Now a case would no longer be argued by using quotations from antiquity, but by expertise in the case itself.

Barthes called the most dynamic state of *ars topica* "a grid of empty forms," and Locke's structured, yet highly flexible commonplacing provided a paradigm for this grid. Even though he refrained from calling them part of an *ars topica*, his written forms were not merely accidental scribblings, but rather the written items of thinking sequences and observation. The relation between *ars topica* and mind had thus reversed after humanism: the *ars topica* was not what was already present in the question or the problem at hand, something that the scholar simply was supposed to locate, but rather the *ars topica* emerged from the scholar's experience of the world in sequences that the scholar turned into a written, even narrated *ars topica*. The *ars topica* had been a given of the subject matter; now the scholar's writing on the subject matter formed the *ars topica*. In the empiricism of the seventeenth century, "topical" was what was noted down as a personal entry on a specific thought, a topos had become a "place" for an individual's subjective writing. During the eighteenth century, however, there were a few remarkable last attempts to reanimate the old *ars topica* with a new focus. The continuity of the topical habit of thought, the need for it as a mode of organization and motivation of the mind, would reappear in narrative prose forms around 1800.

Topica Aesthetica *and the* Ars Topica *of the World*
While Locke was still too close to humanism and hence in need of differentiating himself clearly from any form of older impersonal topical practices, one generation later Vico could again refer to the notion of an *ars topica* by combining the humanist ideal of studying the ancients with the empiricist's concepts of studying and understanding the world directly. His *On the Study Methods of Our Time* (*De nostri temporis studiorum ratione*) of 1709 showed an interest in education similar to that of Locke and was originally an inaugural address to new students at the university of Naples.[79] Before dedicating sections to subjects such as law, medicine, and physics, Vico compares the study methods of the ancients with those of the moderns, taking a moderating position in one of the most crucial debates

about formal aspects of the arts in the seventeenth and eighteenth centuries. Mostly praising the art of criticism — the Cartesian ability "to discover whether there is any truth in a subject" — the moderns have "utterly disregarded . . . the art of 'topics,'" he writes.[80] Criticism's focus on judgment had caused this dismissal of the *ars topica* as a practice that seemingly competed with that of judgment, which, according to Vico, reflected a Cartesian misconception of knowledge. Judgment, he argued, can occur only after elements of knowledge, the topoi, are found, "since the invention of arguments is by nature prior to the judgment of their validity."[81] In general, thoughts occur through inventive processes such as the *ars topica* not simply because they allow for logical argumentation, but rather occur in the sense of Locke's "common-place," where thoughts are instruments to convey any content from the world to the mind.

The *ars topica* was therefore responsible for the genesis of ideas. It exercised thought as well as eloquence, neither of which can be learned through criticism alone. Vico could arrive at this combination of humanist and Cartesian epistemology because he was not defending paradigms, but he already historicized each approach so as to allow students to use both methods according to their practicality. In this approach, Vico was already following his own amalgamation of the *ars topica* and criticism, presenting both methods in all regards so that the flaws of each could be eliminated. His proposal was to have students first learn the richness of arguments through the *ars topica* and afterward learn the art of judgment through criticism, a rule that he narrowed down to the sentence, "Criticism enables us to achieve truth, while *ars topica* makes us rich [in words and thought]" (*ut Critica veraces, ita Topica nos fieri copiosos).*[82]

For his mediation between the ancients and the moderns, Vico referred to Cicero for the classical method of *ars topica* and to Antoine Arnauld and Pierre Nicole's *Logic, or the Art of Thinking (Logique, ou l'art de penser,* 1662) for its modern dismissal. Arnauld and Nicole's *Logique,* which contained a chapter titled "Topics, or the method of finding arguments. How useless this method is," argued that not the *ars topica*, but "nature, the attentive consideration of the subject, and knowledge of various truths" help find the general terms of a subject, and thus logical reasoning as such is derived from this ability.[83] The *Logique* therefore took the most explicitly antitopical position, but Vico only seemingly contradicted this. His use of the *ars topica* as a companion to criticism was not meant in the logical sense. He was not doubting the project of the new *Logique*, but rather used "topica" in the sense of the transcendental observation of the subject. Very much like criticism, the *ars topica* for Vico was not bound to any specific, formalized discipline such as law, logic, or rhetoric. Rather, it was the ability to comprehend, collect, and combine all types of mental data. For that matter, in his *New Science* (*Scienza Nuova*, 1725) he adapted his earlier argument to a theory of culture, going so far as to claim that it was the *ars topica* that gave the first humans their initial thoughts before later ages separated and criticized them: "Providence gave good guidance to human affairs when it aroused human minds first to topics rather than to criticism, for acquaintance with things must come before judgment of them. Topics has the function of making minds inventive, as criticism has that of making them exact. And in those first times all things necessary to human life had to be invented, and invention is the property of genius."[84]

Implied is the notion that an *ars topica* is in essence an ontological "acquaintance with things," for which he coined the term "sensory topics" (*topica sensibile*).[85] Vico did not save the old *ars topica* from the new criticism, but rather understood the *ars topica* as a cognitive habit that he applied to a new idea of logic, reasoning, and perception — whatever is posed by the mind is part of this new *ars topica* before it is processed, judged, and criticized. The logical relations Aristotle and Cicero had listed as topoi were now to be discovered in perception itself. A topos was no longer defined as a matter established and proven to be significant and persuasive to thought. To the contrary, what a mind considered to be a significant and persuasive thought and that was perhaps even written down and shared with others, that must be called a topos. Where Aristotle found that a commonly accepted *endoxon* can exist only in its embodied state, Vico goes further in claiming that any "embodied" view must necessarily be subjective before it can be common.

This approach prefigured the question of the *ars topica* as a discipline of aesthetics, rather than of logic, a transfer that would surface a few decades after Vico in the founding document of the discipline of aesthetics, the *Aesthetica* (1750/1758). In a central section instructing those seeking "beautiful cognition" how to conjure up the richness and manifoldness of a specific aesthetic material — for example, for use in writing poetry — Baumgarten distinguished the (old) *topica logica* that helps to find arguments for reasoning from the new *topica aesthetica* that contribute to sensitive cognition.[86] Baumgarten confirms Vico's intuition about replacing traditional knowledge with subjective perception and further explains it. He argues that the *ars topica* was never addressed to universals and should therefore not be seen as forming its own system. Instead, it was to be applied pragmatically, to exercise the mind and to subsequently to find specific material for use in literature, the arts, or philosophy. Truth was no longer what regulated *ars topica*; rather it was the subject's psychology that did so. That is, the configuration of the mind itself was now able to judge easily whether the topoi found through the *topica aesthetica* applied to the task at hand. In a seminar, Baumgarten elaborated:

> We would like to add another rule to the aesthetical topics [*ästhetische Topik*].... Whoever ... is a psychologist, which I consider very necessary for various reasons, will quickly look over his theme [*Thema*], if I may say so, judging it in advance, by examining it according to any sufficient catalogue of the sensitive capabilities of the soul, for instance with the questions: Have I often perceived a given theme [*Thema*]? Much in it? Enough that's worthy? Probable? In the light, so that I may present it sufficiently vivid? Etc.[87]

Sensitive intuition and even emotion were the instruments of this new *ars topica* and allowed the matter at hand to be judged without the complicated formalist rules of the old *ars topica*. In his lectures on the *Aesthetica*, Baumgarten provides one concrete example for exercising such an aesthetic *ars topica*, or a "special topics," as he calls it there. This example is composing one's own curriculum vitae:

> Were I to draft, for example, my own curriculum vitae [*Lebenslauf*], even just to amuse myself, I would first ask: How rich he may be, how large is his family, which variations will appear in it, further, how important are they, what kind of truth, what kind of probability, what kind of liveliness is there? Where do I have to place the full light? Where shall I move? That is the special topics [*die besondere Topik*] that we propose for the first exercises.[88]

From all possible exercises of writing, Baumgarten considered writing an autobiographical curriculum vitae the one that most vividly exemplifies the function of an aesthetic *ars topica* because the aesthetic *ars topica* not only lists topoi of an individual person's life, but also provides the art of conveying that life, of turning those topoi into the strongest, most truthful, and most aesthetically pleasing narrative.

In this example of an *ars topica* of the self, nothing was left from the old *ars topica* of a universally applicable set of argumentative forms. Whereas a curriculum vitae is a highly fixed form of narrative, each particular case will cause a different *ars topica* that conjures up the particular arguments for its particular narrative. After the *ars topica* had turned, since Locke, from being a practice of tradition to a practice of the self, it was not surprising or coincidental that Baumgarten's only example was the curriculum vitae. The *ars topica* of the world became identical with the *ars topica* of the self. In any *topica aesthetica*, *topica universalis* and Bacon's *topica particularis* were united.

However, at the very moment that Baumgarten left behind the difference between a universal and a particular *ars topica* and completed the radical change from the general laws of discourse to the discourse of the individual subject, the *ars topica* ceased to exist. If each instance of thinking, speaking, and writing requires its own set of a specific *ars topica*, the whole concept and method of an *ars topica* as such becomes obsolete. On the surface, only topoi remain — birth, education, and death, in the case of a curriculum vitae, for example. Yet below the surface, the history of the *ars topica* became the history

of a poetics of specificity; the specific *ars topica* of an aesthetic experience coincided with the form of the perception of that experience.
Behind the particular draft of a life's story, an aesthetic *ars topica* can
determine the form of each sequence of this particular story. With
the same intuition, Gottsched had used the exact example of composing a curriculum vitae (*Lebenslauf*) to dismiss the old *ars topica*,
arguing that no life could be narrated by naming its topical circumstances, such as name, family, origin. "If a speaker consolidates a
detailed curriculum vitae of a human by using good moral perception," he argues, "then he will need no further topics [*So wird er keine
fernere Topiken brauchen*]."[89] The humans of modernity were no longer
"topical humans." Their lives were no longer topical lives and could
no longer be accurately grasped according to topical rules.

The Afterlife of the **Ars Topica**

Instead, the poetics of specificity characteristic of the lives of humans
in modernity appeared as narratives. Narratives can elicit events, and
not only in empirical research, as Locke claimed. A motto used in the
early twentieth century by the art historian Warburg to describe his
research, "God dwells in minutiae" (*Der liebe Gott steckt im Detail*),
contains this awareness.[90] Based on Gottfried Wilhelm Leibniz's
notion of "*petites perceptions*," it evokes a psychological notion stemming from the post-topical empiricism Leibniz shared with Locke
according to which accidental details on the margins of one's consciousness can turn into hints and suggestions that lead right into
the central issue.[91] Warburg did not elaborate much on the method
behind this motto, yet his student William Heckscher, calling them
trouvailles (windfalls, or lucky finds),[92] showed its relevance for art
history[93] and more generally for its function in what could be called
the hermeneutics of the everyday. Neither facts nor knowledge, but
the meeting of two realities by virtue of a detail-induced narrative
causes the post-topical trouvaille.

A less epistemological version of this trouvaille is Joyce's description of the same effect for literary composition. Sudden structures of

perception and coincidental appearances of certain details in the midst of the bleak everyday captured Joyce, and he decided to represent them in highly compact, strongly stylized brief prose narratives. This type of experience, but also the prose genre it induced, were termed "epiphanies" by Joyce for the sudden arrival of transcendent meaning in the profane everyday.[94] The almost seventy epiphanies he wrote remained with him for decades in various ways, as Chapter 6 will discuss in detail. He implemented them in other works and also modeled plots of his stories after them, treating them as his personal *ars topica* in the sense of guiding narrative plots that form the content of his stories.

Another way to describe this replacement of the discursive system of an *ars topica* through the discursive system of short prose narratives is to say these brief narratives do not represent the whole of a life portrayed in an indivisible unity of life as such, but rather only the individual aspects of that life, the granularity of the everyday. More broadly, they propose that life cannot be represented as a whole but can be grasped only one experience at a time, instance after instance. While the novel in its ideal type can be understood as "a compendium, an encyclopedia of the complete spiritual life of an ingenious individual," as Schlegel argued, the short story, the novella, the fairy tale do not address the transcendental infinity of the individual but the immanent presence of the listener or storyteller.[95] Benjamin's opposition between the author of a novel and the storyteller reflects this difference. The eternal truths of history or *historia*, the discourse from which the novel form stems, are not addressed by these shorter prose forms. They correspond to the "storyteller's diverting reminiscences" (*kurzweilige Gedächtnis des Erzählers*) that constitute the afterlife of the *ars topica*.[96] Narratives do not assume and address, in Benjamin's words, "the meaning of life" (*den Sinn des Lebens*) but evoke instead "the moral of the story" (*die Moral von der Geschichte*) by installing themselves as discrete acts of narration.[97] Asking about the meaning of life is a symptom of the loneliness of the subject to which the rise of the novel correlates without being able to pose a response.

Completely different from the novel, a short prose narrative uses the potential topicality of the individual's lifeworld — the probable logic of the individual's own opinions, its own commonplaces — and provides them with the narrative form that grants exemplarity to the single fact. Against the solitude of life and the infinity of the world, this exemplarity can oppose a concreteness and a particularity. Against the dead system of topical knowledge, the act of narrating vivifies details, things, observations, or anecdotes. What Benjamin bemoans about storytelling traditions of past times he also suggests might be returning: prose narratives can become agents against the hyperindividualism, contingency, and alienation in modernity.

Barthes has made similar observations suggesting that the everyday is a phenomenon of mythic mediatization whose background structure is a subroutine that adapts an *ars topica* of life. We can see in his essays in *Mythologies* but especially in his last seminar, *The Preparation of the Novel* (*La préparation du roman,* 1978–80) — his observation that the "short form" of literature, most notably the haiku, is the minimally required narrative that can create such a device active within the everyday. Like Joyce's epiphanies, the haiku is the smallest narrative entity that occurs from the everyday, when writing turns the quotidian into a microstory. Haikus provide clarity, ephemerality, and subjectivity while at the same time culminating in a moment in which the reader identifies with them, struck by how the minimal narrative alters the momentary perception of the day, an effect that Barthes calls the moment of "That's it."[98]

After the *ars topica,* that is, after the end of the form of life that lives through content-based, material topoi, it is finally left to short narrative forms to create an "instantly meaningful event" that has "at the same time no pretention to a general, systematic, doctrinal meaning."[99] Truth is created in these narratives — not epistemic truth but aesthetic truth. These short narratives neither explain nor instruct. Instead, their form conveys lifelike scenes that create meaning within the ahistorical present of the reader's life. While many studies exist that share the common goal of understanding the capabilities of new short forms developing in modernity outside the canon of medieval and classicist genres such as fable, exemplum, or idyll, these studies either employ genealogy for their ideological agenda, such as Jolles's 1930 *Simple Forms*,[100] or lack a genealogical comprehension that could explain the transitions between these two traditions.[101] Reconstructing this genealogy by extending the influence of the *ars topica* beyond the eighteenth century, the chapters that follow show how the life-guiding, life-simulating capabilities of literature in modernity have grown from absorbing the topical practices of premodernity.

Form of Life and Literary Form

Two moments of its lineage stand out during which the *ars topica* had a specific double function: at its beginning in Aristotle and at its end in Baumgarten. In both cases, the content of the discourse is identical with the form in which they are presented. The *ars topica* of the curriculum vitae in Baumgarten *is* the course of life itself, and the *ars topica* of a discussion in Aristotle *is* the whole discourse itself. In both cases, the *ars topica* does not function as a universal storehouse but is bound to its application and can be useful only for a specific pragmatic situation, discussing one-on-one or writing about one's own life. The form of life corresponds to discursive form. Only in the moment of its surfacing and its disappearance does this congruence occur between the method of *ars topica* and the realities it addresses.

The period between Aristotle and Baumgarten needed a way of visibly organizing and renegotiating the relation between knowledge and experience, between life as such and the moments of life in the everyday. Reinhart Koselleck has argued that by around 1800, historical knowledge was considered increasingly useless for meeting the challenges of the present as revolutions, globalization, the natural sciences, industrialization, and other cultural changes created new lives, or rather, a new form of life that no longer found guidance in what the former lives handed down to it.[102] As the topical storehouse of historical knowledge was rendered invalid, life could not look back at history for guidance but instead could discover the *ars topica*'s ability to provide contentless forms that could be filled with meaning by an individual when they are related to their singular life. Emptied of material topoi, the *ars topica* thus became a way to organize collective discourses through forms of narrative, which would have the same life-guiding function as the old, content-transporting *ars topica*.

However, there were problems that followed from this development. The afterlife of *ars topica* poses the question of relevance in the modern lifeworld.[103] How can the relevance to a life of one item, fact, or sentence of experience be reliably more significant than any another? If everything has the potential to become a topos for me, the original Aristotelian question of the *Topics* — "What to say?" — returns again, with the addition of a reflexive "I" that is concerned about addressing its own here and now in a present banned from relying on history or the future. The question in this lifeworld made of topoi is "What can *I* say?" Or "What *should* I say?" Which item of my world can I turn into something topical, meaningful?

In this dilemma, as we will see, the solution is to give a specific form to any utterance of speech, independent of what its content might be. This act of formalization can single out, combine, and narrativize selected bits of this aesthetic lifeworld, but only because it tends to lend them the ability to stand out, to address this new life in its here and now. The short narratives that are the result of the afterlife of *ars topica* could and can relate to this new form of life because only they are able to create the relevance necessary to address it, to function like the topoi of the old *ars topica*.[104]

CHAPTER TWO

After the *Ars Topica*:

The Failed Return of the Fable

in Modernity

In *Aesopic Conversations*, Leslie Kurke's study on the influence of Aesopic fables and Aesopic discourse on early Greek prose, the classicist employs a motto from Hegel's *Lectures on Aesthetics* as her prompt: "In the slave, prose begins" (*Im Sklaven fängt die Prosa an*).[1] Aesop, the supposed inventor of the fable and the trickster slave of the *Vita Aesopi*, stands, for Hegel, as the most primitive of storytellers, furthest away from the praised novels and novellas of Hegel's own time. Kurke still finds this Hegelian misrecognition of the fable to be true in a system in which art seeks transcendence and has forgotten the immanence or worldliness that dominated ancient Greek literature. Her interest is not only to read classicist scholarship against the grain by showing the deep influence the Aesopic fable had on the prose of Herodotus and on Plato's *Sokratikoi logoi*, but to show as well that Hegel's seemingly primitivist view of the fable marks the necessary egalitarian condition of prose: "Hegel's apothegm is exactly right as a characterization of one strand in the Greeks' own conception of mimetic prose."[2] Kurke's project has at least two aims: to correct literary history and to address the undervalued role of the fable in modernity before and after G. W. F. Hegel. Working in the same direction as Kurke, but on a larger scale, the following three sections exhibit the relevance of the fable form and fabulatory discourse for cases of both literature and philosophy after 1800.

While the argument of Chapter 1 regarding the disappearance of the *ars topica* and the void it left behind operates primarily on a historical level, this chapter investigates this void more directly through close readings of texts that attempt to fill the void by establishing new, post-topical narration. The matter of each text is the appearance of the genre of the Aesopic fable at two specific thresholds of modernity. A few symptomatic cases will be examined — Hölderlin and Kleist around 1800 and Blumenberg around 1980 — that render visible the transformation of the fable from its early modern use as didactic example within a logical frame to an act of storytelling with immediately pragmatic effects.

Since Aristotle, the fable had been defined as having the function of a mere example that could be evoked for informative and moralistic use, very much as a genre within the *ars topica* but the lack of any need for such examples after the end of the *ars topica* left the fable with little of its medieval and early modern purpose. In this suspension of the Aristotelian definition, Hölderlin and Kleist, as well as Blumenberg in retrospect, rediscovered the fable's older, pre-Aristotelian definition as what was called *ainos*. The concept treats what we now call "fables" as the telling of a brief story in such a way that the telling itself comes with pragmatic intent, not with mere rhetorical or didactic calculation, and immediately prompts reactions from listeners and interlocutors. The notion of *ainos* conceives of a fable as an agent directly involved in ongoing social interaction.[3] As will be discussed below, Homer described an Aesopic tale as the active agent of an *ainos*, a designation quite distinct from the later Aristotelian concept of *logos* (meaning "account" or "discourse") or the Latin term *fabula*.[4] The close readings and discussions that follow will trace how the end of the *ars topica* is reflected in the failure of this classicist fable tradition to respond to the shift from a rhetorical to a more practical impulse, a development made even more vivid because Hölderlin, Kleist, and Blumenberg resurrected the agency of brief prose forms using ideas that closely resembled the original *ainos* notion of Aesopic tales. This chapter thus examines the fable in modernity as a symptom of the missing *ars topica*. While such attempts to regain the fable for modernity failed, the rediscovery of the fable's *ainos* quality is itself an indicator what is missing in prose literature.

Praising What Is Present: Ainos *in Modernity*

Hölderlin's so-called *Pindar Fragments* emit a particular trust in the world, as if they were a center in his later attempts to discover a genuinely modern form of poetic speech, that is, the attempt "after the Greeks . . . once more to sing indigenously and naturally, with proper originality" (*seit den Griechen, wieder . . . vaterländisch und natürlich, eigentlich originell zu singen*).[5] Having survived only as quotations by other writers, Pindar's Greek originals bear no titles, and Hölderlin provides conceptual captions for all nine of his renderings. These captions set the tone under which the Pindar translations and Hölderlin's own commentary resonate with one another. It is unusual that Hölderlin wrote the Pindar commentaries as a clean copy, which has survived, and thus presented them in a well-developed state, nearly ready for publication or at least circulation.

The internal organization of the nine pieces is by no means accidental, and neither is their order. This course of poems and prose is initiated by a piece Hölderlin titled "Unfaithfulness of Wisdom" ("Untreue der Weisheit"), a wording that seems to announce a set of warnings. However, "unfaithfulness of wisdom" turns out to be a cautiously trustful maxim aimed at recognizing the ambiguous nature of wisdom in modernity. Hölderlin's rendering of the six lines from Pindar reads:

> O child whose love most clings
> To the pontic game beast's skin,
> The rock-enamoured, with all cities mix,
> Praising, with good will,
> That which is present,
> And differently think when the times are different.[6]

An adult is speaking to a child about wisdom by comparing the child's human mind to the nature of the polyp or sea anemone ("the pontic game beast"), which can never leave its rocky location once it has settled and become attached to the ground. In this immobile state, protecting itself is possible for the polyp only by mimicry of its "skin," by adapting its appearance to the surface color of its environment.

After establishing this analogy between human and animal as Pindar proposed it, Hölderlin chooses to translate the second half of the fragment against the grain of usual interpretations by turning it against the first half and installing a new, antithetical tension at the heart of the poem. Instead of implying that the polyp's form of life is an appropriate analogy or even a model for adolescence or human life in general, as other translations generally do,[7] Hölderlin opposes the human way of adapting to a new environment to the polyp's method of growth:

> O child...
> ... with all cities mix,
> Praising, with good will,
> That which is present,
> And differently think when the times are different.[8]

The polyp has no real method of adaptation because it can settle only once and never again, whereas humans must continually find a new understanding of their environment, at least as long as their environment is changing. Bringing out this contingency of life is precisely Hölderlin's interest in this fragment, and in the prose commentary, he develops a clarifying argument deduced from his translation:

> The lonely school's [der einsamen Schule] capacity for the world. The innocence of pure knowledge [reines Wissen] as the soul of intelligence [Klugheit]. For intelligence is the art of remaining faithful in changing circumstances, knowledge the art of being sure in one's understanding in the midst of positive errors. If our understanding has been exercised intensely, it retains its strength even in diffusion [im Zerstreuten]; inasmuch as it easily recognizes alien things [das Fremde] by its own honed sharpness, and so is not easily confused [irre] in uncertain situations.[9]

This untraditional — or better yet, antitraditional — reading of Pindar's verses is achieved by misreading them, perhaps even consciously so, and Hölderlin thus performs a symbolic act of "unfaithfulness of wisdom" against the wisdom of Pindar. His practice of translation inverts the trust in the wisdom of age asked of the child and turns it into a general mistrust in the authority of knowledge, be it an experienced adult authority or that of Greek antiquity.

To praise benevolently what is present is the deepest and most crucial concern of this fragment. The result is a plea to respect both of the forms that intelligence (*Klugheit*) can take because it sometimes allows adaptation yet at other times causes "diffusion" and distraction. Hölderlin develops awareness for the doubleness of experience; the experience of the present here and now, while it can be sharpened, might also be lost completely in every changing instant. Only by praising what is present, with a benevolent temper and without being distracted by knowledge, or by what is not knowledge, can world and human be brought into contact. Especially for the poet, who like Hölderlin is in the process of breaking with the classical tradition and its model of a preexisting spiritual relation between mind and world, the question of how to establish this contact again through poetry becomes crucial, against the grain of traditional intuitions and despite the modern dominance of knowledge. Pindar's original version of this central line reads, "τῷ παρεόντι δ' ἐπαινήσαις ἑκών" (*tō pareonti d' epainēsais hekōn*)[10] and might be translated as "readily praise the person who is present"[11] or as "*assentiens autem ei quod praesens est*,"[12] as Hölderlin found it in the Greek-Latin edition he used as source. In that crucial line, the central function of "Praising . . . / That which is present" is carried by the word ἐπαινήσαις, *epainēsais*, which is derived from *epaineō*, meaning "to praise, to commend."[13] A paraphrase of the core interest of the fragment could thus be "to investigate the conditions of how to praise the present, that is, hearing and speaking to the here and now." Everything else in Hölderlin's rendering of the fragment is arranged to serve this investigation.

To understand the concept of praising, however, it is necessary to remember that the Greek term "to praise" is derived from another concept that denotes a certain genre of speech, namely the idea of *ainos*, a concept that originally denoted the telling of a brief story such as a fable at a specific occasion and with a particular purpose. With this linguistic relation between *ep-ainos* and *ainos* in mind, giving praise can be recognized as the most important instance of an *ainos*, of a story that interacts with those that are present. Given this etymology, it is worth noting that in Pindar's fragment, the use of *epainos* points precisely to the older sibling of *ainos*, in that Pindar reduces praise to situated awareness. It is this poetic awareness that Hölderlin underlines and amplifies as what we would call "situationally aware speech." The significance of the act of praising is shifted from more content-based approval or admiration to a mode of communication whose form signals responsiveness or responsibility in the face of the present. Whether consciously or not, Hölderlin evidently recognizes Pindar's indirect allusion to this etymological root of "to praise." Thus, the semantic root of *praise* or *epainos* becomes the central argument for the new translation, that is, "words spoken in response to the present."

If humans were like polyps, Hölderlin's translation reasons, they would never experience "alien things" (*das Fremde*), "positive errors," or "diffusion," suggesting that in Pindar's antiquity, perhaps the opposite of these modern experiences were true; for example, familiarity, positive intentionality, and calmness of mind. The mental sensations that Hölderlin lists in his prose commentary therefore define the state of the modern mind as opposed to that of antiquity. Being untrue to Greek wisdom, Hölderlin can oppose polyp and human, emphasizing that with the end of such Pindaric analogies between human and nature also has come the end of a Pindaric relation between mind, language, and world. Modern humans are not sedentary, nor does the world itself allow "knowledge" and "intelligence" to be obtained by learning the wisdom of the ancients. By attempting to find the wisdom of the ancients in their poetry, the moderns deprived themselves of the ability to use poetic speech according to their own minds and their own world.

Between 1802 and 1805, the years of writing the *Pindar Fragments*, many instances can be found in which Hölderlin strived to find a form of poetry that not only abstractly praises what is present — that speaks to a presence, whatever this would mean — but is also able to address what is physically and contemporaneously present. Besides his pointed mistranslation of the Pindar fragment and the subsequent return to the original meaning of *ainos* as a poetic tale told specifically for the here and now, during that period Hölderlin made two other uses of the ancient *ainos* idea of telling a fable, thus differentiating it from the task of the modern storyteller. Before turning to these other cases, a short look into the state of the fable in Greek antiquity is helpful to understand Hölderlin's gesture.

As noted earlier, *ainos* could be translated as "fable," yet this merely denotes a genre, especially Aesopic fables, and suppresses the situative, pragmatic meaning contained in the early Greek term.[14] Using the language of the late twentieth century, the classicist Gregory Nagy has pointed out that "it is better to think of the *ainos* as a mode of discourse, not as a genre."[15] This function as a "mode of discourse" is still present in Homer, who provides the following specific and very tangible example of an *ainos* in the *Odyssey*.

When Odysseus has already returned to Ithaca after fighting the Trojan War, but is still in disguise, he meets the swineherd Eumaeus, his former servant. They sit around the fire eating and drinking, and as it gets dark, a starry and cold night sets in. Odysseus has no coat with him, and in order to test the hospitality of Eumaeus, as well as to obtain a blanket, he tells a tale from the Trojan War. On a very cold night, he begins, he once begged the great Odysseus, next to whom he was sleeping, to give him some cloak or coat so he could cover himself because he had mistakenly left his own by the ships. In response, Odysseus sent away one of his men on a pretext of needing reinforcements. In his hurried departure, the man left his coat, which could now be used as cover against the cold night by the speaker, that is, the storytelling Odysseus in disguise. After he ends his brief story that already had begun by paralleling one cold night with another, the tale immediately establishes its intended function. Eumaeus responds by saying, "ὦ γέρον, αἶνος μέν τοι ἀμύμων, ὃν κατέλεξας" (ō geron, ainos men toi amymōn, hon katelexas) — "Old man, the tale [ainos] you have told is a good one,"[16] that is, he decodes the message of the story (ainos) based on the situation in which it is told and offers his visitor a blanket so that he can sleep comfortably. The *Odyssey* employs *ainos* here precisely in the sense of the living function of a tale or fable as Nagy defined it, as a mode of interactive discourse.

When suggesting that inventing fables is one way a rhetor can argue by way of an example, Aristotle's *Rhetoric* does not use *ainos*, but already uses *logos* as the term for Aesopic stories, when he writes "λόγοι, οἷον οἱ Αἰσώπειοι καὶ Λιβυκοί" (logoi, hoion hoi Aisōpeioi kai Libykoi) — "fables [logoi], such as those of Aesop and the Libyan."[17] Without going into further philological detail, one can see what this replacement suggests. The use of prose speech or poetry was distributed by Aristotle into general categories of occasions, uses, and genres, but the pragmatic role of the *ainos* as something employed as situationally aware speech contingent on particular occasions and for contingent ends is too complex to fit into this taxonomy. In fact, Aristotle was the first to speak extensively about the use of examples as *paradeigmata* with regard to fables, as a kind of informal logic by which an example is used to deploy a general rule, thus separating the use of fable from the uses for which fables always had been employed.[18]

The effects of Aristotle's estrangement of the *ainos* quality of short narratives only increased over time. This can be grasped particularly from the most important Roman treatise on rhetoric, Quintilian's *Institutio oratoria* (c. 95 AD). Fables now were ordered into an even stricter taxonomy than Aristotle's, one that displayed even less consciousness of the fable's pragmatic potential. Practically eliminating any residue of their *ainos* function, Quintilian allowed himself to evoke the use of fables only through a second-hand example that was in itself historical (e.g., Menenius Agrippa's use of the Aesopic fable of "The Belly and Its Members"), rather than providing a full first-hand example himself.[19] This dismissal of prosaic storytelling in favor of controlled, rhetorical *narratio* would influence the decline of the *ainos* quality in the subsequent centuries.

As indicated by Hölderlin's intuition, this loss of the fable's agency from Homer's *ainos* to its systematic suppression in rhetorical treatises had grown into a central problem for the state of poetry and literature around 1800. While drafting his *Pindar Fragments*, Hölderlin simultaneously jotted down an idea for an article he would never write — "On the Fable of the Ancients" ("Von der Fabel der Alten"), in which the term *fable* pertains not exclusively to the Aesopic fable, but also to myths and the general meaning of fable as fiction, plot, or topic of a fiction. The sketch lists a number of concepts and abstract ideas and does not specify which ancient authors Hölderlin had in mind. But one can still understand "On the Fable of the Ancients" as an attempt to pin down the lost state of the fable or other fictional narratives in which such stories carried a relation to the world that was immediate because their interpretation was not a theoretical question, but a physically, corporeal reaction. Stating the features of this lost actuality of fables, Hölderlin's list includes:

System
Relation. Movability
Different forms which these, despite the necessity of their formation,
    suffer as principles
Mythological content. / Heroic / Purely human
Higher morals
Connection between humans and spirits
Nature; as it takes effect, history[20]

Despite their fragmentary nature, these thoughts allow us to trace Hölderlin's attempt to sketch an *ainos*-like idea of fables.

In the speculative genre of prose poetics that Hölderlin sketches here, literary speech appears to be formed after principles that keep it in a kind of spiritual contact with both gods and humans while remaining dynamic and intuitive enough to be fully in touch with the occasion of its telling. As a direct recourse to the *Pindar Fragments*, this list also includes the term "infinity of wisdom" (*Unendlichkeit der Weisheit*) and shows us Hölderlin at work on the first half of an essay that in its final state very likely would have tried to repeat his argument from the *Pindar Fragments* by defining a philosophy of epic literature. This opposition between ancients and moderns would presumably have hinged on the fact that the ancients' fable existed in an "infinity of wisdom," whereas Hölderlin himself was still in search of a poetic language that indicated the "unfaithfulness of wisdom." Echoing directly what he had written earlier, this would be a mode in which the moderns could be "untrue" to the ancients in order to regain the ability to speak to their own present. Because "fable" is a term not usually related to the largely lyrical poet Hölderlin, his use here shows even more how his idea of reinventing a German poetry as a modern poetry was paralleled by an interest also in reinventing the genre of poetics in general, a project that is more apparent in Schlegel's works and notes from the very same years.

Hölderlin's other use of the word "fable" depicts the concept much more clearly as a desired, yet for now impossible form of literature. It occurs in the third version of his late hymn "Patmos," in a stanza concerned with the impossibility of singing a *Fabel* as the ancients had done:

> John. Christ. This latter now I wish
> To sing, like Hercules or the island which
> Was held and saved. . . . But that's
> Impossible. A fate is different. More marvelous.
> More rich to sing. Immeasurable [*Unabsehlich*]
> The fable ever since.[21]

Like the mythologies that tell of Hercules's refuge from a storm on the island of Kos, Hölderlin would like to tell of the refuge that John found on the island of Patmos. But "Immeasurable / The fable ever since": that is, in the age since Christ, any fiction of that kind has become increasingly impossible. *Unabsehlich* literally means "unpredictable," unforeseeable, both out of sight and incalculable.[22] The end of this old model is definite, as Hölderlin couldn't have put any more clearly than by saying, "But that's / Impossible" — a verdict spoken among those who know they must be looking for another way to tell and sing to their time.

In "On the Fable of the Ancients" and in "Patmos," Hölderlin sought an idea of the fable that tries to come to terms with how literature and poetry have become irreducibly unsituated, that is, temporally and physically out of touch with the world and its human speakers, readers, and listeners. Understanding a fable had now become necessarily an intellectual procedure. In the existing genres of fictional speech, it was no longer possible to interpret a story with a reaction, as Eumaeus did in the *Odyssey*. Hölderlin's excavation of the hidden Pindaric reference to *ainos* as "pragmatic fable" in "Unfaithfulness of Wisdom" further clarified this lack. The fable is Hölderlin's boundary concept marking in retrospect the threshold of the end of the age of the *ainos* while at the same time pressing for its return in modernity. Hölderlin's poetic intuition is an indicator for the general need around 1800 to understand how a here and now could be addressed through literary speech. His rigorous work on lyrical and narrative forms, as well as on poetic concepts, marks literature's lack of awareness about what must be spoken of, about what and how its present needs to hear. Like Hölderlin's method when articulating the *ainos* concept, this lack in modern literature runs below philosophical discourses, literary theory, and the history of ideas, surfacing at first only when emerging within other texts and contexts.

A Here and Now in Poetics

One such case in which a fable develops an *ainos*-like agency is in an essay by Kleist. But first, a brief look into the state of the Aesopic fable around 1800 will show what is at stake when Kleist allows the fable to regain some of its ancient potential. As we've seen, a dialectical relation exists between the rise of Aristotelian systematicity and the disappearance of the *ainos*. Although Hölderlin sensed this dialectic around 1800 and tried to open the space for a new and different mode of thinking about *ainos*-based poetics, Lessing's famous *Treatises on the Fable* (*Abhandlungen über die Fabel*, 1759) and Johann Gottfried Herder's *On the Aesopic Fable* (*Von der Aesopischen Fabel*, 1787) were not yet able to go this far.

Lessing and Herder were no longer approaching the fable as La Fontaine had in the 1680s, as an ancient genre updated into a pleasing poem for the moderns, but by locating it within a taxonomy of fictional literature.[23] However, this approach led them to doubt the fable's place in this modern system, most vividly in Herder's remark "that to me any such distinctions of the fable appear as futile efforts... and that it cannot interest us from which compartment of the Linnean system of nature the creatures of a fable are taken."[24] Both Lessing and Herder also criticized the Aristotelian differentiation of the "real," factual example from history as opposed to the "invented" examples of parable and fable. Against the exemplary truth of history, they remark that a certain historical situation is highly unlikely to occur twice, which makes the practical persuasiveness of historical examples close to zero.[25] The quality of the real must hence be transferred away from historical anecdotes to the fable. Whereas the comparison made by the parable is concerned only with the possibility of a relation, writes Lessing, the fable addresses cases with both its "inner probability" (*innere Wahrscheinlichkeit*) *and* its representational reality.[26] Herder equally noted that the parable perhaps puts forth a probability, yet only the fable can add an "inner necessity of the subject itself" (*innere Nothwendigkeit der Sache selbst*), which makes it reach the necessary force to truly convince. Ethel Matala de Mazza has summarized this argument with a similar attention to the afterlife of the *ars topica* in narration: "The higher realism that Lessing grants the fable originates from a reality effect [*effet de réel*] of a fiction that acts as if there were no fiction and that creates the as-if of such real presence [*Realpräsenz*], the easier and the more manageable the respective case is and the less the narrative has to lose itself in the details of historical circumstances."[27]

Persuasion is thus dismissed in favor of truth in narrative prose, which is convincing for its inner logic and its necessity of succession. While such dismissals of traditional rhetoric and rhetorical analyses show a turn toward describing a pragmatic force of literature in its ability "not just simply to persuade [*überreden*], but by virtue of the presented truth itself to convince [*überzeugen*]" (Herder),[28] they were still dependent on the terms and categories of the Aristotelian and Quintilian tradition to arrive at this differentiation. Lessing even located himself within this genealogy of theories of the fable when he argued that the "amusing" fable of La Fontaine should be rescued from this misuse and returned to the didactic purpose it had for orators.[29] Lessing and Herder undoubtedly shared Hölderlin's intuition that a prose form such as the fable could touch a here and now in a way comparable to the classicist poetry or prose in its timeliness and pragmatist effect. Yet contrary to his intuition and theoretical argument, Lessing's own fables very much followed the traditional model. This paradox between the theory and practice of fables could perhaps be grasped by saying that *asking* for a new place for the prose fable in life is the signal for the impossibility of *using* fables this way at the same time.

A way to resolve this paradoxical tension, which Lessing can only identify, was put forth by Kleist. Instead of simply declaring that the fable is untimely because of its classicist, unrealistic form since La Fontaine, Kleist did not theorize about it but rather used the fable in order to talk about prose itself. He achieved this in his essay "On the Gradual Production of Thoughts while Speaking" (*"Über die allmähhlige Verfertigung der Gedanken beim Reden"*), which is commonly known as being concerned with the various settings and emotional conditions in which the movement of thought heavily depends on the simultaneous utterance of speech. However, if we examine Kleist's text not in those terms or in terms of its declared interest in rhetoric, but instead by focusing on the use it makes of the fable and other prose narratives as examples, his essay reveals its real interest: prose poetics. Aristotle's *Rhetoric* reduced the fable from the *ainos* to mere exemplary use;

Kleist's essay intends to reverse this development and regain the ability of the fable to address the here and now.

As Lessing's and Herder's fable essays had done, Kleist's text first approaches the fable within the Aristotelian didactic limits of presenting it as an example. To illustrate its main thesis, the essay draws on seven examples of various types, including a fable. In chronological order, these examples are an autobiographical anecdote with Kleist's sister; a historical anecdote of Molière and his maid; a historical anecdote, Mirabeau's "thunderbolt" speech; a scientific analogy using the electrical "Kleistian jar"; La Fontaine's fable about the animals ill with the plague; the liveliness of speaking in company; and finally the scene of a public oral examination. Given this dense succession of diverse material, the text does not resemble a treatise. Its experimental incorporation of smaller prose texts can more accurately be described as a prose montage. The argument runs only along the seams of its examples and breaks up their presentation, at times producing a rapid oscillation between the narrator's voice and that of the quoted speaker. In fact, the essay's narrator speaks directly only in a very small number of lines, some of which are written only by formal requirements or to prompt quotations, such as the epistolary opening that addresses the essay's dedicatee, Rühle von Lilienstern, or a reference to the allegory according to which an axle exists that connects the wheel of thought to a wheel of speech.

Since this is neither a dramatic text nor a representation of a fictive dialogue but an essay ostensibly about what language can do, the ensemble of quotations with different speakers at first appears to be a patchwork of prose texts that each force their own form and genre onto Kleist's text. The first objective of this montage is, of course, to provide various scenes of spontaneous speaking as rhetorical examples, such as Kleist's own anecdote about talking to his sister as a means of accelerating his thinking or the sudden unfiltered burst of words that occurs when speaking in a lively atmosphere. From these content-specific examples, the text deduces arguments such as the following, which advances its general hypothesis step by step: "It is a strangely inspiring thing to have a human face before us as we speak; and often a look announcing that a half-expressed thought is already grasped gives us its other half's expression."[30]

It seems at first that the Mirabeau anecdote and the La Fontaine fable are used in the same way, as complementary cases in which the gradual production of thoughts while speaking can be observed. Yet in the form of the essay — the way prose is montaged into one cohesive draft — these two examples stand in significant opposition to the other examples. First, they are the only examples containing direct speech, which they signal by quotation marks that doubly verify that the reader is not only being confronted with live speech, but that this live speech is an exact quotation from historical (Mirabeau) or fictive live speech (La Fontaine). However, Kleist only partly quotes word for word. In fact, he freely alters these external texts, exchanging, for example, the wolf in La Fontaine's fable for a fox. Rather than marking these insertions accurately as citations, his goal is to produce the effect of an external voice speaking in his essays. Second, and even more powerfully, Kleist interrupts both the anecdote and the fable by fragmenting the quoted direct speech via interjections by the narrator. Similar to modernist montage techniques, this mutual interruption of different layers and voices has the effect of a stylistic intensification through formalization, including the modernist phenomenon of momentary confusion that the reader has to sustain. Here is an example from Kleist's rendering of the Mirabeau anecdote:

> "Yes," Mirabeau replied, "we have heard the King's command" — I am certain that beginning thus humanely he had not yet thought of the bayonets with which he would finish: "yes, my dear sir," he repeated, "we have heard it" — as we see, he is not yet exactly sure what he intends. "But by what right" — he continues, and suddenly a source of colossal ideas is opened up to him — "do you give us orders here? We are the representatives of the nation." — That was what he needed! "The nation does not take orders. It gives them." — which launches him there and then to the highest pitch of boldness. — "And to make

myself perfectly plain to you"—and only now does he find words to express how fully his soul has armed itself and stands ready to resist: "tell your king we shall not move from here unless forced to by bayonets."—Whereupon, well content with himself, he sat down.[31]

Even if what is in quotation marks was the original wording of Mirabeau's speech which it is not, we would still need the narrator of the essay to intervene with his comments to reach the suspense necessary for understanding that something significant for the argument of the essay is happening in this statement.

That is to say that this anecdote does not actually convey an example on the level of content. All Kleist knew was that Mirabeau had provoked the king's ambassador with his actual comments, not whether they were spontaneous. Including the anecdote in the essay implies that it draws its purpose from being a self-contained form, which in return affects the form of Kleist's text itself. Hints about how this strange relation between the essay and the anecdote unfolds are contained in Kleist's syntactic and diacritical arrangement of the words of the essay's narrator, which cut in on those of the speaker in the anecdote. These reciprocal interruptions are the necessary result of the essay's attempt to incorporate an autonomously functional anecdote about a historical speech act of political significance. The main text can achieve this only by interrupting and adapting it, effectively working to sustain its own coherence against the strong form of the anecdote.

When presenting La Fontaine's fable "The Animals Ill with the Plague" ("Les animaux malades de la peste") one page later, Kleist then repeats this effect of mutual interruption between main text and incorporated text. It becomes clear that the two are related not only on the level of their textual incorporation, but also as the only cases of political speech in Kleist's essay. More than the somewhat unclear origin of the recorded version of Mirabeau's speech in a posthumous volume of his works that Kleist used, however, La Fontaine's fable exists in a printed, canonically fixed form.[32] And more than in

the case of the anecdote, the fable submits its independent, autonomous form to the essay, which can neither distract from nor eliminate this form, but can only structurally incorporate it and make use
of its preexisting formedness. It does so by recognizing that the fable
requires being interrupted — even more than the anecdote did — in
order to produce the desired argument: the fox did not know what
he was supposed to say when he addresses the lion and wants to avoid
being identified as the most evil animal:

> "Sire," says the fox, wishing to ward the lightning off himself, "in your zeal
> and generosity you have gone too far. What if you have done a sheep or two
> to death? Or a dog, that vile creature? And: quant au berger," he continues,
> for this is the chief point: "on peut dire"; though he still does not know what?
> "qu'il meritoit tout mal"; trusting to luck; and with that he has embroiled
> himself, "etant"; a poor word but which buys him time: "de ces gens la", and
> only now does he hit upon the thought that gets him out of his difficulty: "qui
> sur les animaux se font un chimérique empire." — And he goes on to prove that
> the donkey, the bloodthirsty! (devourer of grass and plants) is the most fitting
> sacrifice. And with that they fall on him and tear him to pieces.[33]

The explanation of this formal agency of the fable in the essay
takes into account the specific *ainos* quality of all fables. Of course,
La Fontaine's original contains no such thing as "a gradual production of thoughts while speaking," but as a fable, it already comes with
the formal capacity to produce the effect with which Kleist's essay is
concerned. The essay's central interest is not the dynamics of what
speech does or can do, but rather the dynamic situative function
already included in prose forms. By breaking up the fable to bring
forth its capacities to convey speech acts, Kleist negated the historical manifestation of a canonical genre and one of its most famous
authors and in turn retrieved the *ainos* capability of "Les animaux
malades de la peste." That is, if it is told in the right way and at the
right time, the fable can convey thoughts and cause reactions in a way
that it could not if one kept it as an integral, untouchable work by La
Fontaine.

The fable enters and affects Kleist's text because of its closed form. Its content is secondary, since many other fables contain similar political and potentially spontaneous speech acts. The essay incorporates this form by interlacing it with its own form, using syntax and punctuation to render separate speech acts where in the fable there is only a monologue and by interrupting and commenting on the fable as if the storyteller who tells it is being interrupted by the frame's narrator. The immediate effect is that the fable's literal prose is turned into a virtual oral speech.

However, there is a second and more consequential effect: this oral speech contaminates the prose of the essay itself, resulting in an altered form of prose. In other words, by breaking up the classicist prose style of La Fontaine with a formally experimental direct speech, Kleist arrived at a new form of nonclassicist prose. This prose speech regained the Homeric awareness of the pragmatic force latent in any short prose narrative by freeing it from its fixed, didactic, and exemplary uses since its classification by Aristotle. "On the Gradual Production of Thoughts while Speaking" is thus a condensed poetics that addresses the prosaic here and now of modernity. Perhaps one should consequently think of Kleist's essay more as a manifesto that tried to reframe prose poetics as a counterpart of rhetorical speech — "The gradual production of thoughts while *writing as if one were speaking*." What Lessing and Herder were able to express only in traditional poetical terms and what Hölderlin could develop only through lyrical poetry, Kleist achieved most convincingly by reducing the fable form to its origin as a tale told with pragmatic intent.

Yet as Hölderlin had intuited, the modern pragmatic tale differs crucially from the ancient pragmatic tale. In modernity, no *ainos* relation can exist between fictional speech and its listeners on the level of content, only on the level of form. Mind and world are caught in dualism, and neither the life form of the polyp nor the fabulous fox can be made to resonate with the human animal. In looking back at the pre-Aristotelian *ainos*, a distinction can be made between the representative and the impressive function. As Francisco-Rodríguez

Adrados writes, "*Ainos* is, then, a 'story', but it may be a story that, rather than having a representative function, narrating something real or fictitious, has an impressive one: to advise, eulogize (and, of course, criticize)."[34] The fable in modernity does not function via representation, and while the impressive function remains, it cannot be established through content; it must be established solely through form. It is its form as a fable that exerts an impressive function on Kleist's text, which incorporates it while talking over it. In this dazzling play between essay voice and fable voice, Kleist's text achieves its own impressive function as an *ainos*. It performs on the textual level what it tries to argue on the content level: that formal interruptions of a text by an external text form have the power to set thought in motion.

Since this argument is made not through actual orality, but rather in an essay that employs the formal *ainos* of a fable, Kleist demonstrates a poetology of prose. Kleist shows that rhetoric no longer includes fables as means of persuasion, as it had since Aristotle, but that modern prose has regained the impressive function *ainos* used to have on the formal level, not on the epistemological level of content. If this assessment is true, Kleist's essay speaks of the susceptibility — or impressibility — of modern life by formal, structural interferences. In short, "On the Gradual Production of Thoughts while Speaking" performs what it argues: just as the fable's form gave an impetus to Kleist's formless essay, any form of prose might interfere and interrupt us and thus potentially support our current argumentation. When Kleist remarks toward the end of the essay, "For it is not *we* who know things but pre-eminently a certain *condition* of ours which knows" ("*Denn nicht wir wissen, es ist allererst ein gewisser* Zustand *unserer, welcher weiß*"), "condition" denominates not only a static situation, but precisely the situation of being interrupted — interrupted by the here and now of a prose form.[35] This condition is the situation in which life is affected by a novella, a proverb, or a fable. And the reason life can be so affected by them is because they have form, not because they have content. Kleist's essay ascribes the function of everyday interference to short narrative prose forms after 1800.

The argument in Kleist's text can be further illustrated by relating it to Koselleck's well-known thesis from his essay "Historia Magistra Vitae," that after 1800, historical knowledge no longer had the power to provide guidance to life because the relation between past and future had become unreliable.[36] Lessing and Herder had dismissed historical examples in favor of the didactic function of the fables and thus sensed the instructive primacy that form had over content. While historical examples no longer could guide life, Koselleck showed that an anecdote could have an influence on modern life because it is a narrative prose form. The mode of discourse that Kleist develops in his essay is a dynamic stream of thoughts and words in which each one ideally provides the formal cause for the next, a formational *energeia* that might spill over from prose into life. Unlike argumentation based on topical knowledge, arguing or writing by compiling series of historical or other examples, Kleist's form-based argumentation provided for an afterlife of the *ars topica* solely on the level of form — form as the teacher of life.[37]

Fabulatory Philosophy

The general argument of Kleist is that one first needs to be affected or interrupted by a prose form before one can speak of the moment and of thoughts occurring right before that interruption. Located at the opposite end of modernity, a wholly different and more explicit case is Blumenberg's last project, which could be called his "fabulatory philosophy." Working with fables and various shorter anecdotes for almost two decades led Blumenberg to excavate the *ainos* nature of the fable. He argued that reading and understanding a fable has the deeply philosophical quality of affecting us in our current life moment while at the same time forcing us to observe ourselves in this very moment.

One of Blumenberg's main criticisms of the 1970s was directed against the academic second-degree philosophy that dealt only with the work of other philosophers, shying away from philosophy's origins, that is, the actual questions posed to humans by the world and their lives. This criticism goes back to Blumenberg's training in the Husserlian tradition that pressed for a return to true philosophical problems. In an initial 1974 text devoted to his fable studies, Blumenberg traced an Aesopic fable through the history of philosophy to show how each reception caused a renarration and thus a slight variation of the fable's plot, accentuating different particularities of the fable each time, a phenomenon in the history of ideas he calls "reoccupation" (*Umbesetzung*). Blumenberg retells the Aesopic fable that is his object in the following way:

> An astronomer was in the habit of going out regularly in the evening to observe the stars. Once as he was strolling through the outskirts of the town with his attention completely fixed on the heavens, he fell into a well before he knew what was happening to him. While he was howling and shouting, a passerby who heard his pitiful tones came up and, as soon as he found out what had happened, remarked, "My good fellow, while you're trying to watch things in the heavens, you don't even see things on the earth."[38]

While this "original" is part of the Aesopic corpus, the philosophical reception history of this fable only begins, Blumenberg remarks, when in Plato's *Theaetetus*, Socrates tells a version of the fable in which he explicitly names the astronomer and the passerby. Socrates turned the Aesopic fable into an anecdote about the very first philosopher, Blumenberg argues, by revealing that it was Thales of Miletus who falls and that the passerby was his Thracian housemaid, who, before responding to Thales directly, first of all bursts into laughter about her boss.[39] Blumenberg clarifies that he is on the side of the fable, and not on the side of the metaphilosopher merely observing the scene of the fable. Like Thales in the fable, he argues, philosophy itself should leave the reality of the common people, rise into heavenly transcendence, and then be brought back down to earth when reality strikes and the laughter of the common folk requires that it accept its inherent worldliness. What is not included in the dialectic of this fable, and hence what remains outside of philosophy itself, he argues, is the observer who conceives of philosophy as a closed scene approachable only from the distance of irony and what he called "theory" in the original sense, the mere remote beholding of a subject matter that excludes any possibility of ever interacting with it.

The reason for Blumenberg's interest in the fable, however, is not only to argue for a return of philosophy to metaphysical questions, given the "humor of pure theory."[40] His interest goes much further because his choice of a fable as object is itself already a methodological demand for a practice of philosophy that remains in touch with the reality of the common people and the everyday. With a similar interest in keeping in touch with philosophy's base, Blumenberg had proposed in 1960 that philosophy begin to understand its own medium of language through a "metaphorology." Metaphors, he argued, while often appearing in opposition to concepts, are equally crucial to thinking through philosophy itself while at the same time offering a position from which the limits of conceptuality could be counterweighed. This return to a liquid, nonconceptual state of philosophy was to be achieved not through theoretical quarrels, but by embracing the metaphorical reality of philosophical poetics. Conscious questions about the world and about the human could thus be brought back to the here and now and kept from becoming irrelevant. Because "absolute metaphors" such as light for truth "prove resistant to terminological claims and cannot be dissolved into conceptuality," Blumenberg writes, they already offer a truly philosophical exercise.[41]

The plan for a metaphorology never came to term, but the problem of language returned to his philosophy when he began working closely with Aesopic fables. This fabulatory phase had its peak in a 1987 book, *The Laughter of the Thracian Woman: A Protohistory of Theory*, and brought about what one might call a fabulatory philosophy, as I will lay out below. Because the book, solely dedicated to this short fable, was one of Blumenberg's last major works, the Thales fable marks both the first and final step of this project. Fables had now become philosophical exercises.

Fabulatory philosophy starts for Blumenberg when a philosophical question resembles a scene in a fable; it further becomes a programmatic statement — and, in fact, a break from accepted methods of philosophy — when this fabulatory philosophy is used to distance oneself from both the questions and, more importantly, the straightforward rational style of academic philosophy.

To understand how far Blumenberg's alternative philosophical practice had taken him, it is necessary to engage with the corpus of fable-related texts he published in newspapers and journals.[42] In one such 1985 *Neue Zürcher Zeitung* piece called "Unknown Aesopica: From Newly Found Fables," Blumenberg proposes a fundamental correction of the whole Thales complex. The Thracian woman's call to a "return to realism" is now the primary function of the fable, and Blumenberg stresses further that this is one of the few Aesopic fables involving humans.[43] He argues that Socrates, in revealing that it was Thales who fell into the well, had not only provided the fable with the historical specificity that turned it into an anecdote, but also permanently transferred it from the realm of storytelling to the realm of philosophy. In addition, Socrates realized that this Aesopic fable contained only human protagonists because it encrypted "the secret of Aesop," that the origin of philosophy is also the origin of the Aesopic tale: "The forefather of all philosophy was also that of all fables."[44] Respectively, Socrates and Plato had recast the Thales fable as the Thales anecdote to ground the whole of philosophy in a lineage of historical names, which allowed them, most importantly, to insert themselves into this lineage: Thales, Socrates, Plato, Diogenes Laertius, and so on. Thales thus stands in as the first philosopher simply to replace the mythical storyteller Aesop, whom Socrates deemed unnamable because he was neither a historically reliable fact nor a philosopher suitable for foreshadowing the dialogical, axiomatic Socratic tradition. Once this lineage had become accepted as both a study method for philosophy and a standard for reception, no one could return to the fabulistic philosophy independent of time and space, or at the least, anyone who did so could no longer be relevant in a post-Socratic discourse.

With this fundamental claim, which reveals a fabulistic philosophy without names as the foundation of all philosophy's known lineages, Blumenberg intends to reconnect his own late modernity to the nameless pre-Socratic and non-Socratic fabulatory philosophy. For Blumenberg, revealing "the secret of Aesop" suggests the opposite of Socrates's and Plato's move, eliminating the historical person from the sphere of philosophy altogether. The universal fable, not the indexical anecdote, conjures up the realism that philosophy persistently needed and needs.[45]

Even Blumenberg's diachronic study of the Thales anecdote in his 1987 book can be reinterpreted within this interest. The study intends to reveal the irreducible presence of the Aesopic fable in each appearance of the anecdote throughout history, exhibiting at each point of reception the persistence of a fabulatory philosophy. This permanence of the fable, in turn, allows Blumenberg to render irrelevant the philosopher who applies it, those historical thinkers who, misled by Socrates' and Plato's method of naming, believed that their use of the Thales anecdote alone secured their place in the history of philosophical thought, when all they did by turning to the fable was to act within philosophy's universal medium. The specificity of the Thales anecdote is hence one of a double deception because it not only deceives its receiver about the true origin of philosophy, but also prevents the fable's autocorrective function within philosophy because the act of naming made an identification with the fable's anonymous, fallen thinker almost impossible. Blumenberg's radical claim can thus be clarified. Since the time of Socrates, the rules of academic philosophy have been erected on the scaffolding of two principles: speaking about a philosophical anecdote and focusing only on the moral dictum attached to a fable. These principles have prevented all true philosophers from wrapping themselves in thought itself, that is, in what the fable has to say.

This historical originality of the fable acquires its methodological groundwork in "The Misunderstanding of the Lifeworld" ("*Das Lebensweltmißverständnis*"), a longer essay from 1986. Blumenberg here engages the idea of the lifeworld, Husserl's concept regarding an imperceptible yet omnipresent background of metaphysical assumption in relation to which all human thought, belief, and culture always already occurs. Because nothing in the lifeworld can be known directly, Husserl hoped to regain fundamental philosophical questions by finding them implicated in the lifeworld. Blumenberg varies this constraint by suggesting that despite the lifeworld's lack of expressivity and predication, it still possesses a form of language. Involving the lifeworld in his fabulatory philosophy allowed him to argue that the language of the lifeworld is what fables are expressing, and given the secret beginning of philosophy in Aesop, his claim could be extended to suggest that fables are the origin or preliminary form not only of philosophical anecdote, but also of logical conclusions, moral maxims, and even of universals and perhaps of any philosophy.[46]

Blumenberg's position confirms the modern ability of short prose narratives developed in Chapter 1 and also confirms the intuitions of Hölderlin and Kleist that the fable as a specific case indicates this historical development. His explanation of why the fable links the analysis of the lifeworld with the practice of philosophy contains the most compact program of his whole fabulistic philosophy. He writes that the lifeworld

> has its stories that might institute pensiveness, but they make thinking as a conditional relationship between question and answer obsolete. To draw a "moral" from a story and attach it to a fable is to us perhaps the sole remaining trace of the transgression of a particular condition [*Überschreitung eines Zustandes*], namely, when it was obvious [*von selbst zu verstehen*] what was meant by a story. That is why long ago we began to be amused by the inadequacy of inherited moral conclusions and the rich meaning of ancient fables to which these morals seem to be attached, like helpless annotations. At some point, transportable sentences were needed that made the story seem superfluous, and then questions about these sentences were needed, to which they [the sentences] could have been given as answers. This procedure might have been shorter and helped save time, since stories always have a degree of circuitousness. But no one could know that the short circuit between question and answer triggered a new and more vast circuitousness, namely, to put all

given answers to the same question in competition, to play them off against each other in order to get closer to the distant goal of the exclusiveness of one single valid answer.[47]

Here, at the end of his essay on the lifeworld, Blumenberg presents a morphology of Western philosophy *in nuce*. He begins with the pre-Socratic Aesopic fable and concludes with the technical ideality of the "short-circuit" relationship between question and answer that Descartes demanded. This genealogy of philosophy ends with a state in which every response to a question must exist independently of time or place and leaves the philosopher diametrically opposed to the storyteller's here and now. In this hunt for perfect definitions,[48] the philosophical fables can cause nothing but laughter: "That is why long ago we began to be amused by the inadequacy of inherited moral conclusions and the rich meaning of ancient fables." Adverse to requiring solitary, straightforward answers, Blumenberg argues that the whole multitude of questions and answers potentially contained in a fable should be posed and restored.

Blumenberg's idea of a fabulatory philosophy thus proposes a return to a speculative, storytelling philosophy that is able to elicit questions from the realism of any life situation. His fable books relate to this project as exercises in which one can study how fables may be discovered beneath the anecdotes we hear of historical people and their deeds. Such a proposal stands in full agreement with Hölderlin's and Kleist's concern with the fable not only as the place where language can reach its full poetico-philosophical potential, but also as the archetype of narrative speech that holds a life-related core within it, and allows it to address its here and now. *Ainos* is not the word that Blumenberg uses to denominate the philosophical, that is, Aesopic, fable, yet the definitions of the *ainos* match the situatedness and immediacy of telling a fable that Blumenberg seeks, as well as a fable's enigmatic quality, which urges philosophical unraveling.

Steering clear of strictly philosophical terminology, Blumenberg selects "nonunderstanding" (*Unverstand*) and "pensiveness"

(*Nachdenklichkeit*) as the two notions that describe the fable's *ainos* phenomenality. Both account for the decisive effect that the condition of thinking through fables creates in the mind. On the one hand, "nonunderstanding" works as the opposite to "obviousness" (*Selbstverständlichkeit*), the Husserlian definition of the pregiven, "always already" perception of the lifeworld. "Pensiveness," on the other hand, closely resembles the Kleistian "certain *condition* of ours which knows," the idle state consisting of passive and active knowing where thinking occurs with interruption but not on methodical paths. Yet "pensiveness" does not denote the activity of "being pensive"; rather, it points to a mood of an insistent, not yet resolvable pensiveness that yearns for answers, as David Adams has accurately translated.[49] With both concepts, Blumenberg emphasizes the actual lived situation when one is faced with a fable — not the mere reading of a text, but the embodied effectiveness of prose narratives as the original scene of a topical conversation. To write the reception of a fable is therefore to write a history of a particular pensive mood.

Like Hölderlin and Kleist, Blumenberg here is acutely interested in following closely how a fable emerges as a semantic agent in the world. The here and now of a fable situation is a middle ground between the edge of the lifeworld and the edge of a life, and only on this ground is insight given into both. The anecdotes and fables Blumenberg investigates therefore cause narrative frictions within the self-evidence of lifeworld as they point to unexpressed contingencies and thus cause nonunderstanding and especially pensiveness in their readers.[50] Blumenberg outlines these founding procedures of his fabulatory philosophy in a short 1980 essay titled "Pensiveness" also initially published in the *Neue Zürcher Zeitung*:

> Humanists and philologists have always been struck by the inadequate or non-existent proportion between these maxims and the stories to which they are assigned. If one has surrendered to the pensiveness that the story induces, then its "moral," the result that is supposedly to be derived from it, is often not only sobering, but dismaying and annoying in its nonunderstanding

[*Unverstand*]. Although almost none of the teachings can be declared completely wrong, they are in themselves somewhat peculiar and inexplicably inappropriate.[51]

Here, nonunderstanding is the refusal or inability to give oneself over to the fable's pensiveness, which is "exhibited in the incongruity between the fable and its moral."[52] But at the same time, nonunderstanding is also the reason for turning back to the original fable itself, posing questions to the nonunderstanding left by former commentators.

Among Blumenberg's various journal and newspaper pieces about fables is also an article called "Of Nonunderstanding: Glosses on Three Fables," which presents three brief essays about three fables that are merely concerned with the possible nonunderstanding that their factual (or imagined) commentators have had.[53] Nonunderstanding thus negatively denotes the space between a fable and its possible answers, an incomprehensibility the fable opens between life and lifeworld that pensiveness can positively occupy. "One of the descriptions of pensiveness," explains Blumenberg, "is that whatever comes to mind is allowed to pass through one's head. Pensiveness is an experience of freedom, especially the freedom of digression." Deeply opposed to this fabulatory pensiveness is well-ordered thought — unless it invalidates existing answers and leads to perplexity and helplessness. Reminding thought of its need for pensiveness is the only function of ordering the mind, "leading thought back to its origin and base in pensiveness."[54] To illustrate pensiveness, Blumenberg can turn once more to a concrete example, the Aesopic fable "The Old Man and Death": "An old man who had travelled a long way with a bundle of sticks found himself so weary that he cast it down and called for Death. Death came straightway at his call and asked him what he wanted. The old man answered, 'Help in loading my burden on my back again.'"[55]

This fable represents for Blumenberg "the shortest possible story" (*kleinstmögliche Geschichte*), the minimum of a narrative prose form that still causes a maximum of friction against the lifeworld. The smaller the fable, the more pensiveness is created. Precisely at this point, Blumenberg's text continues to rely on the fable's *ainos*, pointing us to the fable's ability to radiate pensiveness that can in no way be described, summarized, or separated from the act of telling. Once a fable is told, it becomes active within the space surrounding those who listened. In this moment, the fable appears as an agent, carrying out something that could be called an act of prose. Through this act, any speaker or listener is addressed, and the fable creates a high tension toward its possible contexts and environments and develops the power to touch on anything that is present. "We think about where we stand because we were disturbed in not thinking about it" is Blumenberg's minimal description of this emergence of *ainos*.[56]

Finally, this alternative philosophy led Blumenberg to write his own variations of fables. His newspaper piece "Unknown Aesopica: From Newly Found Fables" contains three short parafables written in dialogue form in which three animals complain to Aesop about the way they were misrepresented in his fables. As the article's title announces, Blumenberg claims that all three are new findings of "unknown Aesopica" that he happened to have come upon. In a postscript, he even adds that he tried offering them for publication to a Frankfurt publisher, who refused them because "Aesop was not a German classic." Taking the position of a fictive editor, Blumenberg is able to remain at a distance from these parafables, which he obviously wrote himself, and thus follows the separation of fables and their author that he had seen as characteristic of a fabulatory philosophy. Since Aesop appears in these pieces, but is not a historically fixed philosopher/storyteller, Blumenberg calls them "intermediate forms between animal fable and anecdote," neither one nor the other. This form conjures the quotidian potential for fabulatory philosophy by its location in the momentary medium of the newspaper. Both narrative and medial form add to pensiveness, telling us that we are in a unique and unrepeatable fleeting contact with the inventor of the fable himself, performing, as it were, the origin of philosophy out of the lifeworld of the reader. Additionally, all three "complaints" have a self-reflexive form that allows each to investigate the rise of pensiveness by causing pensiveness about the way fables are written.

In the first parafable, a fish complains to Aesop that he is never included with the other animals in any of his fables, to which Aesop responds that the proverbial "mute as a fish" must have some truth to it, since the fish just wasted his only chance to say something relevant by complaining about other animals. Similarly, a wolf complains in the second parafable that Aesop constantly misrepresents him as being very talkative whenever he is just about to kill and eat another animal. Aesop responds by reminding the wolf that this false portrayal is of course the necessary condition for his appearance in the fable to begin with. The third parafable, "The Fox's Complaint," is different because the plaintiff here, as in Kleist's rendering of La Fontaine, uses his wit to speak so thoroughly that his arguments reach beyond the limits of the text itself, revealing most strikingly how fables work:

> The Fox, too, complained to Aesop. He made him look ridiculous with all the cleverness he imputed to him. "I am not smarter," the Fox said, "than I need to be in order to survive."
>
> "In return you are preventing others from surviving," Aesop pointed out to him. "Think about the chickens you are stealing."
>
> "They have their own art of survival," the Fox protested. "They have invented the easiest procedure to reproduce — they pursue it while seated."
>
> Aesop did not want to let the Fox get away with that. "You are confusing two things there. The chickens that you feed on can no longer make their kind by sitting. But you live on each time, and even better, meal by meal."
>
> The Fox did not relent. "But for my devouring chickens, the world would be full of chickens, as easy as it is for them to become many."
>
> Aesop took the objection in good grace. "That wouldn't be bad. Then even we slaves would have our daily egg and our chicken on Sundays."
>
> "But," the Fox triumphed, "you could no longer invent fables, because the interpreters and exegetes think they have recognized that your little stories are cryptic outcries of a slave's misery."

From Aesop's own hand we find the addition: Here Aesop was silent. He never told of just how clever he really had to find the Fox to be.[57]

Aesop's own fable creation amuses him so much that he falls silent — or, better yet, falls into a pensiveness, not so much about his own fable, but about his own life before the background of his lifeworld. This parafable collapses the name-based history of philosophy into ephemerality, but also provides us with the scene of a double *ainos*. The storyteller is struck by the way his fable points him to the condition of his own storytelling, just as we are struck by the fact that this story points us toward how a philosophy of storytelling should and could be developed.

As the self-reflexivity of this example shows, Blumenberg limited publishing such examples of a practiced fabulatory philosophy to cases in which they stand in for their own theory. To follow his own premise that fabulatory philosophers may not be named would have meant to publish all such fables under a pseudonym, or at least in similarly intricate editorial framing. From this perspective, most of his fable studies are fabulatory philosophies in which the author Blumenberg is simply the fictive framing avatar for an unknown, unnamed thinker whom the reader gets to observe as he or she is thrown into a pensiveness over revealing the "unknown Aesopica" at the substratum of the history of philosophy.

Kleist's concern was how prose can once again reach the formed, informed life in modernity, a problem his essay solves by help of the *ainos* of a fable that interrupts it and thus puts in practice what the essay itself could not set in motion through pure theory. Blumenberg's concern, and hence his turn to the fable, is different because he is not trying to regain the production of prose, but the relevance of thought itself. This brings out the responsive side of the *ainos*, the pensive captivation that prosaic richness exerts from minimal stories. Both sides of the *ainos* — setting a prose form in motion and bringing to thought a nontheoretical, prosaic space — arise out of Kleist's and Blumenberg's intuition that reviving the fable can address the here and now of life in modernity. For both, the moment of interruption or "disturbance" is crucial in this regard because it never merely signifies distraction or disturbance, but the intervention of what is relevant, similar to the significance Hölderlin had found in the calculated "caesura" (*Cäsur*), which can reveal "a pure word" (*das reine Wort*).[58] Blumenberg's pensiveness is the interruption of the *vita laborans*, forcing the individual to break from this modernity and to transport themself into an intermissive *vita contemplativa* in which the Kleistian "condition" arises. In an essay about the pragmatism of rhetoric, Blumenberg pointed out that speech is a substitution for action ("rhetorical substitution in the compulsion to act"),[59] yet in his fable phase, he inverted this observation in order to relate fable and action.[60]

Three genuinely modern narrative prose forms — the novella, proverb, and fairy tale — occupy the space thus held open by the fable as a placeholder in the afterlife of *ars topica*. The three chapters that follow render more tangible how these narrative prose forms cause a pensiveness that can influence actions by halting and altering life. In modernity, any ponderer — anyone who allows such interruptions and formal interferences of their lifeworld — can unearth the Aesopic discourse that it takes to recognize the relevance of topics. This is what is required of literary speech after the *ars topica* for it to elicit the action that matters in the *vita activa*, to use Arendt's definition, whose relation to short forms will be analyzed in Chapter 6.

CHAPTER THREE

Form: The Novella and the Agency

of Short Narrative Forms

The afterlife of the *ars topica* is to be found in the pragmatic potential of short discursive forms. For Kleist, as we saw, it is the formal properties of the fable as a narrative prose form that give it a purchase on modern life because after 1800, the mere content of exemplary texts increasingly failed to speak to the era and its rapid changes of mind and world. And later, Blumenberg, in seeking retrospectively to recover the *ainos* qualities of the fable for modernity, stressed the effect on its readers: the stimulation of "nonunderstanding" and "pensiveness," the subjective postures fundamental to the pursuit of thinking genuinely in the present moment. The novella offers many of the same pragmatic and affective potentials, but a simple, yet critical feature distinguishes the novella: the phenomenality caused by its form.

Since Schlegel's studies of the novella in the late 1790s, the novella has been contrasted with the anecdote to understand its genre. An anecdote merely reports an incident — a tailor is mistaken for a count because of his fine coat, for example. A novella looks *through* the incident to tell a story about the world. Yet one could also imagine the anecdote about the tailor belonging to a different genre, such as a case history — a quasi-literary, quasi-scientific, legal, or medical genre of writing. It could have been the case history of a mentally disturbed, schizophrenic man who had begun to believe that he was someone else or of a sociological experiment about the function of clothes in social interaction, for example.

In following Schlegel's intuition about this difference, however, this chapter will show that the primary feature that distinguishes novella from anecdote is how it is received. This turns on the kind of role played by its narrator. In an anecdote, the narrator's role is minimal, barely noticeable, barely adding to its event-based interest. But in a novella, the narrator makes us feel that we are no longer listening to an anecdote that lives off a proximity to historical truth ("perhaps it actually happened this way"); in so doing, she defers — or rather, dissolves — the question of truth into the literary quality of the story presented to us. Schlegel calls this exchanging of truth for fiction the story's ability to create "interest" in the reader; using what is at hand, the novella narrator seeks to capture our attention. The moment the narrator speaks, she makes a vow: to create interest — and verisimilitude — compelling enough to compete with the reader's interest in the reader's own sensed world. A novella is thus not a fairy tale, it is the world in itself. But the novella does not create an *alternative* reality, as does the novel, as we will see below; the novella's reality seeks to replicate, in literary form, the reality of the reader.

As this chapter will show, Schlegel was the first to analyze the novella as a literary form and as the archetype of the literary prose form of modernity. He argues that for the novella, it is irrelevant whether the anecdote from which it sets off is true or false, whether it has stayed close to proven facts or has completely rewritten or even invented them. What is highly relevant, however, is that the novella has taken over the event-based form of the anecdote. The unexpected, singular event that is the cause for the anecdote provides the narrative framework for the novella. In every novella, this specific condition is created by a chain of actions that lead to a crucial turning point, and it is this force field, surrounded by the narrator's frame, that is the form of the novella and that provides us with an idea of literary form as such.

Foucault makes similar use of these qualities of the novella for an archaeology of modern literature as a discourse of power. Foucault

is interested in how the novella's inner, event-based form is modeled
to direct attention legitimizing the narrator's speech. One could say
that seen from the outside, the novella is a self-justifying speech act.
Its form can be paraphrased as trying to express something like,
"Listen to me! — And if you do, you will find out why you needed to."
This trait alludes to the novella's close relationship to the newspaper
article, the semantic and etymological sibling of its original Italian
title, which can be translated as "news" because both provide us with
a new, unheard story. From the news story, the novella has retained
only its need for attention in the form of a news-telling narrator who
produces a variation of the newspaper effect. However, the novella
replaces the news story's focus on factual, historical truth with a
focus on immediate, literary narration. The case history, news, and
the novella all originate in the anecdote, but the novella is the only
form that relies on the literary to distinguish itself from the anecdote. The news pretends to be a medium of truth and dissimulates
its narrativity; the case history is written for a case-based, casuistic
system such as law or medicine, and its intent is to accentuate the
anecdote's knowledge so that it suits this casuistic system (hence the
original meaning of the term casuistry as the application of theoretical rules to particular instances). The novella uses neither of these
aids but takes its form from the anecdote format, transposing the
anecdote's model story to the realm of narrativity and therefore of
literature.

Comparing anecdote and novella emphasizes the differences
between the former's more or less accidental form that is derived
from oral accounts and the latter's clearly artistic form that wants
to distinguish itself from the accidental accounts by making it clear
that its form is not only the condition, but also the cause for its being
told. You hear of Keller's novella Clothes Make the Man because the
anecdote about the tailor mistaken for a count is rewritten into a
strictly formed novella that is no longer about the tailor, the count, or
his coat but, as the title states, about a specific correlation of clothes
and people in general. The title's identity with a canonical proverb

signals this awareness of the universal quality of the novella.[1] *Clothes Make the Man* thus conforms to the novella's general intention of providing a formalized understanding of the world through a particular human conflict. After the long nineteenth century of novellas, from Goethe's *Conversations of German Refugees* (*Unterhaltungen deutscher Ausgewanderten, 1795*) to Mann's *Death in Venice* (1911), Jolles provided one of the most compact definitions of the core features of a novella in his extensive 1921 preface to the canonical work that coined the novella in the first place, Boccaccio's *Decameron* (1350s). Jolles not only touches on the primacy of form over content, but also deduces the consequences that follow in an exemplary definition:

> As novella we understand the depiction of an incident or an event of haunting and powerful significance that appears true to us [*die Darstellung einer Begebenheit oder eines Ereignisses von eindringlicher Bedeutung, die uns als wahr anmutet*]. The novella demonstrates this event for us in such a form [*Form*] that it appears more important to us than the people experiencing it. It all comes down to what happens [*Auf das Geschehene kommt es an*]; the psychology and the characters of those acting and suffering do not interest us in themselves, but only inasmuch as what happens is caused by them. This is how the novella differs from the novel. Goethe's *Werther* and Merimée's *Carmen* both show in content how a man is ruined by his love, but Goethe's novel depicts the man, Merimée's novella the ruining; one offers a human and his fate, the other fate and a human. . . . In the novel, adventures surround the image of the hero; the novella has no heroes, its characters are important only as far as they cause incidents, only well depicted as far as they render an event truthful. The same applies to descriptions of the conditions and the environment; they, too, come into consideration only as far as they make the events more comprehensible or contribute to their appearance as real.[2]

Jolles's characterization clarifies that the novella is perhaps the paradigm for a literary genre whose form is strong enough to structure the majority of its content. In a novella, a protagonist is merely a semantic vector in a force field capable of ordering a context so that its narrative chain reaches the singular, crucial event, which will justify and anchor the whole story. Jolles clarifies that the novella is written with only one event, chance, or incident in mind; everything else is guided or directed toward and from this point. In light of this simplicity, rigor, and directedness, the novella could be described as the paradigm of poetically formed prose literature. In turn, whatever can be called a novella merely exemplifies what literary prose form means because each novella contains an indirect consciousness of the relation between world and literature. For this reason, the novella offers the clearest look at the consequences of the short form in literary prose.

For the novel, Blumenberg has defined two conditions in which literature can "tell the truth," that is, when literature can be truly conceived and trusted: "First, when it is claimed that literature refers to a given outside reality [*Wirklichkeit*] — whatever that reality may be; second, when literature is said to create a reality of its own."[3] Neither relation to reality applies to the novella, but that does not mean that the novella has no category of truth. Unlike a novel, a novella does not need to distinguish itself from other realities or adapt to them because it has no interest in creating an autonomous reality of its own. Novellas have no interest in simulating artificial realities. Unlike novels, novellas are interested in intervening in existing realities, no matter whether they are already marked as artificial or considered to be real or true. Instead of simulating a new reality, a novella uses parts of an existing reality merely as discursive material for its plot, as an environment in which it can stage its particular intervention in this existing reality. In contrast to Blumenberg's definition of the truth claims of a novel, novellas are therefore not concerned with simulating a truth but with creating an attention that interrupts a currently valid reality. This quality can be called the particular agency of a novella. Novellas thus are *textual acts*, analogous to what J. L. Austin and others have called "speech acts."[4] They can develop their own activity and agency in the world, which crucially distinguishes them from larger forms such as the novel.

This agency of the novella, as well as its being focused only on events and action, also entail a specific plot economy. Novellas are short because the goal of their narrative economy is to achieve a feasible, truthful intervention with the least necessary means, that is, with the most compact and shortest story. Rather than being potentially infinite, like a novel, which can always add to its world more characters, events, or descriptions, the number of sentences in a novella must be great enough to depict its truthful incident or action, but not so great as to compete with the existing reality of the reader. Hence, the length of a novella is kept in a range so that it can be read in a single sitting, fitting like a single, erratic incident within the tapestry of discrete events in an afternoon's or evening's experience, a temporal interruption now collated into a reader's lived reality. This temporal economy inscribed into the novella form means that novellas come with an inherent impatience that is exhibited by its limited character development and the fast pace of its plot. They have to be quick enough to make an incision in our world by bringing us in contact with an unheard-of event.

The phenomenological difference between novel and novella developed from Blumenberg's definition of the former, the difference between simulation of a world and intervention into a world, could thus also be described by the novella's "thatness": "*What* happens in these texts often seems far less important than *that* it happens."[5] For these reasons, the novella is the paradigmatic example of the specifically disruptive and thus *active* manner in which brief narrative forms can enter and provoke the reader's reality. While not all novellas or short narrative forms fit this definition, the ability to interfere actively in existing realities is the most consequential outcome of their formal existence. They demonstrate the interventional power short narrative forms can develop when they are specifically constructed according to their interventional economy. With that ultimate act in mind, a fictional event in a text can be transformed into a true occurrence in a life when it provokes *questioning* a truth deemed unquestionable.

This chapter will develop what could be called the phenomenality of the short prose form. It will do so by analyzing the novella form in three steps. The first part of the chapter draws on Foucault's comparison of the novella concept with a particular paraliterary seventeenth-century and eighteenth-century small prose form used by Parisian authorities, the so-called *lettres de cachet* — literally, "letters of the sign/seal" — in which he finds not only the beginning of literature as we know it, but also the intensity, force, and autonomy of literary prose forms as such. Besides this alleged nativity scene of modern literature in proximity to state power, Foucault's work also provides a reduced but rich insight into how short prose forms behave *in actu*, that is, when performing autonomously as protagonists in their own right. Foucault's argument about the prehistory of modern literature can therefore be extended to a general level of literary phenomenology because he delivers further arguments for a prehistory of the activity of literary forms.

The second part of the chapter follows up on the insights gained from the *lettres de cachet* by examining the first actual theory of the novella, formulated by Schlegel in the last years of the eighteenth century. This theory is scattered in notes and fragments and across different essays and so far has received little, if any attention. Surprisingly, in these writings, Schlegel not only agrees with Foucault's superposition of novella and *lettres de cachet* when he discovers that the novella is the first prose genre of modern literature, but in an insight that proved decisive for the rise of literary scholarship as such, he is the first to realize that the distinct form of the novella offers a position that the literary scholar can take up in order to observe the function and behavior of literature. Affirming and clarifying the insights gained through Foucault, this section on Schlegel illustrates why the novella is the paradigm of literary form itself. To the reader, the novella exhibits literature's active engagement with lived reality, and to the scholar, it delivers at the same time a blueprint of the way prose can form vectors that are directed at the world.

Finally, the third and last part of the chapter places these insights regarding the growing independence and agency of formed prose writing in the eighteenth and nineteenth century next to Storm's last, famous, and, from the viewpoint of a phenomenality of short narrative forms, most revealing novella, *The Rider on the White Horse* (*Der Schimmelreiter*). Storm, who throughout his life was outspoken in his resistance to switching from writing novellas to writing novels, is the author who perhaps most programmatically favored the novella form in the nineteenth century. As an effect of this particular poetic intuition, his last novella disregards what since Schlegel had been the consensus about the relation between protagonists and plot in a novella. Storm planned to merge the novella's incident-centered plot with the biographical life narrative of the work's main character, Hauke Haien, which exceeds the novella's capabilities and would have meant turning *The Rider on the White Horse* into a novel. This tension of genres and respective plot arcs, however, is taken up and resolved by the novella itself in an act that could be called autoactive and self-formatting. This reaffirmation occurs on the level of content and fortifies the form of the novella, allowing it to regain control of itself by limiting its span and reinforcing its event-centered plot. By exhibiting the novella's force and ability to transgress even itself and to eliminate its narrator, this last part of the chapter will make earlier arguments tangible through reading a case of what I call "novelistic action."

Thus far, no novella theory specifically has looked at the active capabilities or textual acts of novellas. Yet a number of theoretical precursors exist who have identified and developed the active potential of the novella. In 1924, Walter Benjamin was the first to point out what could be called the pragmatic potential of the novella form when he famously opposed the novella *The Marvelous Young Neighbors* (*Die wunderlichen Nachbarskinder*) to the novel in which it is incorporated, Goethe's 1809 *Elective Affinities* (*Die Wahlverwandtschaften*). In the novel, Goethe conjures up the seemingly harmonious world of a couple, Eduard and Charlotte, enjoying a peaceful, yet remote life on an estate, a life that begins to deteriorate once they invite

Eduard's friend Otto and Charlotte's orphaned niece Ottilie to live with them. Both spouses suddenly feel drawn to the newly arrived guests, leading temporarily to the formation of two new couples, but eventually to chaos and a tragic end for all. Before this decline, a visitor by the name Mittler ("Mediator"), attempts to ease the new tensions. Among other things, he entertains the four by relating a story within the novel, *The Marvelous Young Neighbors*, in which contrary to the creeping reorientation of their relationships, a sudden realization guides the protagonists: two long-estranged and now otherwise engaged former lovers suddenly meet again when he rescues her from a suicide attempt, causing them immediately to rediscover their love and, consequentially, shed their existing relationships for what they recognize as truer commitment. The pragmatic argument of the novella, however, does not reach the characters in the novel, rendering both genres insoluble in one another.

Benjamin argues that this novella within a novel is the inversion of the novel on the level of content because it allows for the eponymous "elective affinities" to happen, a concept Goethe derived from chemistry, that is, the quality of two compounds or relationships is increased after the involved pairs mutually switch partners. By allowing the law of elective affinities to unfold, the novella helps establish a fortunate outcome of its protagonist's fate, an outcome that the novel denies its own protagonists. Despite the ability of the characters in the novel to enact their double switching of partners, learning about the potential of changing their partners from the novella only accelerates the fateful end of each of their lives. Benjamin argues that the novel itself falsifies the notion that the law of elective affinities is applicable in the world of the novel. To underline this claim, he treats Goethe's novel as a frame for the novella similar to the fateful frame narrative of Boccaccio's 1350s *Decameron* or Cervantes's 1613 *Exemplary Novellas* (*Novelas ejemplares*). This argument allows Benjamin to assign the most crucial role to the novella, a role he says that only this short form could fulfill.

The novella, *The Marvelous Young Neighbors*, is not merely an exemplum in the novel; it is also a narrativized case taken from the world of the novel and left for the listeners in the novel to judge how they will carry over its meaning into their own lives. Novella and novel enter a paradigmatic relationship because to the novel, the novella can appear only as advice leading to what cannot be attained. In contrast, the reader of the whole work must conclude that she should not fall into the inaccessible, parallel world of the novel, but should be receptive to the advice given by the novella. Our real world is the origin of the novella form, explains Benjamin: "The characters in the novella come forth closely surrounded on all sides by their human environment [*Mitwelt*]," while on the contrary, "in the life [of the characters of the novel], seclusion prevails, which completes the guaranteed freedom of their actions."[6] Where the novel creates its own independent netherworld, the novella takes and narrativizes exemplary content from this world and thus suggests to its readers the necessity to act and judge for themselves.

Benjamin's insight into the specific inclination of the novella to the world is clear: while the novel poses another, independent world, the novella has the ability to act and elicit actions in this world, even if these actions would initially cause disenchantment of an existing reality. But this claim can be made without the immediate novel-novella comparison that *The Elective Affinities* necessarily evokes. The novella can be understood as one early phenomenon of the independent agency of short literary forms in general, forms indebted to a new function of literary narratives that emerged around 1800.

Andreas Gailus has argued that novellas always "take place . . . in a border zone."[7] In Goethe, this is the border zone circumscribed by the two alternatives facing the young anonymous man in the novella within the novel: either elect and rescue the partner you know you should have been with in the first place or watch her commit suicide while staying in your current relationship that you never fully embraced. Classifying various novellas according to their location in such border zones of ambiguity, contingency, or difference, Gailus concludes, "The novella then is quite literally a *border genre, where the border is at the same time the site of a conflict between incompatible forces.*"[8]

The border, in other words, is always a border in reality, a real-world conflict, a border zone to which the novella transfers us, releasing us finally with a plot in mind that we can apply to our own reality in our own world. In Benjamin's words, this is the pressing agency of novellas: "From the outset [of the novella] everything, sharply contoured, is at a peak" (*Alles steht* [*in der Novelle*], *scharf umrissen, von Anfang an auf der Spitze*).[9] More theoretically, this incentive could be described as the novella's ability to single out border conflicts from the world, amplify these conflicts by shaping them into a suggestion for action or perception, and finally project the novella back on the world with the purpose of influencing and altering the condition of the world.[10]

In addition to such a direct, active effect, novellas' origin along edges and convergence points of conflicts allows them to encourage a metadiscourse. Novellas provoke reaction. The motivating way a novella outlines conflicts always calls for emotional, contemplative, or theoretical responses. This can be seen primarily through various historical lineages of novellas, which show that the novella genre received significance in social settings in which the learned public sought to readjust the habits, politics, and ontologies of their lives. From Boccaccio's and Geoffrey Chaucer's efforts to affect the politics of the fourteenth century, the novella retained the quality of forcing readers to question practices and laws of their societies. Similar interests continue in the various folkloristic and prosaic spin-offs that ran parallel with novella collections throughout the sixteenth and seventeenth centuries, crystalizing again in works such as Marguerite de Navarre's *Heptaméron* and Cervantes's *Exemplary Novellas*. This provocative character, which often pointed toward potential changes in the role of the citizen, reached its peak between the French Revolution and World War I, from the question of a continental Europe in the aftermath of the French Revolution in Goethe's *Conversations of German Refugees* to the representation of fantastical, social, aesthetic, and psychic beliefs in the figure of the citizen by novella writers such as Tieck, Dorothea Schlegel, E. T. A. Hoffmann,

George Sand, Gogol, Poe, Flaubert, Maupassant, Adalbert Stifter, and Arthur Schnitzler.

In the opposite direction, the metadiscourse of the novella also has the potential to speak about the capabilities of literature as such. This quality has been seized on not only by Schlegel, Jolles, Benjamin, and Foucault, but also by other critics since the eighteenth century.[11] As the second part of this chapter will show, Schlegel's studies of the novella fueled his project of a history and scholarly examination of European literature, as well as the groundbreaking literary theories of his brother, August Wilhelm Schlegel, and Friedrich Schleiermacher. Particularly because of its form or poetic formedness, the novella also played a crucial part in a second bloom in the discourse of literary scholarship, in the movement of Russian formalism, whose prose studies can be seen to originate in Boris Eikhenbaum's 1918 text on a novella by Gogol, "How Gogol's *Overcoat* Was Made," and to continue through the analyses of the novella by Michail Petrovsky, Aleksandr Reformatsky, and others.[12]

By 1923, the novella had turned from a fashionable literary genre into a concept for discussing narrative form as such. It was Viktor Shklovsky who detached it from literature early on to use it heuristically as a cinematic conception in an essay on the narratological similarities between literature and film.[13] Similar formalist works on the novella were written in German by Lukács (1909), Erich Auerbach, Jolles, and Benjamin in a very short time, all 1920 to 1922.[14]

With the success of structuralist scholarship in the 1960 and 1970s, a third wave of theoretical works appeared in which novellas offered the principal understanding of the ontology and function of literature itself. Tzvetan Todorov's 1969 attempt at writing a *Grammaire du Décaméron* formalizes the archetypical Boccaccian novella down to its syntax. In a similar way, the chapter "1874: Three Novellas or 'What Happened?'" in Gilles Deleuze's and Felix Guattari's 1980 *A Thousand Plateaus* uses the novella form to extract a formalization of life that is justified by the truism that "we are made of lines."[15] Meanwhile, it is a famous novella by Melville that offers Giorgio Agamben the influential formulation of potentiality in his 1993 essay "Bartleby, or on Contingency." These and other works were among the first to reintroduce the novella's theoretical potential in the second half of the twentieth century. In the most recent phase, the novella has been approached more frequently for its pertinent mode of conceptualization, for example in regard to the semantics of its form,[16] its genre poetics,[17] media theory,[18] poetics of knowledge,[19] and its relation to law and literature.[20] These and other appearances now account for the metadiscursive potential of the novella.

The form of the novella and the theories about it show that it is not merely a genre, but a narrativized demonstration and figuration of a problem that can arise out of discursive, political, or metaphysical tensions. The novella is not an invented art form, but rather a symptom of the potential of modern literature in general and of short forms in particular. This further suggests that its formedness is predestined to represent such tensions in a formalized and pointed shape meant to continue on the level of literary discourse. The following three sections examine from different perspectives the novella as a formed scene of interplay between narratives and the world, spelling out its political, literary, and formalistic capabilities.

Force

In the later phase of Foucault's work, which primarily dealt with state apparatuses and the evolution of madness, sexuality, and disciplinary measures, there is a brief, but significant return of the literary. In his research on the early modern French state, he had discovered the *lettre de cachet*, a "sealed letter" sent to the king that contained a short narrative by means of which a citizen defamed and accused another citizen of being a threat to society. While these *lettres* were written solely with the administrative intent of incarcerating the defamed, Foucault's essay "Lives of Infamous Humans ("La vie des hommes infâmes") cannot help but analyze them as novellas in bureaucratic disguise. Both share the quality of setting action in motion through short, self-contained narration, which is why Foucault's theory of the *lettre de cachet* allows for a crucial insight into why the modern novella still functions as a textual act.

The risk of embarrassing himself, Foucault tells us in this 1977 essay, kept him from describing his captivation while reading early eighteenth-century records of internment for the first time at the Bibliothèque nationale de France in Paris. His essay makes this confession years after he had first come in contact with these texts during his work on the *History of Madness*. Foucault's text shifts the analytical mode with which he first encountered them toward attempting to grasp the inner astonishment that a reader experiences with these files and records. Into which category of sensation do these feelings fall that he is so embarrassed to recall for us, Foucault asks himself. Is it his immense captivation, his anger, or his neutrality during the hours he spent with them? Clearly, he felt struck by them, struck in a way that any academic discourse cannot and should not strike a reader, a fascination that led him to initiate a project to publish these texts as narratives, since no discursive framing could convey the sensations he felt. The essay that was meant to be a preface to this project, "Lives of Infamous Humans," changes the register of discourse analytics, governmentality, and biopolitics that Foucault had put forth in the 1970s to that of literature, the form of art that cannot exist without sensations such as embarrassment and captivation. In the voice of an editor, Foucault tells us that he has "excluded everything in the way of imagination or literature" from the collection, but in the voice of a reader, he goes on to explain that "none of the dark heroes that [imagination or literature] have invented appeared as intense to me as these cobblers, these army deserters, these garment-sellers, these scriveners, these vagabond monks."[21] Despite his intentions to remain outside the literary domain, Foucault is not able to avoid referring to the literary canon altogether and returns to it in the voice of the literary scholar: "Novellas" are what the accounts he found resemble, novellas because they combine a quickness of narration with the reality of the narrated events.[22] "For the things said in these texts," Foucault writes, justifying this comparison to the novella, "are so compressed that one isn't sure whether the intensity that sparks through them is due more to the vividness of the words or to the jostling violence of the facts they tell."[23]

Foucault's text investigates the phenomenological appearance these "novellas" lend to the "encounters with power" they are disclosing.[24] In addition, it acknowledges that the only possibility to access this phenomenality is by describing the intense sensations encountered by the reader. Neither the archival, historical, and philological facts presented in the texts nor their unique relation to a discourse analysis of a history of prisons and of madness suffice for Foucault to grasp the specific force and intensity they produce. It is therefore a crucial fact that he cannot help but refer to the novella. Surprisingly, no scholarship has recognized that Foucault's text functions in this way, even though Foucault's own interest — describing the literariness of the *lettres* — is structurally dependent on his appraisal of the novella.[25] The goal of what follows is to understand the implicit agency of novellas on which Foucault's argument relies.

The problem Foucault faces here is that of negotiating the vocabulary of historical account and literary text, or that of objective fact and subjective fiction. Consider this passage of a *lettre de cachet* that he provides in his essay: "Mathurin Milan, placed in the hospital of Charenton, 31 August 1707: 'His madness was always to hide from his family, to lead an obscure life in the country, to have actions at law, to lend usuriously and without security, to lead his feeble mind down unknown paths, and to believe himself capable of the greatest employments.' "[26] What is the necessary condition for Foucault that a criminal, medical, or psychological case such as this can be described only as novella? Is it enough simply to say this is a combination of a particular case written in a particular style, both of which can be employed to shed light on the state of a related whole, for example, on the whole of French society around 1700, of the history of madness, or of the common practice in 1700 of writing patient reports at hospitals? Generally, texts such as these fall under the category of the case history, a quasi-scientific, medical, or legal genre, which poses the question why Foucault chose to put them in relation with the novella. Which specific features did the novella genre signal for him that lie outside of what is usually associated with a case study or case history? What does the comparison to the novella add to these internment records? Besides the reference to the novella and despite the shortness and particular interest of "Lives of Infamous Humans," Foucault's text contains further references to other genres of short texts, underlining both his dependence on analogies to short-form prose genres and the novella's critical role among these genres.

Before Foucault even introduces the "novella" form—he always keeps it in quotation marks—as a genre comparable to the internment records or *lettres de cachet* in the collection, he relates those texts to the genre of the exemplum. He hesitates to apply the term, since the *lettres de cachet* "are examples that convey not so much lessons to ponder [*leçons à méditer*] as brief effects whose force [*force*] fades almost at once."[27] These two sides of the exemplum—a sample to consider and a snippet chosen for intensity—roughly outline the two roles that have been assigned to the example since Aristotle. The exemplum's function, however, changes from being a narrative proof or means of persuasion, of "saying something in another way,"[28] which is tailored and addressed to a specific purpose and place in speech or text, to becoming more and more unspecific, reducing its function merely to introducing external content into the present context.[29] In underlining the "force" of the exemplum, rather than its lessons for pondering, Foucault seems to have recognized that by the twentieth century, there was no common range of possibilities for what an exemplum could or could not do. This change makes any sort of applied example, *tertium comparitionis*, or specific illumination unreliable, rendering the idea of an exemplum useless for Foucault's own intention of situating the collection of *lettres de cachet* he is about to publish. Instead, he evokes the exemplum in order to dismiss it as a category that is inapplicable to his "anthology of existences."[30] More appropriate, however, are the poetic qualities of "intensity" and "force" that he evokes in opposition to the factual, informative, and epistemological function that the exemplum used to fulfill. In a similar way, he brings up the term "anecdote" only to refuse its use for describing the *lettres de cachet*, which are not ephemeral, accidental, or merely irrelevant snippets from biographies.[31] Their nonanecdotal quality in turn brings forth their active, significant, and often lethal role in the actual course of the lives of which they speak.

The fourth premodern genre of writing Foucault proposes is that of the legend. Comparable to the popular medieval collection called the *Golden Legend* (*Legenda aurea*), whose vitae of saints had informed much of the Western culture for centuries, these early modern "black legends," as Foucault terms them in contrast, are based on a "purely verbal existence"[32] that created "a certain ambiguity between the fiction and the real" (*une certaine équivoque du fictif et du réel*).[33] The only source these legends have for an agency is not the facts they contain, but their status as independent, closed narrative forms, untouchable by science, history, or politics. "Whatever its kernel of reality," continues Foucault, "the legendary is nothing else, finally, but the sum of what is said about it [*la somme de ce qu'on en dit*]." Legends are defined by their ability to summon magnificence, foremost by the form of their narrative, not by lining up a selection of specific deeds that are features of a saint. This formal aspect of the legendary narrative leads Foucault to assign it one more self-perpetual feature in remarking that the legend "is indifferent to the existence or nonexistence of the persons whose glory it transmits."[34] A legendary person is not a mimetic rendition but is exclusively a consequence of a particular narrative that will set up this person in a realm whose rules of conduct do not relate to the concepts of fiction and reality. This narratological condition is described as "historical thickness" (*l'épaisseur historique*) and depends on the brevity of the accounts, since "it is rarity and not prolixity that makes reality equivalent to fiction [*réel et fiction s'équivalent*]."[35]

Quasi-historical density is not an effect of the richness of description, but of the scarcity of the words of which it consists. Foucault uses the radical smallness of the texts not only to illustrate the disproportion between the irrelevant lives they refer to and the mighty power of the state that responds to them but also to imply that especially the short, intrinsically formed text is designated to summon and elevate the vernacular, low lives that "no literature in that period could have accommodated."[36] Although this could make one believe that literature after the seventeenth century would gain this ability, especially since at that point it would become "literature in the modern sense of the word," to Foucault, the emergence of modern literature means that life is turned from its infamous smallness (black legends) or famous glory (golden legends) into a narrativizable, mediated, flat prose.[37] Neither the improbable hero nor the improbable brute could exist in the quotidian evenness needed by the prose of literature for its discursivity of the everyday.

Finally, a last premodern genre is evoked by Foucault to illustrate this suppression of improbability from literature. Before the rise of the literary imperative that all of life be made sayable, the moments and incidents of life that were narrated were given attention because they fell into the genre of the fabulous. Only events "marked with a touch of impossibility" became expressible, he remarks, a typical trait of the fable's ability to remain exemplary for something above or below the flatness of the everyday.[38] To narrate quotidian life realistically, as the modern novel would later develop it, could at the most cause laughter around 1700 over its banality and the ridicule of even bothering to speak about it. While being more commonly didactic than the untouchable legends of saints, the fable works through the same ambiguity between true and false. "Hence," summarizes Foucault, "literature belongs to the great system of constraint by which the West obliged the quotidian to enter into discourse."[39] The fable, with its rise to a central role in the moralization discourse of the seventeenth and eighteenth centuries, thus marks the last high point of narration that openly undoes categories of reality and fiction. The threshold opening toward modernity is fashioned by the rise of the novel in the eighteenth century and the perfection of its realistic prose, from *Don Quixote* to *Robinson Crusoe*. For Foucault, Abbé Prevost's scandalous 1733 novel *Manon Lescaut* seems to be the last major work that bears traces of the seventeenth-century *lettres de cachet*; it is a text that begins to assimilate the specificity of the *lettre de cachet* into literature, providing modern literature with the same origin, the immediate "action . . . of power on lives" (*le travail . . . du pouvoir sur les vies*).[40]

Foucault's typology of premodern short prose genres shows that the intensity of the *lettres de cachet* precludes them from fitting into the canon of accepted literary forms while at the same time showing that they can still be nothing else than a (secret) form of literature. These letters are not simply notes or diaries, but the narratives of unnarratable lives forced into the form of the sayable, reduced into "the sum of what is said about it." This double exclusion is precisely what provoked Foucault's early embarrassment: neither the canon of literary forms nor the norm of historical occasional prose allowed the *lettres de cachet* to be included. The captivation they exert on the modern reader is one of form, less one of knowledge, and it is precisely at this fact that Foucault attempts to hint in approximating these *lettres* to the novella. Among exemplum, anecdote, legend, and fable, the novella sticks out as the last of premodern forms, that is, also the oldest of modernity's forms, because in the seventeenth century, the novella tradition had a hiatus between the Renaissance and modernism. It would take the modern absorption of the reprinted, retranslated, and repopularized novella cycles such as Boccaccio's *Decameron*, Marguerite de Navarre's *Heptaméron*, and Cervantes's *Exemplary Novellas* in the eighteenth and nineteenth centuries for the novella to emerge as an individual form fully emancipated from its frame narrative, reaching its widest modern range between Kleist, Joseph Conrad, Zweig, and Samuel Beckett. Foucault asserts that since "none of [the *lettres de cachet*] will ever measure up to the least tale by Chekov, Maupassant, or James," the relation of the two genres is that of an impossible encounter prevented by the genrelessness of the *lettres*, which we therefore should term "paranovellas."

This fundamental difference in terms of genre, however, is opposed by a similarity on the level of narrative form. Bypassing the question of classifying these short narratives according to (literary or nonliterary) genre allows us to see the specific literary quality of such a *lettre de cachet* novella, which arises solely, as I will go on to show, from the form of its narration, and not from its typical or canonical characteristics. When Foucault draws the *lettres de cachet* near to the novella, he is not interested in the genre-poetical definition, but he finds that the novella develops the very response in narrative that a *lettre de cachet* develops, given its situative function between literature and the dispositives or systems of power:

> Literature occupies a special place within that system . . . it has the duty of saying what is most resistant to being said — the worst, the most secret, the most insufferable, the shameless. . . . But it should not be forgotten that this singular position of literature is only the effect of a certain system of power [*dispositif de pouvoir*] that traverses the economy of discourses and strategies of truth in the West.[41]

Novella and *lettre de cachet*, in other words, resemble each other as phenomena, where they have absorbed specific systemic tensions between laws, rules, norms, expectations, and so forth and have developed a formal, narrative solution consisting of prose in order to conserve such tensions and to allow for their voicing and actualization upon reading. Also according to Gailus, the novella's relation to its generic system functions this way, where novellas "serve to externalize a tension that the system can no longer hold and thus must project to the world outside as a conflict."[42] For Foucault, to read a *lettre de cachet* is to experience literary agency, the effect or force exerted through a text, the same experience that comes from reading a novella. His "Lives of Infamous Humans" guides the literary mind to recognize a literary quality that the nonliterary or paraliterary text can develop, which in turn becomes detectable in literature when looking beyond the definitions of genre and canon. The *lettre de cachet* is a case of literature outside of literature itself, an exception to the rule of literature that hence allows for an analysis of the literary.

A selection of cases or dossiers of *lettres de cachet* from the Archives de la Bastille, each containing three to five requests, denunciations, and personal accounts that petition the king to incarcerate a particular person was edited in the book *Disorderly Families* (*Le désordre de familles*, 1982) by Foucault and the cultural historian Arlette Farge a few years after the publication of "Lives of Infamous Humans."[43] When going through the hundred or so cases, one gets the sense of the paraliterariness of these texts. The letters addressed to the authorities do not present a description of the denounced person but rather narrate a brief story about him or her through a succession of characteristics, misdeeds, violations, and even mere opinions, solely for the purpose of creating the worst possible image of a detestable human whose only appropriate place would be the Bastille, the Salpêtrière, or an expulsion to the New World.

In their antidescriptiveness, the letters narrate according to a formulaic plot of condemnation that has its climax in the petition for police intervention. This formulaic story reads like this: "My husband is coming home at the latest hours of the night, often without his hat and with dirty or even torn clothes, he has lost his manners, is drunk most of the time, and speaks in crazy ways; furthermore, he is also involved in all kinds of debaucheries; I call on your highness that he be taken away to the Bastille for the well-being of the house and the family." In most cases, no specific law has been broken or evoked, nor is there any reference to other prior police activity, but the narrative tries to stand in for an etiological analysis; that is to say, it tries to illustrate the origin of the accuser's adverse feelings toward the accused through a chain of incidents and observations. The purpose of each letter is to initiate police actions by making the accused appear to be an incorrigible scourge to their own and the petitioner's environment. In short, the plots of the letters intend to summon the most evil through the most simple tale of everyday life. All the features of this person are deemed necessary causes for their evident inappropriateness of a free life in society.

Here, on the level of narrative form, it is not the novella that helps explain the *lettre de cachet*. Instead the *lettre de cachet* itself must be analyzed to take seriously Foucault's intuition about the *lettres*' abilities to create "force" and "intensity." Take for example the following *lettre de cachet* from 1728 regarding the young man Louis Henry:

My Lord,

(1) Louis Henry apprentice locksmith of twenty-one years of age, (2) has been so disturbed over the last three or four years that because of his libertinage and his debauches, he could not stay with any master to finish his apprenticeship: (3) he traffics with a band of vagabonds and libertines, he goes roaming with them after dark, often staying out all night, and when he returns to his father's place after eleven o'clock or midnight, he is so drunk that he will not hear reason, he curses and renounces God and (4) threatens to kill his sister [*menace de tuer sa sœur*], which he attempted to execute on the 24th of last month, having armed himself to this effect with a fireplace shovel that his father took from him by force. (5) Who knows where he gets the money to supply his debauches as he does not work, and his parents are in no state to give him any: several times he has been convicted of theft from the houses of masters to whom he had been apprenticed, and he even pushes his unruliness so far as to carry off what he can from his father's, threatening him and telling him that he will put to the test which of the two will be the stronger. When they threaten to have him locked up and to complain of this to Mssrs. the magistrates, he brazenly replies that he would like to be in Bicêtre, but that he does not fear or suffer any man. (6) This is why his father and his mother most humbly beseech My Lord the Lieutenant General of Police that he might wish to give this his attention.

Signed Henry.[44]

This first letter was followed by a second addressed to the Cardinal de Fleury, which consists of almost identical, yet rewritten content and has the following concluding additions:

The petition is signed by the father, by the mother and by three masters whom he robbed.

M. Thoru signifies that this said Louis Henry leads a most detestable life and requests that he be locked away;

the Vice Principal of the Collège des Quatre-Nations also requests that he be locked away.[45]

After providing the profession and age (1), and looking back at the past years of Louis Henry's life (2), his bad behavior, contact with vagabonds and libertines, and blasphemy (3), the letter reaches its narrative peak in the lines in which it tells of the incident where the father has to stop his son from killing his sister with a coal shovel (4). We can see the two holding onto the metal shovel, pushing and pulling it while yelling at each other, Louis perhaps drunk and aggressive, the father in fear for his two children, with Louis's sister in the background, scared to death. Despite the bureaucratic intention of the letter, we are experiencing what it tells us as a lively scene. The plea switches into the literary, which marks the encounter with the coal shovel as the most strongly remembered point of events, a crisis, the point at which the parents of Louis became convinced they needed to approach the police.

This passage of crisis most strikingly bears the "intensity" of the letter that Foucault located between "the vividness of the words" and the "jostling violence of the words."[46] It displays the madness of Louis Henry while also justifying his parents' urge to write it down, therefore becoming the *Urszene* of both the text of the letter *and* the legal consequences it aims to set in motion. Given this double purpose, we have to locate the source of this intensity in the narrative form of the letter: in the short narrative that develops (1, 2, 3) into its catharsis (4), whose turning point retroactively not only provides the framing for laying out the further problems (5) and the final plea (6), but also explains the necessity of the very letter that makes its case.

The triggering quality of the catharsis of events is here and in many other *lettres de cachet* the intention of future harm — he "threatens to kill his sister" — that is, the cathartic scene of the letter presents one hitherto unforeseeable event in the most vivid description and aims to prevent further events of the same kind. This expression of unpredictability is the modern, already partly literalized form of the improbability that Foucault had found to be so decisive for legend and fable. Paradoxically, the letter tries to prevent tragedy by bringing alive the most crucial tragic moment of the past, giving its prose the form of a brief biographical arc. It varies not only from the literary genres mentioned earlier, but also from the related legal genres of petition or supplication, whose sole purpose is humbly to ask the party in charge for a specific action, deed, or favor. As I have reiterated, the *lettre de cachet*'s purpose is to portray somebody's unfavorable character through actual events so that the following request to incarcerate that person appears as a necessary consequence. In the afterword to their collection of *lettres de cachet*, titled "When Addressing the King," Farge and Foucault describe this plot of the letter: "It is a strange theater in which violence, misery, and tribulation were expressed through the ceremonial obligations owed to authority. Poor people took the stage, sometimes beggars, but more often simply shabby, put on costumes, struck poses, declaimed loudly and grandiloquently in a way that to them seemed necessary for supreme power to deign to throw a glance their way."[47]

Whereas in the petition (or *genos enteutikon*), speaker and addressee are members of the same political or diplomatic realm, the *lettre de cachet* communicates from the lowest member of society to the highest, traversing practically all legal distinctions and barriers, from the unrepresented, muted citizen all the way to the omnipotent, divine emperor.[48] Given the disproportion of this intention, their narrative is written according to the attention economy of the state apparatus, which eventually leads up to the police lieutenant of Paris and the king. "But if these [events] were being recounted," Farge and Foucault write, "it was because the king, or at least one of his representatives, was being addressed.... One staged oneself for him [*On se met en scène pour lui*]."[49] Even though these letters partly follow the style and models of the scribes who took them on as commissions, each of them does its very own damage to the life or lives of the accused. "All at once the secret had been told to the king, the insignificant had suddenly become larger than life [*l'insignifiant devenu à ce moment exorbitant*]. Once in the king's hands, it could only function in an outsize and strange manner and no other."[50] Despite their goal to prevent harm, their initial urgency to denounce and their competition for attention from the officials produce a force in their narrative form that will prove uncontrollable, unpredictable, and disastrous once it is received and translated into legal instructions and police procedures.

Foucault's hesitation to sort the *lettre de cachet* into one of the canonical genres of short literary forms, approximating them only to the novella, pointed to their double exclusion—they are neither just literature nor simply historical or legal artifact. However, their literariness is evident, and their double exclusion points ahead to what would become the story of a medical or legal case by the end of the eighteenth century. Whereas a *casus* or case history is defined by both the internal particularity of the individual story and its framing and external use within a larger knowledge-based matrix of argumentation (law) or treatment (medicine), the *lettre de cachet* is oriented inward and remains a closed single transmission. It aims to get the king's attention in order to entangle his omnipotence in its particularity and make it even more singular, that is, continue the unfolding of the individual story as incomparable. The fate of Louis Henry remains his very own story, no matter whether anybody besides the lieutenant or the king has read the *lettre de cachet* or not. Foucault's interest and initial embarrassment about reading the *lettre de cachet* happened thus with respect to discovering a system of power that was never meant to be taken as a whole by the experts or scholars, unlike the legal or medical casuistry, whose whole interest is to advance a dialectic discourse.

While the Bastille's archive of *lettres de cachet* appears to be a collection of precedents within a legal case-law system, the letters were never meant to relate to one another or to be added to the king's summary of procedures. A legal or medical case, on the contrary, is brought into its respective discourse in order to add specific arguments to that discourse, and its narrative form must therefore differ from the narrative form of a *lettre de cachet*, which is meant to develop its force and provoke actions independently and autonomously. No third option exists; either the king listens and acts, or he does not.

This difference might not be highly visible when comparing a *lettre de cachet* with a case history. But from the perspective of their generative difference, on a fundamental level, the *lettre de cachet* displays more narrative force than a case history can. A *lettre de cachet* acts only on its own behalf and has only one ideal addressee, its omnipotent reader, while the case history has to preaffirm the rule to which it relates and thus needs to be comprehensible by anyone who wants to question or apply this rule. If this casuistic environment is left out, the story of Louis Henry remains a translation of the tensions between life and state power into pure narrative form that is meant to gain its effect on its readers solely from its narrative. Exactly because of this self-reliance, the *lettre de cachet* is the paradigm for understanding the way small prose forms develop their agency.

Form is also the distinctive quality of the eighteenth-century case histories that have gotten much attention in the recent years for their ambiguous status between science and literature, most prominently perhaps, through the stories collected and published by Karl Philipp Moritz in his *Journal for Empirical Psychology* (*Magazin zur Erfahrungsseelenkunde*, 1783–93). Many scholars have written on the various aspects of case histories, most notably Nicolas Pethes, who concludes, "The case report can neither be regarded as a scientific sort of text nor as literary genre."[51] Pethes suggests that the case history is both science and literature and that literary applications from Moritz to Poe and Georg Büchner show "how the narrative schema of the case is able to confuse the border between the discursive registers of science and literature because of the immense overlap of the respective representational interests and forms." In Pethes's view, the prehistory of scientific observation and literary narration can be traced to such case histories. Keeping in mind the nonsystematicity of the *lettres de cachet*, however, I would argue that narrative form is independent from the knowledge contained in the case history and its predisposition to a discursive setting. The question of whether facts or fiction or both are presented in a *lettre de cachet* is irrelevant for the narrative form and the cathartic crisis it evokes. The epistemological and the narrative are not necessarily dependent on each other — one cannot be deduced from the other nor does their combination prove the significance of the case history for both literature and science. On the contrary, the case history often bears a strong narrative drive and plot that lends it a force that allows it to act with a self-perpetuating agency. Farge and Foucault had described the uncontrollable, "exorbitant" developments that occur once a letter elicits actions, and this effect is a result more of the gesture of its narrative than of the facts it conveys. Only small forms of prose can become devices that act on their own behalf when entering new fictional or nonfictional contexts in a more or less unforeseeable manner.

The novella is perhaps the paradigmatic case of such a self-empowering brief narrative in the ensemble of smaller prose genres. Both the *lettre de cachet* and the novella bear this ability much more than a case history, whose narrative has become secondary to the knowledge it must convey to a legal or medical system and its rules. As much as combining literature and epistemology can emphasize the omnipresent poetical condition of experiencing language, the truly literary quality of the novella is not the applicability or usage of a specific knowledge it contains, but rather the independent, autonomous character it receives from its form. Novellas are devices because they follow a plan with the particular purpose of directly addressing their reader. Because of its contained narrative and its external brevity, the novella is found in various contexts and thus might appear as an instrument of knowledge or an epistemological agent; its activity lies in the fact that it behaves, as a narrative, *as if it knew* something particular. The outrageousness of its plot discourages any questions about its truthfulness. The *lettre de cachet* regarding Louis Henry might be incorrect or correct when it comes to the facts it states, yet its form is definitely correct and correcting, that is, successful in committing Louis Henry to prison.

Autonomy

What I have attempted to outline could be described as a phenomenology of short prose forms, deduced from Foucault's pairing of the *lettre de cachet* with the novella. The very first scholar who recognized and dealt with this phenomenology by analyzing the novella form directly was Schlegel. He was not only the first literary scholar in Germany, but perhaps also the first theoretician of the novella, having initially described the novella's crucial features and thus having helped elevate it to the status of a genre that was necessary for its wide popularity in the nineteenth century of Goethe, Tieck, Stifter, and Storm,[52] finding in Goethe's *Conversations of German Refugees* (1795) the first German work continuing the novella tradition, conscious of Boccaccio's *Decameron*. In Friedrich Schlegel's fragments regarding the novella (1797–1803), which culminate in his "Dialogue on Poetry" (1800) and his Boccaccio essay, "On the Poetical Works of Giovanni Boccaccio" (1801), one finds the novella's original genre theory, which was initially spread by his brother, August Wilhelm Schlegel, by Tieck, Schleiermacher, and the other members of the Romantic circle. But it is highly doubtable whether Friedrich Schlegel truly planned to identify or reinvent a genre. Instead, what can be called his theory of the novella is concerned with pointing out the specific simultaneity of form and content that the novella embodies, namely, to represent "something objectively peculiar ... with a subjective tendency" (*etwas objektiv Merkwürdiges ... [in] subjektive[r] Anneigung*), as he describes it in the Boccaccio essay.[53]

Schlegel's focus throughout his novella studies is the historical development of the form and its narratological consequences. In Schlegel's theory, the narrator of the novella is an agent who has chosen an "objectively peculiar" content in order to perform the "subjective tendency" of that content by narrating it in a certain form. Giving a strict form to a particular, limited content is the primary quality of the novella. "How, indeed, would it be possible to listen with attentive interest to any narrator," Schlegel explains, "supposing his histories to be devoid of internal connection [*inner Zusammenhang*], either with history or mythology, unless he inspires us with some dawning interest in himself personally?"[54] Novellas require a narrator who performs them, that is, a narratological agent who lends form not only to their outside, like the narrator figures in the frame story of Boccaccio's *Decameron*, but also to the development of their inner story. Only after an explicit or implicit narrator (the outer form) catches the listener's interest, Schlegel writes, can there also exist an "internal connection" (the inner form) of the novella.

Schlegel obtains this strong role of the narrator from the rhetorical speaker, underlining in a number of his notes that he ascribes the origin of the novella to rhetoric, even suggesting at one point that the Aristotelian classification of the three genres of rhetoric is unified by the novella form: "The novella is so very much rhetorical that it divides itself into *dikaniké, epideiktiké,* and *symbouleutiké.*"[55] He seems to intensify this assertion a short time later: "Absolute rhetoric a goal for tragedy and also for novellas — but in a very different manner. For the novella the epideictical, for the former the dikanical."[56] But in Schlegel's motion of thought, such changes reaffirm their common denominator; that is, they prove that the novella is highly rhetorical, and more specifically, "epideictic" or demonstrative. The novella's fundamental difference from rhetoric, Schlegel continues, is that the narrator of a novella — its inner frame — has almost always *nothing* to say, no actual knowledge to convey: "In the novella, the story must be as much nothing as possible. Epideixis about and from nothing in order to make a good story" (*In der Novelle muß die Geschichte so nichts sein wie nur möglich. Epideixis über und aus Nichts eine artige Geschichte machen zu können*).[57] To create interest for something of no political, historical, or timely value, something that does not refer to a recent war, a pressing political decision, or someone's death, is for Schlegel the decisive feature of the novella. The effects of the form, which created the novella genre in the first place, are responsible for making something out of nothing, creating meaning out of irrelevance by creating a prose text that by emulating a narrator, tells a story about a particular event.

The 1801 Boccaccio essay, which in many ways is a condensation and culmination of Schlegel's thoughts on the novella, defines the role the narrator plays within the novella form in the following paragraph, which is at the core of the essay:

> The novella is an anecdote, a story [*Geschichte*] as yet unknown and narrated as one might in society narrate it; a story that must be interesting entirely in itself, without any reference either to time, national feeling, or the progress of humanity and its relation to education. It is a story [*Geschichte*] that, strictly speaking, belongs not to history [*Geschichte*] and that, even in its birth, brings with it into the world a foundation for irony. Because it must create interest, the form has to contain something that to many will appear remarkable or pleasing. The art of narration may only elevate it a bit higher, and the narrator will try to show this art by entertaining deceptively with an agreeable nothingness an anecdote that, strictly speaking, would not even be an anecdote, but he nevertheless knows how to amplify that, which as a whole is a nothingness, with all the fullness of his art, so that we yield ourselves willingly to the pleasing deceit, indeed even let ourselves be seriously interested by it.[58]

"Yielding ourselves willingly to nothing" summarizes the paradoxical form of the novella, and in ascribing to it a "foundation for irony," Schlegel relates it to his concept of Romantic irony. "Irony is the form of the paradox," as Schlegel famously said,[59] and Socratic irony contains the "indissoluble antagonism between the absolute and the relative, between the impossibility and the necessity of complete communication [*Notwendigkeit einer vollständigen Mitteilung*]."[60] Being captivated by someone who has nothing to say places the novella in the irresolvable conflict between the necessary and the accidental but outside of a distinction between logic and knowledge in the realm governed by form. It is the form of the novella that ensures "complete communication," in the sense of an absolute disclosure. This phenomenality of the novella that Schlegel had called "absolute rhetoric" he later rephrases by saying that the novella begins *"with an absolute positing of pure narration"* (*mit einem absoluten Setzen d.[es] reinen Erzählens*).[61] This "positing" marks the outer form of a novella as the absolute beginning of narration and leads to a set of consequences for the semantics and ontology of the novella that Schlegel expresses with the definition "most novellas are true."[62] That is, they are not concerned with truth, since they might even only *appear* as a quasi-anecdote, as the Boccaccio essay put it, "an anecdote that, strictly speaking, would not even be an anecdote." Instead, narrating a story in a novella form means the story achieves an independence from its context and from the world. It *becomes* true. Being captivated by such a narration means that the categories of true and false are invalidated. The reader, having been "in" the story, can do nothing else in the end than agree to having been exposed to a truth. Whereas like the anecdote, the novella was "originally history" and once acquired its truth from the verisimilitude required from historical discourses, its narratological truth now is generated exclusively by itself. Novellas appear as cases of narration, not as verifiable facts from history. In fact, they touch on their historicity as a rhetorical effect, drawing on the historical circumstance of the event they tell in order to exclude themselves from actual history. Schlegel writes, "The novella originally [is] history, even if no political or cultural history, and if it is not [history], this must be considered as the permitted, perhaps also necessary, but always only single exception."[63]

Without the necessity of following the conditions for historical accounts, the novella has gained autonomy about the way it draws and directs tension and attention, what Schlegel called its "subjective tendency" and what we would perhaps call plot. This emancipation leads Schlegel to attach the existence of a narrator to it, which can be seen as his way of associating a "figure" with the autonomous agency provided by the form of narration in a novella. Overall, Schlegel tends toward an understanding of the novella as a single phenomenon, going beyond its textuality and bypassing its mediality, which leads him to see in Boccaccio's coining of the novella form a necessary result of the strong subjectivity of all of Boccaccio's writings. Anyone as concerned as Boccaccio was about giving his writings a very subjective influence, Schlegel argues, must have sooner or later arrived at writing and inventing the novella as we know it. The short prose literature that finds its genuine form leads to the novella as a genre; the author Boccaccio is only the vessel for this emergence:

> I will begin by trying to summarize the tendency of the poet, who is rightly considered the father and founder of the novella, in one idea [to see] whether it may shine a light on the deep peculiarity of the genre.... The subjective quality or relation of almost all works of Boccaccio strikes the eye. Let us now assume that this is not erroneous, but that it was in fact the actual and right tendency of his art to bring to light the subjective with the deepest truth and intimacy or to suggest it with clear allegories [*mit klaren Sinnbildern*]...and if we manage to put the character of the novella in context with this concept of the artist's tendency, we will have found a midpoint and a common viewpoint for all his works.[64]

Boccaccio's tendency to write highly subjective works culminates in the form of the novella, which in turn can be defined along the same lines: "I assert the novella is very suited to represent [*darstellen*] a subjective mood and notion [*Stimmung und Ansicht*], namely, the deepest and most curious ones indirectly and at the same time allegorically [*sinnbildlich*]."[65] The questions that follow, for example "in which novella Boccaccio, for instance, has most completely expressed his individuality," all lead back to the earlier short definitions of the autonomy and independent agency of the novella that Schlegel at some point had simply summarized in the following elliptical line: "Individuality [is] the essence [*Wesen*] of the novella," rendering the nature of the novella as that of an individual being, that is, a singular appearance or phenomenon.[66]

The most striking of Schlegel's observations about the phenomenology of the novella, however, is an argument that exhibits his attention to the combinatorics or the connectivity of the novella. For him, the qualities that I have outlined above, namely, the novella's form, rhetoricity, and individuality, all build up to a particular ability of novellas: they coagulate and form series, cycles, or other, even more intricate systems. Already, his first 1797 notes on the novella show a strong attention to the fact that true novellas almost never appear isolated but are often elements of a larger structure:

> Systematized novellas are connected like tercets in the prophetical [*wie Terzinen im Prophetischen*].[67]
>
> Don Quixote is rather a chain than a system of novellas. — Many novels are actually only chains or wreaths of novellas. — The novella is a romantic rhapsody.[68]
>
> The oldest form of the prose novel is a system of novellas.[69]

Contained in these observations is a seeming contradiction to the analyses of the individuality of the novella, since their individuality suggests that novellas remain singular and separated. Yet precisely this individuality, which the rhetorical, closed form of the novella evokes, is a condition for it to appear next to other novellas or inside a novel without having to give up its autonomy. Schlegel clearly recognizes this aspect and remarks that a story is not a novella if it appears only as novella within a system of the same stories.[70] Singularity is the primary quality of the novella, and the tendency to systematize is secondary to this, which renders novellas the perfect discrete unit in a larger narrative structure. "The combining of several stories very much belongs to the art of novellas," he writes, revealing his phenomenological attention to the novella; the novella as a form affects neighboring areas and other forms in larger structures.[71]

For this reason, the novella elicits the attention not only of the literary historian Schlegel, but also of the literary theoretician Schlegel. In his "Dialogue on Poetry," he had disclosed a hypothetical outline for a theory of the novel, a theory that had yet to be written, an idea resulting from his studies of the literary phenomenality of the novella. In *Athenaeum* Fragment 383, Schlegel declares that "an understanding of pure novellas has practically ceased to exist," and he supports this claim with the fact that Goethe's *Conversations of German Refugees* are often misunderstood in their form and intention.[72] Still, in the *Dialogue on Poetry*, when speaking about this hypothetical theory of the novel, Schlegel seems to have in mind the function that the novella plays in Goethe's *Conversations* when he writes:

> In my historical research I came upon several fundamental forms which are not further reducible. Thus, in the sphere of Romantic poetry, for instance, novellas and fairy tales seem to me, if I may say so, infinitely contrasted. I only wish that an artist would rejuvenate each of these genres by restoring them to their original character. If such examples became known, then I would have the courage for a theory of the novel [*Theorie des Romans*] which would be a theory in the original sense of the word; a spiritual viewing [*geistige Anschauung*] of the subject with calm and serene feeling, as it is proper to view in solemn joy the meaningful play of divine images [*das bedeutende Spiel göttlicher Bilder*].[73]

Novella and fairy tale are the two forms that Goethe's *Conversations* famously and paradigmatically juxtapose. Writing about an *"Anschauung"* of the "play of divine images," Schlegel therefore certainly speaks about a phenomenology (*Anschauung*) of literary forms — or better, of novellas — when he supposes that these forms can be observed in their essence while they combine serially into a cycle and perhaps even further into a novel. There is no doubt that Schlegel's famous allusion to the possibility of a theory of the novel is grounded on a phenomenology of the novella. Its form, individuality, and self-perpetuity lead novellas both to bind together and to coalesce into the novel as a larger form. What Schlegel has in mind is obviously neither an analysis of a particular novel nor a program for writing a novel. Rather, he envisions a theoretical mode in which the nature of modern prose literature can be theorized, that is, described on the phenomenological basis of other modern prose forms. Both the theory of prose and the concept of literature itself hence originate in Schlegel's studies of the novella.

Schlegel's phenomenology of the novella, in other words, invents a theory of literary forms while at the same time discovering the independence and autonomy of these forms. His argument that rediscovering the "pure understanding" of novellas is a condition for coining the future poetry of the Romantic nineteenth century, in fact, has to be inverted. Romantic transcendental poetry is not the poetic result, but the theoretical precondition for a phenomenology of literature. Conceiving of ideal literary forms, as Schlegel does when writing his novel *Lucinde*, leads to a consciousness of the autonomy of literary forms. Though this consciousness is historicized when turning to Boccaccio, Cervantes, or even Jean Paul, it also helps to rediscover the quotidian, life-related origin that a form such as the novella first had. In a way, one could say that Schlegel does not so much discover as revives the novella from the everyday around 1800 and the contemporary Enlightenment actuality of literature. This leads to several consequences that would be decisive for the novella in the nineteenth century, but that also became paradigmatic for establishing the agency that is ascribed, felt, or simply enacted by small forms of prose.

Schlegel's theory of the novella poses three fundamental theses about the function of form in short prose. First, the form of the novella is defined by two factors: inner narrative and outer environment. The inner narrative provides the primary frame, from the inside, as the inner limits of the novella are defined by closing the plot. The novella's outer frame is secondary because it is defined by the environment of the novella, its appearance in a cycle, collection, journal, novel, or as a free-standing text. Its narrative frame, media environment, and poetic embedding thus all define the novella form from the outside.

Second, because of this narrative and environmental demarcation on the textual, motivic, and media-technological level, the novella becomes a self-conscious literary form aware of its agency. Defined by its inner autonomy and its outer contextuality, the novella appears as a phenomenon in a structuralist sense: regarding its inner and outer structure, it seems to have "something" in mind that reaches beyond its own content. The novella can act on the minds and the everyday life of its readers by eliciting actions, judgments, ideas, feelings, and so on, and it can thus reach into history, into politics, and into other texts and other arts.

Third, in this phenomenality of the novella, Schlegel recognizes an exemplary status for the capabilities of literary prose forms in their relation to life: unlike poetry, whose scarcity of words always already has form and gestural appearance, and unlike epic prose's unformed, virtually infinite discourse, the novella is the self-conscious condition of modern literature. In many ways, it can be described as a literary vector, a quantity having direction as well as magnitude, what Schlegel called its "epideictic" quality. The novella is epideictic literature: while telling a story of an event, it presents itself as literature.[74] Its quality lies in the ambivalence between fictional imagining and factual, actual gesturing that Schlegel called "true."

Gert Mattenklott has also observed this self-consciousness of literary forms in Schlegel's idea about the organic relativity of art, which occurs "between the represented and the representing" *(zwischen dem Dargestellten und dem Darstellenden)*, as Schlegel says in *Athenaeum* Fragment 116. This positioning between the signifier and signified elevates the novella from sign to form, appointing it to the gap "between the raw material of reality [*Wirklichkeit*] and the forming power of artistic productivity," Mattenklott explains. The result of this operation is that "the contingent particles of reality [*Wirklichkeit*] are being melted into the consistency of experienced life [*erfahrenen Lebens*]."[75]

Self-Formation

Schlegel assessed the novella before authors such as Christoph Martin Wieland, Kleist, Goethe, Joseph von Eichendorff, Annette von Droste-Hülshoff, Conrad Ferdinand Meyer, and Keller refined it as one of the most prominent genres of nineteenth-century German literature. It would become, among other things, a catalyst for realism's social sensitivity and would thus reaffirm Schlegel's symptomatic attention to the novella's potential to lend representations of prosaic life the urgency of artistic significance. Located toward the other end of this peak era of the nineteenth-century novella are Storm's late works, especially the novellas *A Doppelgänger* (*Ein Doppelgänger*, 1886), *Beneath the Flood* (*Aquis Submersus*, 1876), and, most prominently, *The Rider on the White Horse* (*Der Schimmelreiter*, 1888). They originate in the post-Schlegelian novella tradition while at the same time announcing that the constraints of the form have become increasingly problematic for creating prose narratives that retain relevance as narratives of realism are slowly being challenged by those focusing on an inner impressionism, mood, and psychology. With Keller and Stifter relieving the novella of its stricter rules and authors such as Gerhart Hauptmann shifting its focus to the highly naturalistic, Storm is the author who most intentionally remained within the novella tradition, from which *The Rider on the White Horse* stands out as a culmination point that contains the most prominent insight into the conditions, effects, and forces that the novella form still bore, in spite of its waning, at the end of the nineteenth century.

Storm not only addresses the crisis of the novella while defending his inclination to it in correspondence with fellow realist writers such as Keller or Theodor Fontane, but he even reinforces the novella's pertinence programmatically in a famous preface, which was written in 1881 but only published posthumously. Storm wrote it in response to another writer's belittling remarks, who criticized the quality of novellas by explaining that they are a lesser form of literature. An author of serious, long, multivolume novels, he argued, may turn to writing a novella but only "perhaps every now and then after work and, as it were, for recreation," rendering them incompatible with a serious approach to literature.[76] In contradiction, Storm emphasizes that the novella can bear content and meaning of the highest degrees, comparable only to the drama's ability to evoke human life from its most intense situations, coining the phrase that claims the realist novella as the "sister of drama."[77] To underscore the relevance of his and other novellas written at the time, Storm distinguishes between the "old" novella's focus on one specific event followed by an unforeseen turn ("incident," *Begebenheit*) and the novellas of "today," which can develop a sense of urgency and deal with the "deepest problems of human life." "Identical to this [human life]," he continues, today's novella "demands for its completion a conflict at its center from which the whole is organized into a most closed form and according to which everything unessential is discarded; it does not only tolerate, it also makes the highest demands on art."[78]

However he may have intended to update the novella for the late nineteenth century, Storm's distinction between the older and the contemporary novella becomes blurred, given that the quoted definition of the newer novella merely transforms the classical, Schlegelian definition of the older. Between the latter and the former, Storm transposes the following three crucial features in his preface. He replaces the "unforeseen incident" with a "central conflict," redefines "brief representation" as "organically organized, closed form," and finally also evokes what used to be called an "unusual case" as the relation of the conflict to the "deepest problems of human life." But such readjustments turn out to be rather minor. In the end, Storm cannot detach the old novella from its Schlegelian definition. In fact, his attempt reemphasizes the continuity of the novella. The fact that Storm famously shied away from attempting to write a novel or even a drama, sticking only with the novella for all of his prose works, shows his indebtedness to the form from the 1840s onward, before distinctions between the Schlegelian and his realist definition would even seem necessary. His attempt to differentiate simply reflects the novella's constant potential to be rejuvenated, reaffirming the urgency and strength of the form, which to the twenty-first-century reader appears to be equally fulfilled by a novella from Goethe's *Conversations* and by one of Storm's late works.

In his 1909 essay on Storm, "The Bourgeois Way of Life and Art for Art's Sake," Lukács stumbles upon Storm's 1881 determination that he is writing a new type of novella, concluding that Storm's formal innovation is to have extensively included the inner, psychological developments of the protagonists, which used to be represented only indirectly through the general course of action. Storm extends the novella structure beyond factual deeds and events toward inner

monologues. The change that Lukács detects and describes, however, is instead a development in the relation between art and the
representation of life, turning realism into naturalism and causing
psychologization, traceable also in parallel developments in art from
Paul Cézanne to Adolph Menzel. In fact, it does not alter the epideictic, devicelike character of the novella form, but rather affirms the
novella's ability to incorporate changing social discourses. Storm's
novellas employ all their narratological means, including psychological scenes and monologues, to sustain a strong form that results in a
focus on a single, central, and often tragic event.

Even Storm's last and most prominent novella, *The Rider on the
White Horse*, finished only shortly before his death in 1888, follows this
classical plan of the novella. The appearance of the ghostly rider on
the white horse, as well as the events that follow from it, culminate
in a fated act of suicide. In opposition to such conformity, Lukács and
others have tried to show why at the time of writing *The Rider on the
White Horse*, Storm had begun to find the novella form unsuitable for
what he wanted to achieve. In the case of this novella, his goal was
not only to convey its protagonist Hauke Haien's destiny, but also
to write a story of a protagonist whose whole life unfolds by struggling with that destiny. When comparing Storm's 1881 characterization of the conflict-oriented novella with the extensive biographical
arc that *The Rider on the White Horse* traverses to arrive at its final
conflict, spanning over 220 pages in the first printing, this novella
poses first and foremost the question of its own form. The novella
is set in an area on the North Frisian coastline that over centuries
had been extended toward the North Sea through an ever-growing
system of dikes. The main protagonist of the story, Hauke Haien,
is the son of a farmer and surveyor and learns his father's trade as
he grows up, later also studying mathematics and geometry with
the goal of improving the architecture of the existing dikes. Based
on his knowledge and ambition as a young man, he soon becomes
the warden overseeing the area's dikes and begins to implement the
changes in the dike form he has been thinking about all his life. The

novella culminates when, during a storm surge a few years later, the dikes whose reconstruction Hauke oversees break at a vital spot and sweep away two villagers, causing him to drive his white horse into the sea, offering himself as a sacrifice to avert more harm from the community.

In Storm's novella, the lengthy description of its protagonist's life signals that the shortness of the novella has become insufficient for presenting deeply psychologized human conflicts in a pointed, formed manner. This hints at the divergence that Schlegel had noted between the form of the novella and its corresponding form of modern life. In comparison, Storm's previous novellas *A Doppelgänger* and *Bötjer Barsch*, do not exceed 130 pages to achieve their desired result. Storm's final novella attempt is thus at the same time his most complicated. It recollects a detailed picture of Hauke Haien's life, spanning various episodes that vividly paint the novella's main protagonist, only to close suddenly with the archetypical novelistic event, Hauke's suicide. At the height of the era of industrialization, Hauke's leap of fate puts to a test both the *ratio* of the *Homo faber* and the superstition of country folk mistrusting modernity's progress. In Lukács's definition, it suffices for the novella to narrate one single episode of a human life in order to convey the totality of that life, whereas the novel can provide this totality only on the level of detailed content. Yet precisely such a holistic understanding of life seems to be the interest of *The Rider on the White Horse*, leaving a reader to wonder with Lukács whether it should be seen no longer as novella and not yet as novel:

> When the content of the novella becomes very deep and subtle, this on the one hand robs the decisive situation of the story of its fresh, strong sensuality, and, on the other hand, shows its characters in such a many-sided way and in so many relationships that no single event is capable of expressing them completely. This creates a new artistic genre, an absurd one—a genre whose form is formlessness. This approach cannot deal with more than a few episodes in a human life; these episodes can no longer become symbolic, as they were in the old novella; and the whole is not strong enough to form an

all-encompassing universe rounded in itself, like the novel. Hence these novel-las are rather like scholarly monographs, or, still more, like rough drafts for such monographs.[79]

For Lukács, the novella and the novel are works of art and there-fore have enduring form, whereas scientific works can become out-dated, obsolete, and forgotten, lacking this form. He leaves open which novella he refers to, but following his description, *The Rider on the White Horse* comes close to such a scientific work, a nonfictional text about the struggles of a life. Lukács must have had in mind a sociological, historical, or psychological work that tries to compre-hend with nonartistic, scientific means the whole of the life of Hauke Haien. "He saw only isolated cases [*Einzelfälle*]," he continues about Storm, pointing to the observation made here earlier with Foucault that comprehending a life merely as a case does not suffice to turn it into a novella and is not analogous with doing so.[80]

Such an objection to Storm's attempt to compress the novel-like life story of Hauke Haien into the novella form has its cause in the alteration of the changes in life forms that novellas speak to in their interest of being timely. However, perhaps an idea of the novella form's inner mechanics can be achieved when one decides to under-stand *The Rider on the White Horse* as a true novella, that is, by tak-ing seriously Storm's conceptual decisions and firm defense of the novella when examining its narrative form. Such a reading will be attempted here, and it will unfold beginning from Hauke's act of fate as its turning point, its definite mark as a novella. Hauke's fall hap-pens when his life's achievement — the system of dikes — is falling and happens at the same location of this achievement. When Hauke hurls himself and his horse into the sea surge that has breached the dike, he is trying either to close the gap of the dam physically or to sanctify the breach by sacrificing himself. In any case, Hauke is put-ting himself in the position of the dike, literally "filling in" for it, and what he is doing in the last scene of the novella cannot be described in any other way but his wanting to become the dike. Not only does he attempt to save his drowning family from the flooded marshland, whether by sacrificing his own life to save theirs or by filling and securing the dike breach with his own *physis*, he also tries to correct the mistakes he made in miscalculating the forces of nature when engineering the dike. If Hauke's body and the dike's body unite, the latter may stay intact, and he will live on through it. A reductive summary of the story could therefore read "inventing, building, and saving a dike." Hauke, in other words, is not in control of the dike, but the dike is Hauke's superior.

When putting this primacy of the dike together with the problematic relation between novella and life narrative, a pressing question arises that goes against Lukács's objections to the form. If *The Rider on the White Horse* is indeed a novella, it cannot be a novella about Hauke Haien, but it must instead be a novella about the dike, about what takes place physically with the dike. The novella is thus not concerned with the life of Hauke Haien and hence is in no danger of turning into a biographical novel. Instead, it is concerned with the existence, the physicality, and the laws of the dike.

As I have outlined earlier, Gailus has shown that novellas are always concerned with border zones. Sometimes these are border zones of ideologies, political power, or genders. Mostly, however — and more importantly — these zones are geographical borderlands from which novellas take their physical beginning, only later acquiring more abstract and refined problems of culture and state.[81] *The Rider on the White Horse* confirms this definition. Hauke Haien's life takes place not in the center of a society, but on its edges — the edges of North Frisia and the edges of his family, of his village, of his childhood, and of his adulthood, consumed as it is by his anarchism in thinking and acting and his solitary personality. Hauke is an isolated character, and this marginal position brings him to yet other edges. The consequences that follow are the rise of superstitious prejudices against him and the strengthening of his own rationalism in response. In short, Hauke's life takes place on and around the historical North Frisian system of dikes — or perhaps

more accurately, his life is possible only because these dikes had created marshlands in protecting them from the North Sea, bringing
a permanence that allowed agriculture and settlements. Not only is
the unnamed village that is his home a product of the dike-drawn
borders between land and sea, his whole life, too, is a function of
these dikes.

What is even more peculiar about the dike is its composition
from a particular soil that had at one time been sea floor, which
renders the body of the dike — Storm in fact speaks of the "body of
the dike"[82] — a hybrid of land and sea, dependent on both. Unlike the
twentieth century's concrete and steel-reinforced dams, the traditional dike of the novella is concerned with what is unmistakably
both nature and culture. Set up against the waves, the protective
layer on the sea side of the dike consists of clay (*Kleierde*), a highly
fertile, thick and sticky soil that Hauke's men dig up from the mud-
flats (*Watten*) at low tide, when the flats become uncovered for a
few hours. From this clay, they sculpt the earthy, soon to be grass-
covered face of the dike, helping its body become alive and grow a
green skin.

This organic, corporeal materiality and natural flesh of the dike,
however, is paralleled by its strong legal and almost political power
on the cultural side. Besides being a local protection against sea-
water and floods, the dike is also a device governing geographical and
political borders. Form and content of the dike are inseparable, that
is, one enables the other, and *The Rider on the White Horse* can function
only by keeping both in play. In spite of what Hauke's official, quasi-
aristocratic position of dike master implies — that the dike is made,
controlled, and ruled by officials representing a legal state — the
novella will confront us with the opposite: the dike is ruled by no
legal body at all. It instead has its own corpus, which is half nature,
half culture. When governing the area between nature and culture,
this hybridity consequentially leads to the dike's being subjected only
to its own laws. Hauke and his calculations do not control the sea, and
neither do the villagers. The dike is a sovereign over this third space.

Its cross-bred corporeality rules over their territories according to its own powers and fallacies.

In a highly charged passage just before the dike is about to give way to the storm surge and flood the marshlands it had created, the text stages the clash of the human and the nonhuman actors in a single, decisive phrase. On one side, we find the human realm embodied by Hauke Haien in his official role as the dike master, accompanied by his willful, overpowering attitude claiming to rule the dike mathematically. On the other side, this power is confronted with the matter-of-factness of the dike, its unapproachable, superior, even cryptic agency, which, with its earthy walls, defines what is land and what is sea:

> Now and again, the dike master's sharp order cut through the splashing of rain and the roaring of wind, and there was no mistaking that he alone wanted to command order here today [*der heute hier allein gebieten wollte*]. He ordered the carts forward by number and sent back those that crowded. "Stop, there!" he shouted, and the laborers down below paused for a moment. Then he shouted the laborers up above, "Straw! Get a load of straw down here!" And a cart up above promptly dropped its load down on the wet clay.[83]

The German word for area, territory, or zone is *Gebiet*, which is derived from the verb *gebieten*, which translates as "to rule," "to command," or "to order." While Hauke's men are working under his harsh, fear-fueled orders, the possibility of losing his dike and his honor and life with it has become real. The more Hauke anticipates his suicide, the more he loses control and the more his commands lose their ground, tipping over into screams. The quotation is taken from a scene just before the construction work is finished, during a November storm that cuts off Hauke's commanding speech. His orders become mere cries, almost curses against the unresponsive wall of soil, screams lacking the might and backing necessary for constructing a dike. In the *Gebiet* of the dike, words are cast to the wind. They have become weak and unintelligible, failing to be *Gebote*, or commandments. The dike itself is left to enforce and to

order. The secret, unvoiced core of the novella lies here. It can be
seen by rephrasing Hauke's quoted sentence, inverting it to bring
out the other, suppressed meaning of *gebieten*: Here only the dike
can *give orders* — "*Hier kann nur der Deich allein gebieten*" — but more
accurately, "Here only the dike can *constitute a territory*."

This overturning of Hauke's human, rational laws by the legal
force of the dike's body politic is not as sudden as it might appear. The
laws of borders, areas, and lines had marked Hauke's marginal life all
along. As a child, Hauke observed his father while he was measuring
fields, and soon after, Hauke began to teach himself how to measure
and calculate, even studying a Dutch book of Euclid's after learning
Dutch with the help of a grammar book. This had been his earliest
approach to the land, and it happened not through lived experience,
but by imitating his father's geometry and indirectly by studying
grammatical, linguistic, and mathematical laws. This exclusion of
the land from immediate perception stands as an allegory of Hauke's
life formation because it would continue until the very end of his life.
Early on, his father is worried by his son's tendency to favor theoretical over practical activities, and in order to "cure him of Euclid,"[84] he
sends him to work at the dike, exposed to its corpus, "where he had
to push the cart with the other workers during spring holidays."[85]
This leads to the initial confusion between Hauke's Euclidean mind
of ideal, Platonic geometry and its practical application during the
summers working with the dike builders out by the sea.

After days of his being caught between labor and thought, this
confusion seems to be resolved in a moment of nearly transcendental
superimposition of the ideal with the real. Thinking again about
Euclid, young Hauke, sitting out on the dike after another day of
physical exertion, stares at the rising tide, getting his feet soaked and
his face sprayed with salt water in the murky zone between land and
sea. In response to this elemental, primal experience of the sea-dike
border, he comes up with a geometric abstraction: "Without looking up, he raised his hand and drew a faint line in the air."[86] When he
arrives home, his father realizes the danger of Hauke's careless time

at the dike-sea border and reproaches him with a warning: "You might have drowned." Hauke responds with complete disrespect for the father's intuition, opposing it with the trust in his own self-education through mathematical idealities: "'Yes,' said Hauke; 'but I'm not drowned!'"[87]

This confrontation is the first of many reminders about the gulf between the real and the ideal that Hauke will face throughout his life, yet he will continue to respond with the same assurance that no life activity is governed by realistic experience, common sense, or precaution, but rather by the normativity of the ideal projection. When still a teenager, he kills a beloved angora cat, the only companion of an old woman who lives by the dike, Trien' Jans, because the cat violates what Hauke views as the rules of a game he has been playing with it. This is a disrespect of his authority, which Hauke takes as the license to turn into a beast of prey (*Raubthier*) himself, now considering his play friend a deadly enemy and choking the animal until it suffocates. Hauke does not see this cruel act as brutal or illegitimate. On the contrary, in killing the cat, he remains the sovereign, following the Schmittian dictum that the sovereign is defined by enacting exceptions to the rule. By maintaining the truth of his ideals even during their exceptions, he is able to despise the reality of animal behavior: "'All right!' he yelled and grabbed it even harder. 'We'll see who's the first one to give up!'"[88] To perceive himself as the "beast of prey" that he has become is thus made impossible by the self-assertion of controlling the force of the law.

With these examples in mind, one can see the novella following a strict structure. It repeats this conflict between ideal and real again and again, each time in another setting from Hauke Haien's life, until he finally can no longer sustain and readjust the distinctions between law and case, between ideal and real. As a result, both realms collapse into one another. This confusion of the ideal and the real is first caused by young Hauke's experience of the dike border, and it will end right there, along with the strategic identity between dike form and novella form. Sitting on the edge of the dike body, in the third space between sea and land, had introduced this threshold reality to Hauke and had caused him to govern it by applying geometric laws. And in the end, it is this same borderline body between land and sea that will finally devour, or rather incorporate, Hauke during his last attempt to govern reality's conflicts through a human-made law.

In the final scene on top of the dike during the storm surge, the novella at last breaks what one could call the inherent laws of the dike body. The inhuman, divine production of normativity is made visible, as is its failure, namely, the constraints, conditions, and consequences of any law applied to reality. Like the ghost of a state, the "body of the dike" applies its own laws and applies them with inhuman force, subjecting the land and its people to its absolute judgment. This breach is also the decisive moment for the genre question of why this is a novella and not a novel. The body of the dike reveals that it is the main protagonist of the story, not only overruling the rules of human law, reason, and engineering, but also showing itself as the true central character of the novella. Where human might fails, the law of the dike emerges in order to embody the cryptic relation between the real and the ideal in a more accurate portrayal than a human character ever could.

From this point of view, the close relation between the laws of the dike-body and the form of the novella become tangible. We can first of all positively affirm Lukács's analysis that Storm's late-nineteenth-century novella "transcends the possibilities of the novella by its content" by understanding it slightly differently than Lukács intended.[89] Storm himself most likely did not plan to transform the novelistic exposition of the ghostly legend about the rider into a story about a maritime threshold edifice. In consequence, this means that it is not the author, but the constraints of the novella form that were actively engaged in finishing the story. The novella's necessity to focus on a single event causes the transformation of what was originally a life story into story about a dike, which in turn appears to occur against or at least without the intention of the author.

How can such a counterintuitive claim be supported on the

formal level? In letters written in 1886, at the time of conceptualizing *The Rider on the White Horse*, Storm declares that his plan is "to put a dike ghost legend [*eine Deichgespenstersage*] on the four legs of a novella without blurring its uncanny character."[90] Having finished the work, however, he shifted this earlier assessment in one significant point that provides insights into this poetical transformation. A letter written by Storm in 1888 a few weeks after completing his "clean copy" (*Reinschrift*), states, "I pulled the legendary material [*den sagenhaften Stoff*] over into the purely human; that was the difficulty during completion; and whatever does not correctly come through in it was held back hereby."[91] Within the framework of the novella form, Storm now mentions the poetic principle of "the purely human" (*das rein Menschliche*), which does not appear anywhere up to this point. Adding the "purely human" as a factor seems to have functioned as an aid in finishing the novella, since the adaption of the "legendary" folktale character into the form of a "dike novella" (*Deichnovelle*) had proven very difficult. Storm's view seems to be that "the purely human" is a necessary corrective in this process, altering the constraints of the novella form more toward the novel and its realistic, biographical, and therefore human possibilities. However, if one sees the "dike ghost legend" and the novella as related in their formalistic principles of narration, as Foucault did in "Lives of Infamous Humans," then adding "the purely human" will only extend its length, but not undo the conceptual form that novella and legend have in common. Increasing the number of human traits, characteristics, and episodes masked the impossibility of changing this fateful novella plot into something else. The novella form, with its centeredness on a single event, cannot overcome its limited capability of portraying the purely human.

Jolles remarked that novellas are not principally stories about their main characters, but "stories about what happened to them [*was mit ihnen geschehen ist*]." One can ask then, what happens to Hauke Haien in *The Rider on the White Horse*.[92] One answer would be that Hauke's engineering project grows beyond its creator, causing him to lose control over it. Similar to what happens in Mary Shelley's *Frankenstein; or, the Modern Prometheus*, the dike is a work of its creator that becomes monstrous and attacks its *ratio*-driven inventor. By adding humaneness to Hauke, Storm has strengthened Hauke's antagonist; that is, he has unwittingly emphasized the nonhumanness and self-rule of the dike. "The purely human" fuels the power of the dike and turns against the human, marking the defeat of the intentions of both Storm and his poetic principle. Ultimately, the form of the novella takes control of *The Rider on the White Horse* through the figure of the dike. Just as the dike governs and frames the life of Hauke, the novella form takes over and governs the novella's capabilities according to its own form.

This opposition between human and nonhuman continues on other levels. In fact, four oppositional pairs can be formed that are deeply at work in the novella, moving from the level of content to that of form: Hauke versus dike, human versus nonhuman, novel versus novella, unformed versus form. Their consequences are not merely found in the unusual length of the text or the burial of the human by the nonhuman. The need of self-formation further plays out in the elaborate efforts the novella takes in framing or demarcating, that is, diking, various zones within itself by nesting one narrative situation in another. Depending on the count, three or four different such areas, or "marshlands" (*Kööge*) exist, which the narrative form of the novella stakes out to demonstrate its formal power over the narrative. The novella's initial narrator (1) says he originally had read (2) the legend as a child in one (2a) or another journal (2b), but cannot find that volume. He thus begins from memory (2c) and retells the legend, speaking in the voice of the former narrator from this lost journal (3), who himself only reports the actual story of Hauke Haien, having heard it on a stormy night at a tavern from an old schoolteacher (4). Each of these frames works like a dike, allowing the speaker within the protected area to tell his story in a seemingly safe setting. Like the novella, each speaker in *The Rider on the White Horse* thus affirms a need for formation, for separation from what is beyond the narratable. Storm's research into the history of dam and dike construction and into the different phases of North Frisian marshland diking since the fifteenth century shows that the novella about the land is a way of letting a palimpsest of geographical exclusions and inclusions speak. The text's focus lies not so much in the accuracy of the historical and architectural details, however. In fact, it wrongfully ascribes the invention of dikes with a slowly ascending sea side to Hauke Haien's eighteenth century. Storm's research is much rather a part of the poetic semantics of form that the novella requires: making the dike become its own corporeal, living being. On the one hand, the dike might be formed by history, engineering, politics, and the law, yet on the other hand, it does not fall under the poetic rules of their realities, as a novel would. As Foucault's alignment of novella and *lettre de cachet* shows, the novella is not so much an effect of poeticizing knowledge as it is concerned with poeticizing and unfolding all implications of its form. The dike in *The Rider on the White Horse* corresponds to the form of the novella. It reigns over the land and its people as the novella form reigns over *The Rider on the White Horse*.

Given these observations, *The Rider on the White Horse* can be understood as a poetology of the novella.[93] In its lengthiness, it appears to be torn between the brief, condensed plot of the novella, "a human life expressed through the infinitely sensual force of a fateful hour"[94] (Lukács) and the long, meandering life narrative of a novel. In the presentations of the hauntedness of the land and the deceiving nature inhabiting all phenomena, as well as in the superstition of the villagers and the complicated, unclear hearsay transmission of its narrative, it seems as if the novella is drawn to a murky, magic world that finally breaks with the paradigm of the literary representability of bourgeois realism. In the same vein, Michael Masanetz has read the uncontainable symbolism in Fontane's 1895 novel *Effi Briest*, which effectively undermines and undoes the realist project completely, initiated by motifs turning into formalistic devices.[95] As seen earlier, *The Elective Affinities*, and especially Benjamin's take on it, must be read in the same direction, as putting an end to nineteenth-century realism before it even started, declaring it to fall apart into formalist practices whose symbolism or form semantics are merely creative tools. From this perspective, Storm must maintain the novella form precisely because a pure realism is not compatible with his goal of presenting the "deepest problems of human life" by "a conflict at its center."[96] His suggestion of concentrating on "the purely human" is perhaps rather a decoy for himself, the author subject. It hides the fact that *The Rider on the White Horse* needs the narratological constraint that the novella provides him with. One must finally conclude that his novella, in relying on the poetology of the dike as a formal figure, is reinforcing its own form. The novella happens neither in a netherworld (which would be the novel) nor simply in this world (which would be a nonfictional reality), but is instead born in a borderland between worlds. It is a third body that opens up the very literary "ontology" in which the story of the rider on the white horse can unfold. However, perhaps only a subtle intuition about the wide-ranging capabilities of the novella can be ascribed to Storm's treatment of the form. Its political and semantic capabilities, as Foucault and Schlegel described them, find their full application in Storm's unshakeable confidence in the genre. Sensing that the novella itself will be at work, structuring the story while he is writing it, Storm yielded again, so to speak, to the process of writing a novella. Hauke's lifelong spur of becoming dike stands as the strongest trace of this drive of the novella; that is, the drive of giving form to a life otherwise already rendered unapproachable in novels.

CHAPTER FOUR

Argumentation: The Proverb

as Micronarrative Agency

Whereas the novella derived its autonomy — and hence its ability to act as an independent narrative agent — from its very strong form, the proverb achieves the same ability through its proximity to the practice of life. Because the proverb was a typical part of the *ars topica* — a direct result of its universal social applicability — we can use it to trace the decline of a type of topos and with it the afterlife that topoi found in the realm of brief narration.

In what follows, the first section will use two sources — Kant's dismissal of the proverb and Flaubert's unique reinvention of it as a literary microform in his half-factual, half-fictional *Dictionary of Accepted Ideas* (*Dictionnaire des idées reçues*) — to sketch out the status and literary potential of the proverb in the first half of the nineteenth century. This first section will set the stage for the second and third, beginning with a look at Keller's proverb-based novella cycle *The People of Seldwyla* (*Die Leute von Seldwyla*, 1856 and 1874/74), whose rich, often exaggerated realist style is the result of Keller's interest in the baroque proverb, both as a stylistic device and as a vessel to integrate high and low culture into vernacular prose. In the third and final part, a close reading of the novella *Clothes Make the Man* (*Kleider machen Leute*) will fully develop the structural dependence of Keller's prose on the proverb on both the intradiegetic and the extradiegetic level. Finally, with reference to the structuralist proverb theory of

Gregory Permyakov, a brief conclusion will synthesize the proverb's overall significance for the post-topical short-form narrative.

The proverb, a common topical genre, managed to survive the end of the *ars topica* tradition (after having endured a period of discredit and abandonment after about 1700) largely by solving a key problem of prose after 1800: how to address the inutility of worldly knowledge while simultaneously depending on this knowledge for narratives. Its solution was to replace the significance of knowledge with the agency of a genre or form.[1] The invention of realism, which grappled with this same epistemological angst, was less a solution to the problem than a suspension of it. The realist novel, in particular, presented itself successfully as a simulated extension of the reader's world because it had perfected the ability to contain knowledge of this world while not actually being part of it.

The training ground for the novel's ability to do this was the increasing circulation of newspapers and journals, which often contained nonfiction and fiction side by side, effectively blurring the distinction between factual and fictive accounts by sharing a medium of circulation and by reflecting, acknowledging, and directly recirculating each other's content. With regard to knowledge, this relation of literature to public discourse has therefore been described as topical in the original sense of recirculating a fixed set of bits of knowledge. This rule is perhaps most explicit from Schlegel's demand that a novel must be "a compendium, an encyclopedia of the complete spiritual life of an ingenious individual."[2] Goethe's *Wilhelm Meister*, which Schlegel had in mind, might be the very idealistic, bildungsroman rendition of this claim because it does not suppress its aim of being a stylized version of the world. Only when the novel had moved from this subjective idealism to a more mimetic, experience-based realism during the 1840s and 1850s did works such as Stifter's *Late Summer* (*Nachsommer*) and Keller's *Green Henry* (*Der grüne Heinrich*) fully relate to contemporary society as an archival repertory. Uwe Hebekus has proposed that these novels thus provide "a topical inventory of [their] own present."[3] Contrary to the disappearance of the *ars topica*, Hebekus's claim suggests that "topical knowledge" still existed around 1850, while only the system that organized it had disappeared. However, keeping in mind that the *ars topica* had come to an end around 1700, as has been argued above, such a claim is nearly impossible to make. Instead, his observation regarding novels as repository of their time should be adapted; when the *ars topica* as a system of discourse and logic disappeared, the knowledge it had organized and allowed to circulate disappeared, as well. This is a matter of a new concept of reality and of changing discursive systems, but not a matter of the quantity or quality of erudition in a specific society.[4] In fact, topical knowledge had never been the catalogue of a contemporary society but rather was a set of continuing tokens of speech and thought that would remain present over centuries, and for that reason, it is very different, for example, from the ephemeral information circulated through nineteenth-century journalism.

The Scene of the Irrepressible Proverb

The rise of journalistic discourse after 1800 is an indicator of the end of any continuity of topical knowledge. In this time of accelerated social upheavals, the exchange of shared knowledge accelerated, as well, and the past no longer informed the present, as Koselleck has argued. However, the *ars topica* found a formal continuation in the literature of the nineteenth century, where topical short forms shaped the plots of realist prose. In the circulation of journalistic writing in newspapers, the old *ars topica* survived as a meaningless chatter. Meanwhile, the function of the *ars topica* was inherited by specific forms of short narrative. The genre of the legal or medical case study, for example, provided the frame for fantastic, Gothic, and criminological stories such as those of Poe, Hoffmann, and Maupassant, and formerly hagiographic and theological genres such as the legend and the exemplum became the formal containers for realist works by Johan Peter Hebel, Flaubert, and Fontane. Another such form is the proverb, whose narrative agency has been often overlooked.

The proverb had its most prominent use, both in fiction and in other discourses, when the *ars topica* was still in full effect from antiquity to the eighteenth century, but it then was discredited together with the whole *ars topica* and disappeared thereafter. "A proverb (*proverbium*) is not a witty saying (*bon mot*), for it is a formula that has become common [*eine gemein gewordene Formel*]," as Kant defines it in his *Anthropology*, confirming this decline.[5] His reasoning is accordingly very characteristic of its time: "Speaking through proverbs is therefore the language of the rabble [*Sprache des Pöbels*], and shows a complete lack of wit in social intercourse with the refined world."[6]

Despite its eclipse seeming like a settled issue at this point, the proverb reappeared after 1800. Yet it was no longer a container of commonsense knowledge or folkloric wisdom, as this chapter intends to show, but a repository of narrative form that would be absorbed by realist literature.[7] Like the fairy tale studied in Chapter 5, the proverb is defined by its very high oral and written circulation, through which it has lost any trace of an author and has become anonymous. Counterintuitively, the general tendency found in proverb anthologies to speculate about the origin or inventor of a proverb only confirms how anonymity is an important feature for the proverb. Unlike the quotation, the anecdote, and the legend, the discursive function of proverbs arises neither from exact wording nor from being attributed to place, time, or a certain individual.[8] Proverbs rely on the ability to remain semantically flexible in a given context and variable in their concrete wording. Their origin is by definition unrecorded, which in turn stimulates their universal applicability, as reflected in their German name, *Sprichwort*, "an utterance that has been said (recurrently)." For this reason, proverbs do not rely on a textual form to survive circulation, as an apothegm, adage, or aphorism would. Kant's definition "a formula that has become *common*" captures this essence and summarizes the proverb's anonymity by defining it as the result of oral and written circulation and, more importantly, of having become simple, even simplistic due to its use by all and everyone.

Proverbs are results of a dialectical process in both the philosophical and the conversational sense, where intent of application to the common requires formalization or even formularization, and, vice versa, formulaic reduction encourages common use. The motto "*E pluribus unum*," as related to the United States, or the phrase "It is a characteristic of wisdom not to do desperate things," from Henry David Thoreau's *Walden*, are therefore also apodicti, or circulating sayings, but they do not qualify as proverbs, for they are neither particularly formulaic, nor do they directly address the common quotidian life; rather merely speak indirectly about related values or transcendental wisdom. Kant's disparaging of the proverb is based on its form of use, and therefore it acknowledges what the conditions for its coining had been and, furthermore, implies that their disappearance was also based on changes in the discursive relation between world and individual. Kant's view confirms an observation from Chapter 1, that the specificity of knowledge gained through reason and direct experience, whether it is autobiographical or proven through scientific or historical methods, had successfully replaced the currency of the common. Topical knowledge, and with it the anonymous wisdom of the people, was no longer applicable to the members of the increasingly learned and well-read societies, which decided to take advantage of rational discourse, argumentation, and scientific study when maintaining their everyday lives.

Kant's declassification of the proverb also confirms the end of the *ars topica*, which had included proverbs as *loci communes* since antiquity. The place remaining for such a former topical form is what Kant calls the "language of the rabble," namely, clichés, discursive debris, and vague parroting. Whereas Locke, as seen in Chapter 1, had still thought the concept of the commonplace to be a container for observations of common interest or discussion, by around 1800, the commonplace finally had become a pejorative idea related to the simple-minded and the illiterate. At that time, new terms for stupidity were needed and were on the rise. Even new ones were coined, such as *Blödigkeit*,⁹ "simpleton," as well as diversifications and neologisms related to the "fool."[10] The German *Dummheit* or *Thummheit*, for example, is defined by the *Zedler Universal-Lexicon* (1732–54) as a person's failure to make informed actions or judgments, directly relating it to the confusing abundance of knowledge in Enlightenment society.[11] This diversification of expressions for stupidity reflects the increasing demand for judgment in Enlightenment society and shows in turn that stupidity could be countered less and less with commonly accepted truths and topoi. In fact, Locke's seventeenth-century rendition of the "topical man," who is learned but unable to make use of his erudition, returns again as the overburdened eighteenth-century ignoramus. In a response that seems unwittingly self-deprecating, collections of those "foolish" commonplaces of the supposedly stupid were made by the learned, at first only as self-reflective notebooks that were also "stupid" because they were unsorted, such as Voltaire's *Sottisier*, literally a "collection of foolishnesses," Georg Christoph Lichtenberg's *Waste-Books* (*Sudelbücher*, 1765–99), and Giacomo Leopardi's *Hodge-Podge* (*Zibaldone*, 1817–32), but eventually, similar collections were compiled and even published.[12]

A later such *Sottisier* was compiled by Flaubert in the form of a notebook of things he heard or read and deemed ridiculous.[13] Two of Flaubert's literary works are direct results of this *Sottisier*, which makes it a particularly good example for the slow return of a formerly dismissed topical genre of knowledge as a formative principle in nineteenth-century prose narratives. It contains entries similar to Lichtenberg's *Sudelbücher* or Leopardi's *Zibaldone*, but as a whole differs significantly from them in that Flaubert is less reflective, aphoristic, philosophical, or scientific. His *Sottisier* is mainly the record of a realist writer's observations of society's superficialities.

Besides using it as a cynical outlet for his disgust about social stupidity, Flaubert went back to the thousands of entries in his *Sottisier* a few years later to recycle them into a separate work that allowed this practice of notation to tip into literary writing. This project he called the *Dictionary of Accepted Ideas*, and it continues the compilatory format of the *Sottisier* in the disguise of an encyclopedia of people's rudimentary opinions about things of daily life. With it, Flaubert wanted both to confront society with its own thoughtless stupidities and to blame the rising nineteenth-century genre of the dictionary for allowing such stupidity to prevail through trust in the short-winded facts it helped establish. Finished in 1850, but published only posthumously, Flaubert's *Dictionary* is itself a "best-of," a florilegium of stupid utterances from the *Sottisier*, montaged into a general picture what "the people" think, from A to Z. Its entries are brief summaries of prejudices, false ideas, and superficial knowledge. The dry, neutral, and consciously abridged style mocks the tone of encyclopedia entries. Flaubert perfects the balance between parodying the flatness of the people's judgments and invoking a reflective distance from them. The entries read, for example:

> ARCHITECTS: All morons. Always forget the staircase in houses.
>
> LITERATURE: The occupation of idle people.
>
> STONES: Should always be brought back from the seashore.[14]

The ambiguity between sincere observation and ironic rendition that Flaubert achieves is the programmatic core of the *Dictionary*. He explains that "the work was intended to reconcile the public to tradition, to order, and conventional morality, and is written in such a way that the reader couldn't tell whether or not we were pulling his leg."[15]

Containing around a thousand alphabetized entries, the *Dictionary* attempts to provide an exemplary inventory of a standard conversation and small talk among the bourgeoisie; that is, writes Flaubert, "everything one should say if one is to be considered a decent and likeable member of society."[16] While "accepted ideas" (*idées reçues*) are not proverbs, the example of the *Dictionary* shows that after the end of *ars topica*, the fixed sentences Flaubert calls "accepted ideas" had replaced the proverb as self-contained micronarratives that transported miniature insights in the life and the world of the French society. By using the term "accepted ideas," he emphasized that the entries are a new genre that emerged after the distinction between argument or proverb, learned or unlearned discourse, that

Kant found essential had collapsed.[17] By presenting the bourgeoisie with the concentrated form of their conversations, Flaubert warned them that they are not safe from using dull opinions the way the rest of society used proverbs. In the era after the *ars topica*, presumably educated discussions are just as unoriginal, repetitive, and mindless as the "language of the rabble."

Flaubert's claim was that no matter who participates in it, social discourse in modernity always relies on clichés, stereotypes, and hearsay. This, however, turned the *Dictionary* into its own literary work, an anthology of parodic social criticism consisting of snippets of realist narration. His entries announced the narrativization of proverbial content into realist fictions, as we'll see in the case of Keller below, because they left behind the content aspect of the old *ars topica*'s proverb or commonplace and kept only its form, inheriting the *ars topica* by turning it into the smallest possible stories. An entry such as "ICE CREAM: Eating it is dangerous" has remained a formal proverb of modernity, as Flaubert intended, while never being truly evoked for any presumably accurate or helpful information. Flaubert lent the commonplaces and especially the proverb their own literary genre, a micronarrative that usually becomes autonomously active, whether in fictive or factual discourses. Its rootedness in the chatter of the public sphere makes the proverb form both the most durable and the most variable of post-topical genres. The proverb form can accompany both folkloric wisdom and educated elitism into the mixture of a prosaic reality.

Like a modernist echo of the humanists' *ratio studii*, Flaubert's decision to compile the *Sottisier* and from it the *Dictionary* was his way of digesting nineteenth-century mass communication through writing exercises.[18] This critical research into quotidian discourses did, perhaps coincidentally, provide the cause as well as the laboratory for a large part of Flaubert's last and unfinished novel, *Bouvard et Pécuchet*. In it, two men move from their jobs as copy clerks in Paris to the French countryside, where their merely bureaucratic, job-related acquaintance with intellectual material turns into a blind confidence regarding the implementation and use of this material. They fever-ishly set out to become politicians, chemists, doctors, or priests after reading scholarship in each respective field, each time suffering devastating and often life-threatening failures. The novel acts out the incongruity between life and knowledge in modernity and thus confirms that a type of know-how of living, as the *ars topica* had cir-culated it, no longer exists in modernity. At the same time, however, Flaubert also pointed out that the area where knowledge and life overlap is vacant and that it could be filled by his own projects, that is, those of literature. The ironic distance that the *Dictionary* created between its silly commonplaces and their neutral rendition provided a contemporary space in which the plot of the novel could take place.

What the *Dictionary* conveyed through its ambiguous entries and its interest in encouragement of the coining of new proverbs, the novel turned into the plot of the never-ending struggle of the two protagonists to separate the truthful from the false, the relevant from the irrelevant, applicable knowledge from useless knowledge. Both literary works confronted discursive knowledge with the impossibility of judging it. The strongest significance of *Bouvard et Pécuchet* arises at the story's end; the impossibility of distinguishing erudition from stupidity reflects the deep contingency that lies in the practice of life itself. Bouvard's and Pécuchet's research and experi-ments leave them incapable of performing the simplest everyday tasks, like someone who would try to use the *Dictionary of Accepted Ideas* as an actual guide to socializing at a dinner party. Stupidity in learned modern society is no absolute value for Flaubert, but it is rather relative to losing the ability to live an everyday life by relying on abstractions and metaknowledge to get through the day. Stupidity was thus an outcome of the loss of the *ars topica*, an effect of discourse deeply ingrained in modern commonplaces, stereotypes, and prov-erbs. Flaubert noticed modern society's desire to shortcut thought and individuality by using fixed stratagems, which Avital Ronell has pointed to by asserting, "Flaubert argues that stupidity consists of the desire to conclude."[19]

Flaubert included even his own commonsense "stupidity" in this critique because he himself was among those struggling to distinguish helpful information from the superfluous. Both *Bouvard et Pécuchet* and his preceding novel, *The Temptation of Saint Anthony* (*La tentation de Saint Antoine*, 1874), were the result of excessive studies of only remotely relevant material costing Flaubert months of writing time to conduct. As necessary leftovers of so much intellectual debris, the insights that Flaubert's proverb-based or commonplace-based *Dictionary* and his analysis of discourse in *Bouvard et Pécuchet* hold is that these micronarratives were intellectually indelible.

The post-topical afterlife of Locke's topical man, who is full of topoi, but incapable of living, returns in modernity. The decline of the *ars topica* meant a decline in the know-how of living, a decline for which only short-form narratives could compensate. What was a proverb with a clear function in the know-how of life in the fifteenth century was stripped of its epistemological value in the nineteenth century, remaining only as a frame for narration. Whereas a medieval health book contains straightforward warnings about certain foods "to aid common benefit" (*dem Gemeynen nutz zu verstand*), such as, "garlic . . . is damaging to the eyes, the head, the kidney and the lungs,"[20] Flaubert's *Dictionary* contains a common warning that nobody takes seriously but everybody repeats, such as "ICE CREAM: Eating it is dangerous." In the post-topical model of language, such a rule is not a fact but a micronarrative that replaces an argument, saves reflection, and is therefore unsurpassed in its value to the practice of life in modernity, despite its nonsense. Proverbs are a field of know-how about life in literary form that allows the Lockeian topical man to live in a way that no longer hides the relations between life and speech from the writer and reader. The proverb exerted such a pivotal influence on Flaubert because it is not related to a specific form of knowledge, be it public or scientific, topical or critical. Instead, the form of the proverb provided a framework for the new literature that negotiates life and discourse in the field of reality, that is, beyond the question of knowledge.

Flaubert's three works analyzed here can be read as meditations on how specific topoi had become meaningless while their forms remain irrepressible in the literary inheritance of *ars topica*. As what follows will show, the proverb would hence return, contained as speech in small literary narratives. In Flaubert's self-reflective processes of writing, the *Sottisier*, *Dictionary*, and *Bouvard et Pécuchet* resembled a dialectical movement from a critique of public discourse to the adaptation of this critique to literary speech and, finally, its simulation as an autonomous reality. Flaubert exhibits the way that premodern forms of discourse remained stable and returned in modernity because they became structural sources for realistic fiction.

Keller's Baroque

At the moment when Flaubert intuitively rediscovered the literary quality of the proverb as he was thinking through stupidity, Keller was much more immediately interested in implementing the irrepressible formal aspect of the proverb into his writing. The individual novellas in *The People of Seldwyla* are paradigms of the formal inheritance of the *ars topica* in short-form narration. Unlike Flaubert, Keller did not see his contemporaneous public sphere as a blueprint or a countermodel for his own realism. Instead, Keller compared the situation of his own society with that of the baroque, relating tensions between bourgeoisie and regular folk, between the educated and the illiterate. For an account of how the proverb became a motor for nineteenth-century small-form narrative, this question is important because Keller's idea that the baroque era was a prefiguration of the nineteenth century lead him into debates about prose style and literary language in which the proverb played a central role. In early modernity immediately after the fifteenth century, he found a model for his realism in the era's attempts to merge low and high literary styles and motifs.

During the sixteenth and seventeenth centuries, whole schools of writers attempted to elevate the European vernacular languages to a more versatile and widely recognized poetical level while also trying to transport motifs usually presented only in one of the national languages to other vernaculars. Against the rules of Aristotelian poetics, prosaic, low, and vernacular motifs and characters, as well as their folklore genres, were now to become part of the means used by the most well-respected writers. Keller identified the proverb as an important focal point of these tensions between high and low, an implicit site of the quarrel of the ancients and moderns because it was both a container of true folklore speech and common sense and the living archive of antiquity's wisdom and maxims. To remain in use in all parts of society, proverbs had to be both diachronically and synchronically quintessential, which meant their use in literature posed for writers both a true problem and a true opportunity when trying to address the audience of a whole language community. A very brief excursus into this crucial position of the proverb in the baroque as a catalyst between low and high literary culture will help explain what was at stake when Keller was among the first to return to this form of micronarrative since the baroque made use of it.

The anonymous French play *Comédie des proverbes*, published in 1633,[21] and Georg Philipp Harsdörffer's German translation, *Das Schauspiel der Teutschen Sprichwörter* (*The Play of German Proverbs*) in volume 2 of his *Ladies' Conversation Games* (*Frauenzimmer Gesprächspiele*) of 1642[22] were only two—but two very prominent—cases in which the quarrel of the ancients and moderns was negotiated through the proverb.[23] Two lineages met here that had developed during the sixteenth century. Around 1500, authors such as Geiler von Kaysersberg, Martin Luther (whose personal proverb notebook survived),[24] and Sebastian Brandt relied on proverbs in their sermons, illustrated broadsheets, and chapbooks, such as the *Ship of Fools*, to communicate directly with their audiences, who were mostly peasants, workers, and merchants. At the same time, however, Erasmus's *Adages* (*Adagia*, 1500–36 in various extended editions) initiated a parallel and competing lineage of the educated, Latinate collection and commentary of proverbs. While noting that a large part of his *Adages* consists of vernacular proverbs used by the people of his day,

Erasmus's interest was to present them as mere translations of coinages by antique authors.

A century later, Harsdörffer would take up these two competing early modern traditions of proverbs. He not only translated the French *Comédie des proverbes*, but adapted and extended it widely with many German proverbs and, in addition, contemplated the richness of the German proverb tradition in a long preface to the play, "Of the Features, Distinction, and Translation of Proverbs" ("*Von der Sprichwörter Eigenschaften, Unterscheid und Dolmetschung*"). This tractate acknowledged the common nature of proverbs as "a common speech known to almost everyone that is usually said or repeated many times," but also refused Erasmus's elitist claims about the primacy and superiority of antiquity's proverbs.[25] In opposition to the classicist genealogy of a maxim such as "Know thyself," whose origin Erasmus unsurprisingly attested to the inscription γνῶθι σεαυτὸν (*gnōthi seautón*) at the Temple of Delphi, Harsdörffer claimed that this proverb, like all others, is based on experience and therefore polygenetic:[26] "The highly famous saying of the Greeks and Romans: Know thyself (*Nosce te ipsum*) may be generously changed and alternated, in almost forty different ways, with so many practicable German proverbs. These are lessons conceived from experience and are orally inherited by the descendants."[27]

The point of his *Play of German Proverbs* was therefore to increase the circulation of German proverbs and to train their recognition and encourage their use. Harsdörffer argued that to refine the German language, an active role was required from its speakers and readers, and the proverb was the most common starting point, in the double sense. "Finally, the German reader may not receive the play idly [*müssig*]," Harsdörffer advises, "but consider and contemplate during all action and acts how the proverbs that were hastily shuffled together could be multiplied, improved, and comprehended so that similar projects in the future may be made into works with ample perfection."[28] As first examples for such a work, he refers to the German parallels to Erasmus's *Adages* such as Johan Agricola's *Three*

*Hundred Common Proverbs that We Germans Use But Still Not Know Where
They Come From* (*Drey hundert Gemeyner Sprichworter, der wir Deutschen
uns gebrauchen, und doch nicht wissen woher sie kommen*, 1529), or Julius
Wilhelm Zincgref's *The German Nation's Memorable Sayings, Called
Apophtegmata* (*Teutscher Nation Denckwürdiger Reden, Apophthegmata
genant*, 1631). Harsdörffer's play is consciously presented as a bare
montage of proverbs whose baroque textual crudeness — "Oh! I'm
doomed to die, if you cut me out of life" (*O! Ich bin des Todts, wenn ihr
mich umb das Leben bringt*) — was apparently meant as subversive plea
to readers to join in improving the stylistics of German.[29]

These are exemplary cases of the baroque era's conscious choice of
the proverb as a point of contact for high and low styles of language,
making the proverb the site of a "work on language" not exclusive to
educated poets. Whereas the development to refine vernacular German took off and succeeded, the proverb was merely a temporary
vessel that got left behind on the way after 1700, sinking again into
the low regions of unrefined speech, where Kant later found it as
"language of the rabble." Just as Flaubert was doubtful of the proverb's easy dismissal, however, Keller recognized the baroque's formal
appraisal of the proverb and the immediate connections it provided
to a divergent multitude of styles, social strata, and genres. Keller's
intuition about high and low levels of prose led him to understand
why the proverb and literature became separated in the baroque:
the requirements for a prose that combined high and low styles were
not met. The goal of his realism was to change this. One thus has to
assume that many of his novellas in *The People of Seldwyla* are based on
the proverb form because Keller recognized, like Harsdörffer, that
focusing on the proverb would take him back to the common center
of literary speech.

Throughout his works, Keller's baroque appears. His novella cycle
The Epigram (*Das Sinngedicht*, 1851) is based largely on epigrams of
Friedrich von Logau, and a whole passage of *Green Henry* is dedicated
to the works of the baroque mystic and poet Angelus Silesius, to
name just two examples.[30] Immediately after finishing his book on

the ontology of the allegorical baroque style, Benjamin also pointed directly to the crucial relation between Keller and seventeenth-century literature. In his essay on Keller, Benjamin observes Keller "often puts the words together with a baroque defiance [*mit barockem Trotz*], just as a coat of arms joins up halves of things."[31] However, this "baroqueism" was not limited to Keller's imagery, Benjamin argues, but the structure of Keller's prose actually rests on the way content and form relate to each other in the baroque. The quality of Keller's style is to conjoin images while not losing a sense for structure, a feature Benjamin characterizes by explaining that Keller's "style of writing [*Schreibart*] has something heraldic about it."[32] The methods of Keller's style could be so allegorical, heraldic, or rich in representing the world as a reality because Keller had trained them on the baroque's attempts to combine high and low, common and uncommon structures of literature. Similar to Flaubert, but more consciously, Keller recognized the proverb as a testing ground to develop new prose and genres that were structurally based on the practical reality of language among the people. The form of proverbs promises realism; knowledge does not.

By analyzing Keller's baroque *Schreibart*, Benjamin pointed to the true basis on which Keller could adapt the proverb's baroque hybridity. As mentioned earlier, the foremost example of this is undoubtedly Keller's novella cycle *The People of Seldwyla*, which not only originated from his study of baroque literature of the 1850s,[33] but features a city that is itself a baroque anachronism: "a small city [that] is still stuck in the same old circular wall like three hundred years ago, and hence continues to be the same hamlet."[34]

Three of the novellas are explicitly based on proverbs. Of these three, the novella *Spiegel, the Cat* (*Spiegel, das Kätzchen*) plainly states its own structural relationship to the proverb from which it stems. The first paragraph introduces the subsequent story as mythical narrative, as both "legend" (*Sage*) and "fairy tale," which explains the origin of the Seldwylian proverb, "He bought the fat off the cat" (*Er hat der Katze den Schmer abgekauft*).[35] The rest of the short introduction transforms what seemed to be an etiology or an ethnological account into a dialectical, yet cyclical, interdependence of novella and proverb: "This proverb is also used elsewhere, but nowhere it can be heard as frequently as there [in Seldwyla], which might spring from the fact that an old legend [*Sage*] exists in the city about the origin and meaning of this proverb."[36]

The telling of the legend is the cause for the use of the proverb and, vice versa, the use of the proverb causes the legend to be narrated. If narration arises from the circulation of the proverb, and proverbs in general originate out of the experience of reality, Keller here provides a direct morphological link between reality, proverbs, and his realist prose. The existence of proverbs, in other words, is the proof that reality is being experienced and thus can be represented.

Given this proposition, it is not surprising that also other novellas, such as *The Three Righteous Comb Makers* (*Die drei gerechten Kammacher*), *A Village Romeo and Juliet* (*Romeo und Julia auf dem Dorfe*), and *The Forger of his Own Destiny* (*Der Schmied seines Glückes*) contain proverbial utterances, structures, and relations with baroque folklore and theater. The novella that most strongly relies on the proverb, however, is *Clothes Make the Man* (*Kleider machen Leute*), which is the result of an excessive unfolding of the proverb in the title that used to be a topos in Erasmus's *Adages* and elsewhere. As the following reading will show, Keller's novella contains a poetology that proves that previous topical forms strongly shaped post-1800 realism and argues and exhibits why this is necessary for the practice of life in modernity. Both the realist narratives of literature and realism as a notion about the world and the mode of living in it rely on the afterlife of *ars topica* in the proverb form.

Clothes Make the Man *and "Clothes make the man"*

There are two very different ways to think about *Clothes Make the Man*. This is possible because the story is very simple and formalistic. The poor Seldwyla tailor Wenzel Strapinski accidentally arrives in the neighboring city of Goldach, where, due to his fine coat, he is mistaken for a prince, a role he first ignores and then accepts with increasing success. This first half of the story is countered by the second half, in which Strapinski's true identity is revealed when the Seldwylians join him and his Goldach bride on their wedding day in the form of a carnivalesque parade and dance, performing the inverted meaning of the proverb "Clothes make the man." In this act, the Seldwylians reveal two truths: that the tailor's work — "People make clothes" — is the necessary condition for the costume effect of "Clothes make people" and that it is the combination of these two abilities, tailoring and masquerading, that makes the story of Strapinski in Goldach possible. In the moralistic end of the novella, Nettchen, the bride of Strapinski, overcomes the shock of this revelation. She realizes that she did not fall for a simple tailor in prince's clothes, but for the human in Strapinski, with whom she decides to start a family.

One way the story can be conceived and has been interpreted is as a classic trickster story with a moralistic point, resembling a modern version of an episode from a sixteenth-century chapbook such as *A Diverting Read of Dyl Ulenspiegel (Ein kurtzweilig Lesen von Dyl Ulenspiegel*, 1515), the *History of D. Johann Faust (Historia von D. Johann Fausten*, 1587), or *The Book of the Lales (Das Lalebuch*, 1597). The wit of the trickster, however, is replaced by the dreamy passivity of Wenzel, who does not set out to trick and who recognizes the role imposed on him only when it is too late to quit, when playing along has become easier than ending the masquerade. This explanation of the story is quite valid and helpful, but it makes the fact that its whole construction is based on a single proverb merely an accidental, ornamental aspect. The alternative interpretation results from shifting the focus away from Strapinski's unmasking to the proverb itself and its formal, initiative function in the story. In this second perspective, which will be developed here, the trickster aspect of the story becomes accidental and does not necessarily derive from the use of the proverb but instead illustrates the power of the proverb.

With regard to the content, the proverb "Clothes make the man" contains the first trickster half of the novella, and its chiastic inversion — "People make clothes" — is the result of a simple logical operation that produces the moral prescribed in the second half of the story. By considering not just one but two sides of this reversible proverb, the novella is therefore primarily interested in the capabilities of the proverb form as such and only as an effect of this investigation of the proverb does it arrive at the narrative meaning of this particular proverb. This central role of the proverb is already obvious from the title, but its true function becomes clear because the whole structure of the novella is based on developing the proverb and its chiasm, interrupted by the carnivalesque scene of code switching at the center. As a consequence, the novella's unfolding of the proverb has an exemplary status. The novella's interest lies in not in *this* particular proverb and *this* particular story, but in the potential arising from the relation of proverbs to realist narratives in general. *Clothes Make the Man* provides a paradigmatic outcome on the purely structural level of narration. The proverb is still visible here both as the problem provided (clothes and persons, appearance and essence, even content and form) and as the structure (the story's symmetrical unfolding announced by the proverb title).

This control over structure, rather than over content, is very much opposed to Harsdörffer's baroque use of the proverb in his *Play of German Proverbs* or even in the context of his story anthology *The Grand Scene of Dismal Murder History* (*Der Grosse SchauPlatz Jämerlicher Mord-geschichte*, 1649–50). Here, the proverb provides opinions or commonsense knowledge, much like an *endoxon*, an accepted opinion, but is not adapted and structurally mirrored in the work as a whole.[37] Keller doesn't use proverbs as commonsense facts to attract the participation of readers, but as the container of narrative form.

His "baroque style of writing" is therefore limited to the dense realist descriptions and images also found in *Clothes Make the Man*, which Benjamin called "put together with defiance." This baroque prose does not take over the structure of the whole novella but informs the diegetic level. It is most vivid in the descriptions of Goldach, the town in which the role of the prince is imposed on Strapinski and where every house is ornamented with allegorical figures, images, and *sententiae*. Goldach appears like an architecture-based ekphrasis of a baroque emblem book. With amazement, Strapinski sees "fine, solidly built houses, all adorned with stone or painted symbols [*Sinnbilder*] and supplied with names."[38] The content and form of these allegories are one; no matter how old or new they are, they strictly stay on the descriptive, intradiegetic level, not affecting the overall structure of the novella. Whatever a house's allegorical sign and inscription states is reflected by its inhabitants and their form of life and profession. The novella lists the house names that Strapinski reads and describes what he observes in the following manner:

> National Prosperity (a neat little house in which, behind a canary cage covered entirely with cress, a friendly old woman with a peaked bonnet sat spinning yarn), the Constitution (below lived a cooper who zealously and noisily bound little pails and kegs with hoops, hammering incessantly). One house bore the gruesome name Death; a faded skeleton stretched from bottom to top between the windows. Here lived the justice of the peace. In the house Patience lived the clerk of debts, a starved picture of misery, since in this town no one owed anyone anything.[39]

Keller's baroque prose is most tangible in this allegorical realism. The baroque relationship between form and content makes the essence of a thing correspond to its appearance, which consequentially also dictates how a thing must be ornamented, inscribed, or represented. As a Seldwylian receptive to costumes and carnival, Strapinski should have the ability to perform and detect such allegorical play, but, on the contrary, he lets himself be misled: "He thought he was in another world . . . that he had fallen into a sort of moral utopia."[40] As a logical consequence of misunderstanding this agreement between content and form, he applies it as a principle to his own becoming a prince at the tavern called the Scale: "Thus he was inclined to believe that the remarkable reception he had been given was related to this correspondence — for example, the symbol of the scale [*Sinnbild der Waage*] under which he lived meant that here uneven destiny was weighed and balanced and that occasionally a traveling tailor was transformed into a count."[41]

In this false conclusion, Goldach's model of understanding the world, in which content and form must correspond, falsely replaces that of Seldwyla, where content and form are not tied to each other. The latter capability is manifested in the Seldwylian custom of carnival, where the structure of the world is inverted, which allows them also to use disguises to reveal Strapinski's disguise to himself, of course without the Goldachers being able to notice the difference between disguise and reality. Here, the story presents two modes of signification: the allegorical mode of literalization in Goldach and the structural, formalist approach of Seldwyla, which causes the inversion of the story and corresponds to the extradiegetic function of the proverb. To deduce content from form or the man from his clothes is tempting, but only as long as this deduction is not turned into a universal law and remains only a particular conclusion.

On the extradiegetic level, these two modes of signification therefore return in the style and the structure of the novella. The Goldach baroque is what Keller's "baroque style of writing" tries to achieve: a realism in which descriptions immediately correspond to a world. The Seldwyla awareness of formalism, however, is what the novella wants the reader to keep in mind at the same time — that the reader's own realism exists only during a finite period of time during which the application of a particular structural principle is temporarily forgotten. The argument of *Clothes Make the Man* is therefore not a particular one about content and form, but rather one about the universality of how structural containers can produce specific relations between content and form — with the proverb as the crucial example for demonstrating this relation. What this novella allows the reader to observe is how someone who is conscious of the fabrication of reality experiences forgetting this fabrication — a Seldwylian going to Goldach — or rather, how a realist text allows us to see how modern realism is based on disguises and how it differs from the literalizations of its baroque predecessor.

For this reason, it is misleading to consider Keller's reliance on proverbs and other folkloristic genres to be "updated poetical folklore studies [*Volkskunde*]," as Klaus Jeziorkowski has argued with a reference to Jolles's folkloristic and partly even "*völkische*," that is, "ethnic-nationalist," idea of "simple forms."[42] The point of the novella is not to reinstall the proverb "Clothes make the man" or any other proverb in the commonsense and collective communications of his readers, but rather to show that proverbs have a structural potential that can become a formative principle for nineteenth-century realist narrative.[43] After knowledge was no longer the shaping principle for narration, whether folkloristic, scientific, or historical, Keller identified structural principles as the forming basis of literature. His relation of the baroque shows this twofold interest that the allegorical, detailed richness of baroque prose is a crucial feature for realism but that this alone does not suffice to make a work of literature relevant for the practice of life. Prose that is truly effective for the reader must shape its realist richness according to a form such as a proverb or a novella, a form that is itself rooted in the practice of life. Keller took realist richness and the mix of style from the baroque *Schreibart* but also identified the proverb, left dormant since the baroque, as the structural principle with the potential to relate life and literature.

Topos *as Form*

While it is difficult to set aside the surface and the structure of realist prose by relating the one to Keller's baroque prose and the other to Keller's discovery of the proverb's structure, there is another, more straightforward relation between the novella *Clothes Make the Man* and the proverb. On the intradiegetic level, the primary function of the proverb for the novella becomes even clearer. Parallel to using the proverb as a formative principle for the plot of the story, the novella has various moments in which Strapinski uses fixed expressions, proverbs, and other commonplaces to keep up his disguise as a prince and extend from a mere masquerade to his true persona. This plays an increasingly large role as Strapinski crosses from passively being misrecognized as prince to actively behaving according to this role. At first, only his appearance and his mute behavior are being interpreted by those in his environment: "Without waiting for an answer, the landlord of the Scale rushed to the kitchen and cried: 'the young man can scarcely open his mouth from sheer nobility!'" Then, however, the story marks explicitly "his first deliberate lie" (*selbst-tätige Lüge*), which is behavioral and still nonverbal, but is followed by "his second deliberate error [*selbsttätigen Fehler*], by obediently saying yes instead of no." While the first ambiguous action might be less binding and could still be explained retrospectively as accident, words here mark the second and less ambiguous degree of compliance. Shortly after this active affirmation to the innkeeper, Strapinski also acknowledges to himself that he is becoming someone other than himself: "'Things are now as they are,' he said to himself.'"[44] One could say that following the earlier observations about the difference between Seldwyla and Goldach, Strapinski begins to literalize his own social role: what his form appears to be, a prince, now begins to take over his content.

This initiates a more engaged process of filling the role projected on him. Strapinski not only avoids objections and obeys rules, but also plays along by actively using his social intuition and skills. Having served in the cavalry, he is able to steer the carriage "in a professional manner" (*in schulgerechter Haltung*), impressing his new Goldach acquaintances with his skills as a coachman when they invite him to join them for a ride to the councilor's estate for a game of cards.[45] During the card game, they try to converse with him through the usual small talk of the bourgeoisie, "horses, hunting, and the like,"[46] and Strapinski is again able to keep up his role because he knows the common expressions, which this time consist of the fixed phrases, proverbs, and commonplaces:

> Strapinski was perfectly at home in this area too; for he merely had to dig out the phrases [*Redensarten*] he had once heard around officers and the landed gentry, and which had pleased him uncommonly even then. He produced these phrases only sparingly, with a certain modesty and always with a

melancholy smile, and thereby achieved an effect that was only the greater. Whenever two or three of the gentlemen got up and stepped aside, they said: "He's a perfect squire!"[47]

When he is asked to sing something in Polish, since he is a Polish prince, he even remembers a folk song from the short time he spent working in Poland, and he begins to sing the song's words but "without being aware of its meaning" (*ohne ihres Inhaltes bewußt zu sein*). This use of a foreign language is completely stripped of content. Neither Strapinski nor the Goldachers understand the words, but the words still function for both sides as intended. By performing the full formal functionality of an actually meaningless language, Strapinski's role-play has reached its fullest extent. The narrator effectively comments that he is now behaving "like a parrot."[48]

Only by using proverbs, commonplaces, and fixed expressions as formal props can Strapinski's empty acting stay in accordance with his social environment. Despite his not being interested in or even aware of the meaning and significance of these phrases and their micronarratives, he knows how to use them strategically. For the Goldachers, the content of Strapinski's verbal utterances is mostly irrelevant, ignored, or even inaccessible (in the case of the Polish song), but it functions as long as it conforms to its respective setting. What allows him slowly to succeed with his masquerade in society is the strategic and formal function of these devices and his intuition about how to use them. Of course, this is a typical behavior of a trickster figure. But as I argued earlier, the novella quality lies in being based on a proverb while showing how proverbs help a trickster.

Keller presents most purely how what had once been a topos can return as a form after the end of the *ars topica*. When life is meant to be affected by speech and narration, signification is not a necessary category; only the schematic, formal aspects of discourse can have an effect. Strapinski's role play exhibits through intradiegetic action the function of short narrative forms such as the proverb in post-topical modernity. This performed definition matches directly the one given earlier by the structure of the novella itself: A commonplace or a proverb is a topical form that carries structural principles. It can either cause narration (on the extradiegetic level) or inform actions and interactions in everyday life (on the intradiegetic level). When a proverb causes both, as in the case of *Clothes Make the Man*, it forms a poetology of the afterlife of *ars topica* in short narrative forms.

~

Flaubert's and Keller's texts are only two of many cases of the realist, post-topical recognition of these structural and pragmatic aspects of proverbs.[49] Yet it wasn't until the 1970s that theoretical research concluded that proverbs are narrative structures and can influence other narrative structures. Proverbs today are still seen mainly as containers of folk facts, traditionalist knowledge, or mythological wisdom. Within proverb studies, Permyakov (1919–83), in particular, has analyzed how proverbs are logical, semiotic structures of text for which a purely ornamental or entertaining function is never dominant. Instead, Permyakov argued, proverbs can be instructive, prognostic, negative, or even magical utterances, but they always and primarily have a "modeling" function. He defined this modeling function by explaining that "a proverb possessing this function provides a verbal (or thought) model (scheme) of some real-life (or logical) situation."[50] The linguists Christoph Chlosta and Peter Grzybek, who applied Permyakov's method, have especially noted the particular modeling function of "Clothes make the man" for its reversibility. Depending on the context, the proverb matches the categories "Production — Non-Production," "Revelation — Non-Revelation," and "Qualitative Superiority — Inferiority of Things." Chlosta and Grzybek conclude that " 'Clothes make the man' . . . appears to be . . . equally applicable for the case of assuming an imbalance between 'external appearance' and actual meaning, as it is for the case of assuming an equivalence between both." Hence, they confirm the polyvalent semantic potential of the proverb on which Keller's novella is built and the chiastic reversibility that is so crucial for its claim of the proverb as the narrative inheritor of the *ars topica*. "For this reason," they continue, "the logic modeling of this proverb heavily depends on which implicit presuppositions one relates to it, and, respectively, which logical emphasis one puts on it."[51] Because of its modeling of realism and its polyvalent structure, *Clothes Make the Man* is a paradigm for the narrative potential of proverbs. Erasmus had already pointed this out in the entry "Vestis virum facit"[52] in his *Adages*, noting as well that this proverb is most commonly used (*"vulgo tritissimum est"*) by the people, even though his declared interest was to establish it as invented by Homer and Quintilian.[53]

Flaubert first moved the commonplace and the proverb from the domain of disregarded chatter to that of micronarrative, where it could ignite writing and narrating as an autonomous microstory shaped by public discourse. This identification indicated the relation between literature and reality in the public sphere, as well as the demand for structural forms by postepistemological narration. Keller then pushed the quality of the proverb one step further. He used it to display the active role that proverbs play in daily life, even after they are no longer regarded as applicable know-how, and at the same time, he framed this display into a novella that relies on the form of the proverb. As Permyakov showed, the logico-semiotic structure of proverbs thus always includes the potential to simulate the real-life situation it is meant to model. For this reason, proverbs also include a model of realism itself; they bear a clear indication of the mode of reality that has shaped them.

By picking up the proverb where the baroque had left it, Flaubert and Keller could paradigmatically establish a reality of forms, not of facts. These formal topoi are intended for interaction with the world, and they acknowledge, address, and direct a view of the other and a view of the world, not that of the self. It is the application and situatedness of the proverb's formal, logical function — not the proverb itself or its content — that create a relation between its speaker and the world. The older Goethe already had made use of this by approximating his "poetry of sayings" (*Spruchdichtung*) to the proverb, using the form of the proverb as a screen behind which the self stores its experiences, as Wolfgang Preisendanz argued in 1952: "The proverb is related to a concrete personal experience; the reaching out for the proverb from this experience is carried out verbally as an act [*wird als Akt sprachlich vollzogen*]."[54] The *ars topica* has its afterlife in an art of topical forms, that is, in the media of the commons. The self doesn't make informed decisions based on the public circulation of knowledge, but rather it impersonates the knowing individual by acting according to the formal aspects of micronarratives that appear as if they knew something. "ICE CREAM: Eating it is dangerous."

CHAPTER FIVE

Perception: The Fairy Tale

as Topical Archive

During the 1920s, several literary scholars discussed for the first time the poetological and formal implications of the fairy tale genre. Among them were Vladimir Propp, Ernst Bloch, and Benjamin, who in sudden and tacit agreement turned to this genre, which had until then been entirely overlooked by theoreticians of literature. This discovery was something more than a sign of philology's nascent acknowledgment of more types of short narrative forms. The theoretical discovery of the fairy tale involved an interplay between literary thought and literary form; the fairy tale posed a formal problem to literary studies that required a new type of metaliterary thought, one that assimilated the far-reaching cultural agency of the fairy tale into an understanding of the agency of literature itself.

This cultural and literary agency still marks the specific virtue of the fairy tale. The fairy tale can enter into different types of contexts on the formal level, first adapting to their basic structural parameters and eventually affecting their surface narratives. This capability allows a fairy tale such as "The Emperor's New Clothes," for example, not only to reveal that bureaucracy, architecture, and the media are imaginary costumes of the state, but also to exhibit at the same time the mechanisms of such revelatory acts.[1] What would be discovered only in the 1920s is that the fairy tale possesses a specific formalistic force, one that is exclusive to short narrative forms because they are built on revealing and repeating the distinction between reality and literariness.

While folk tales in general had been collected since early modernity across different languages, *Märchen*, or fairy tales, were turned into a specific genre only in the 1780s by J. K. A. Musäus and in the 1810s by Wilhelm and Jacob Grimm. However, this folkloristic and editorial achievement did not add the fairy tale to the field of literary scholarship and thus prevented it from becoming the object of formal and genre-specific analyses, although its autonomy as a literary genre was already backed by Herder's theories of folk poetics. Presented with a growing number of anthologies, nineteenth-century literary thought could accept the fairy tale's most outstanding feature — its nonrealism — only by downgrading fairy tales to the status of children's literature or by elevating them to a fantastical Romantic version of the *Kunstmärchen*, not folk tales but artfully composed imitations, both of which deflected the fairy tale's theoretical recognition. To Propp, Bloch, and Benjamin in the 1920s, this avoidance appeared as both a lack in literary scholarship and a systematic refusal of nonrealist literature that was related to modernity's focus on realisms such as historicism, positivism, and economic progress. By turning to the fairy tale, these scholars sought to discover the formal, even formative aspects of this little-known genre and to recalibrate the general understanding of literature and reality to eliminate the effects of their predecessors' blind spot.

Especially in the case of Benjamin, whose extensive fairy tale studies remain practically unknown, the antihistorical, nonsubjective narratives of the fairy tale promised to solve, on an immediate, noncritical level, a set of problems of history, perception, language, and epistemology that were central to the crises of modernity, but that still lacked solutions.[2] Besides igniting new literary thought, fairy tales, it turned out, are able to teach a formalist mode of seeing the world that promises to reorganize perception and cognition at large. Instead of being based on Aristotelian, Cartesian, or Kantian notions of cognition, the fairy tale's cross-cultural persistence linked it to essential, deep structures of humanity that do not follow teleologies or intentionalities of understanding. Fairy tales cannot be adapted to match specific types or states of cultures. Instead, they offer an abstracted genealogy of relations among agents of society across traditions, whether they are inanimate or animate, human or nonhuman.

It is this unique applicability to almost any place, time, and situation that Propp, Bloch, and Benjamin recognized and developed. Fairy tales are not simply fantastic stories of short length. They are narratives reduced to formal schemata consisting of a limited, recurring set of variables, protagonists, and conflicts. Continuous retelling and rewriting, largely undocumented and untraceable, have condensed them over centuries to their most reduced versions such as those edited by the Grimm brothers. While Propp's *Morphology of the Folktale* (1927) was interested in a quantified meta-analysis of various fairy tales to identify common features between them, and Bloch's various observations pointed to a general hidden and yet-to-be-developed critical potential of the fairy tale, it was Benjamin who recognized the full form and structure of the genre and developed the consequences most radically, using it to widen the concept of literature. While examining their formalistic conditions, he not only arrived at a specific concept of the fairy tale and at specific readings of different tales; his studies also contain thoughts about the effects that the nonrealist fairy tales could have for the understanding of realist literature and even for that of the construction of reality itself.

Benjamin's project is unlike the other two because it goes beyond the literary and develops fairy tales as containers of human knowledge about social cohesion and cohabitation. It is perhaps Benjamin's most difficult, though never completed, undertaking to make visible this social capacity through a literary archaeology of the fairy tale form, and despite its enigmatic visibility throughout his work, this understanding would have a decisive influence there. For these reasons, this chapter will limit itself to tracing in detail Benjamin's little-known work on the fairy tale as an exemplary case of reclaiming short prose forms in a critical response to modernity. This is a *pars pro toto* for the fairy tale work of his contemporaries Propp, Jolles, and Bloch, which will only touched on only briefly toward the end. The wider consequences and contexts of Benjamin's reclaiming of the fairy tale are developed at the end of the chapter after examining his *Fairy Tale Book* project and his readings of Goethe's "The New Melusine" and Tieck's "The Fair-Haired Eckbert."

Fairy Tales versus Legends

That Benjamin was a lifelong reader of fairy tales and *Sagen* (legends) is evident by the references to these tales that are scattered throughout his work and by the central place that children held in his work. He relived his own childhood by observing and documenting his son Stefan, spent a decade writing the various versions of the *Berlin Childhood* — a kind of autobiographical fairy tale book — studied infant phenomenology, wrote radio plays, riddles, and stories for children, as well as reviews of children's books, puppets, and toys, and owned a unique collection of rare historical children's books.[3] In addition to his training in philosophy, literary criticism, and media and cultural studies, this personal fascination with the child made Benjamin particularly well suited to produce groundbreaking work in the field of fairy tales and *Sagen*. Perhaps one could even go so far as to argue that his interest in the fairy tale as a conundrum of literature — sculpted by storytellers over centuries, overlooked by literary studies, and truly honored only by children — provoked a large part of Benjamin's interest in the child.[4]

An exception to the always hovering, but rarely spelled-out presence of the fairy tale in Benjamin's work is a brief period between 1924 and 1928 during which, as heightened references suggest, his notes (now mostly lost) on the fairy tale had reached a critical mass and ranged from folklore fairy tales to the Romantic *Kunstmärchen*. From this core fairy tale period, more than a dozen letters remain in which Benjamin outlines his intentions to write a *Märchenbuch*, a book on fairy tales.[5] According to one letter, this book, which was planned for the time after finishing the *Book on Mourning Plays* (*Trauerspielbuch*), would have consisted of several critical chapters, each focusing on a single fairy tale. Benjamin planned chapters on Goethe's "The New Melusine" ("Die neue Melusine"), Tieck's "The Fair-Haired Eckbert" ("Der blonde Eckbert"), the Grimms' "Clever Else" (Die Kluge Else"), and "The Three Lazy Sons" ("Die drei Faulen"),[6] and, among others, S. Y. Agnon's "Tale of Rabbi Gadiel, the Infant" ("Maaseh Rabbi Gadiel Hatinoq"), translated by Gershom Scholem.[7] While Benjamin mentions early on that he is already bound by contract to write this book, no manuscripts of the project have survived. This is the case as well for its sibling, which was proposed at the same time, a subsequent project on the *Sage*. In relation to the critical essays of the *Märchenbuch*, this second project, appropriately called *Sagenbuch*,[8] would have consisted of a republication of crucial *Sagen* material with an afterword, supplementing the *Märchenbuch* both in genre and type of content. Benjamin was aware of the Grimm brother's parallel work on fairy tale and *Sage*, for each of which they had published two volumes in the short span from 1812 to 1818. Benjamin planned the *Sagenbuch* as an anthology that addressed "for the first time since the Grimms the whole complex [of legends] unrestrained by local or historical limitations," as he explained to Scholem.[9] But despite the fact that the *Sagenbuch* project was fully envisioned — Benjamin already had gone so far as to secure a contract for the book with the Verlag Bremer Presse after Hugo von Hofmannsthal put him in touch with its editor, Willy Weigand — the project never left the stages of conceptual planning.[10]

On the chronological, biographical level, these two book commitments emphasize how significant the fairy tale had become for Benjamin during a phase in which he still considered himself an academic scholar of literature and philosophy, having almost completed his second academic habilitation project on the baroque mourning play. What remains of the *Märchenbuch* and the *Sagenbuch*, however, are only singular remarks, separate observations, and various cross-references to the aggregate of fairy tales and *Sagen* made during the following twenty years of his life, so this chapter will attempt to retrace the lines of these scattered splinters to reconstruct what could be called Benjamin's theory of the fairy tale. Although it began before Benjamin turned away from his academic career, it remained with him as he became a freelance literary critic and author. This continuity makes the fairy tale project very likely the most committed and sustained of Benjamin's attempts to elevate an analysis of literature to a full theory extending to politics, philosophy, history, and culture while at the same time specifically retaining its roots in literature.

Right from the beginning, Benjamin recognizes a general lack of relevant and critical scholarship on the fairy tale, despite its specific position in literary history and its unique quality as form of schematic narration. While preparing the *Märchenbuch* he writes, "I secretly entertain the opinion that there must be new and surprising things to say about the beauty of fairy tales. Hardly anyone has as yet delved into this matter. In addition, this particular form of intellectual productivity is beginning to fascinate me as a form removed from all subjectivity and all self-assured productivity."[11]

Crucial for his formalist approach, Benjamin understands fairy tales as abstract formations of cognitive productivity that bear no trace of an author. They are separated from questions of subjectivity and reflexive individuality and instead are results of the ongoing mental processes of narration. Fairy tales are remainders of placeless, oral, and undocumentable traditions of storytelling, as Benjamin would say later. They evade historical categories, which also distinguishes them from their sibling, the *Sagen*. As reflected by his two complementary book projects, he distinguishes strictly between the two genres. The Grimms had prepared for this opposition in their introduction to the *Deutsche Sagen*,[12] but Benjamin defines more clearly what distinguishes them: "The fairy tale is . . . a waste product, perhaps the most powerful to be found in the spiritual life of humanity: a waste product that emerges from the growth and decay of legends."[13] From this difference Benjamin deduces many more arguments. Whereas *Sagen* are always linked to certain points or phases in history, as well as to specific geographical locations, the fairy tale explicitly refuses such limited relations and subsequent dependencies. Anchored in space and time, *Sagen* undergo the evolutionary processes of history and of language, which do not touch the fairy tale, according to Benjamin. While outlining the *Sagenbuch* for Hofmannsthal, he further sharpens the difference and now opposes the two genres as *form* (fairy tale) and *style* (*Sagen*):

> For I envision a definition of the fairy tale that will derive many essential aspects from the specifics inherent in its form. And it is here that the comparison with legends most forcefully suggests itself to me. I envisioned the style of the legend—in many ways different from that of the fairy tale—to cite Grimm, its "epic integrity" [*epische Lauterkeit*], as one of the most sublime and undervalued possessions of the German language.[14]

A few weeks later, his linking of language and *Sagenstil* has evolved further, also affecting the fairy tale form. Regarding the *Sagen*, he explains to Scholem, his interest has developed toward

> the formulation of a motif, always in the most laconic manner, combined with its most important *linguistic* variations. What concerns me here is the mystery of the *formulas* of legends [*das Geheimnis der Sagenformeln*], and the different and significant way in which legends know how to intimate things [*anzudeuten verstehen*]. . . . In short, what I have in mind is an attempt . . . proceeding from the linguistic nature of the legend [*ausgehend vom sprachlichen Wesen der Sagen*].[15]

Sagen are defined by their relation to history and reflect this through the historical evolution of language itself, despite the continuity of their motifs. In contrast, fairy tales contain a core untouchable by time, which perhaps even remains outside of historical evolution. This distinction continues on the level of content, where fairy tales have a particular narrative form and not a particular motif, scene, or formula, as *Sagen* do. For this reason, *Sagen* display a unique, "perfect and entelechial prose" (*vollkommene und eigengesetzliche Prosa*)[16] and are hence the results of language sediments and not of "intellectual productivity" (*geistige Productivität*),[17] like fairy tales. *Sagen* motifs are incentives for a particular state of language to manifest itself in each version of a *Sage*, allowing this state of language to become conserved. Using a concept coined by Blumenberg, one could think of the *Sage* as conserving a folkloristic, preliterary "speech situation,"[18] a scene of language specific to both a certain historical time and a certain geographical locale. Whoever is able to analyze the "style of *Sagen*," to single out "formulas of *Sagen*," or to describe the "linguistic nature" of a *Sage* is able to understand a particular state of a language, which has been recorded by shaping the *Sagen* motif and thus has been made transportable beyond the historical and geographical limits of its genetic "speech situation." In Benjamin's view, *Sagen* contain a specificity of language and narrative that points to their original time and space. This quality of *Sagen* suffices for him to plan his *Sagenbuch* only as an anthology of republications with an afterword, but no extensive analysis.

Conversely, the fairy tale's disregard for history evades historical strata and variations of language. This is possible because the fairy tale consists of story forms fallen out of history, that is, forms that were historically timeless. In this sense, Benjamin can consider fairy tales as unfinished or ruined *Sagen*, leftovers, or waste, because their forms had already fully decayed and could no longer be used during the "growth and decay of legends." That leaves them as "perhaps the most powerful" by-product of humanity's mental production, erratic narrative formations that withstand historical gains and losses.

This nonrelation of the fairy tale to historical discourses is countered by a universal relational potentiality when it comes to various synchronic contexts. Clearly, Benjamin understands that modernity's obsession with the contemporary and its invalidation of historical knowledge has first suppressed the acceptance of the fairy tale, but now offers a powerful tool whose theoretical implications signal that noncontemporary literature can, in fact, have a forceful agency in any modern present if it is able formally to break open this limitation and tell a human, life-related story.

Disappearing

This whole complex occurs to Benjamin early on, in 1921, when he reads Goethe's "The New Melusine" for the first time, and would stay linked to it until his death. This fantastic fairy tale by Goethe is in fact an adaptation of a partly folkloristic and partly literary story. In the original fairy tale, a man falls in love with a woman who in reality is a mermaidlike figure. She allows him to marry her on the condition that he cannot see her taking a bath, that is, he cannot know her true figure. Once this taboo is broken, the man's curiosity and misbelief are gone, but the price of the revelation of the secret and this return to reality is the fateful arrival of destruction and misfortune in the man's life. Goethe changes the story by a double reduction: he reduces the story's extent to its minimum, leaving out the legendary or chroniclelike aspects of medieval versions, such as the most famous telling by Jean d'Arras, but he also changes the woman's secret. In Goethe's version, she is a tiny, dwarflike creature who can appear only from time to time in the disguise of a full-sized human woman. In Benjamin's 1921 reading of Goethe's version, "The New Melusine" revealed two crucial concepts to him, one about Goethe's text and one about fairy tales in general.

Benjamin read "The New Melusine" for the first time in February 1921 while working on his *Elective Affinities* essay. At the end of a fairly dense letter to Scholem, he tries to set apart how "The New Melusine" figures as both a particular fairy tale and a literary text that causes what he calls "philologische Interpolation." Here is the passage from Benjamin's letter that ends with the reference to Goethe's text:

> I have given some thought to philology (even back when I was in Switzerland). I was always aware of its seductive side. It seems to me — and I do not know whether I understand it in the same sense as you — that, like all historical research, philology promises the same joys that the Neoplatonists sought in the asceticism of contemplation, but in this instance taken to the extreme. Perfection instead of consummation, the guaranteed extinction of morality

(without smothering its fire). It presents one side of history [*Geschichte*], or better, one layer of the historical [*eine Schicht des Historischen*], for which a human being may indeed be able to gain regulative and methodical, as well as constitutive, elementary-logical concepts; but the connection between them must remain closed to the human being. I define philology, not as the science or history of language, but as the *history of terminology* at its deepest level. In doing this, a most enigmatic concept of time and very enigmatic phenomena must surely be taken into consideration. If I am not mistaken, I have an idea of what you are getting at, without being able to elaborate on it, when you suggest that philology stands close to history from the side of the chronicle. The chronicle is fundamentally interpolated history. Philological interpolation in chronicles simply reveals in its form the intention of the content [*Gehalt*], since its content [*Gehalt*] interpolates history. A work has made vividly clear to me what the nature of this way of working could be. This work seized me most deeply and inspired me to interpolation. It is Goethe's "New Melusine." Do you know it? If not, you absolutely have to read this story [*Erzählung*], embedded in *Wilhelm Meister's Travels*, as a separate entity, i.e., without the frame that surrounds it, just as I happened to do by accident. Should you be familiar with it, I may be able to suggest a few things about it.[19]

Several problems regarding the activity of reading and thinking through literature are touched on in this passage, but it seems Benjamin's core question has to do with identifying the approach to literature that would be necessary to understand "The New Melusine." Benjamin favors philology over interpretation or analysis because philology can tempt the reader with a promise to "contemplate perfection" — a reward quite different from mere complete comprehension. This promise of philology is especially compelling regarding a certain historical knowledge that cannot be represented in the completeness sought in comprehension by Kantian epistemology and Kantian concepts. As Peter Fenves has shown, Benjamin's idea of philology is a direct effect of his Kant studies and responds to the limitations of philosophical concepts laid out by Kant that he had discussed with Scholem in Bern.[20] Benjamin returns to the question of the philological mode in the letter and defines philology as the understanding of the deep history of terminology that is at work before concepts have entered knowable history. He calls the type of activity, or *Arbeit*, that such an idea of philology causes "interpolation," a term also taken from earlier discussions with Scholem. Benjamin then hints at what this "philological interpolation" could look like by employing the examples of two very different historiographical genres: that of the chronicle and that of Goethe's "The New Melusine." The chronicle, he explains, is already interpolated history: the chronicler is the philologist who fills the gaps of historical events with stories, which frees the reader from having to comprehend the history through a more or less complete set of facts. Instead, the chronicle allows the perfection of history itself to be contemplated. To reach this contemplation, however, the philological interpolation of the chronicler must be repeated by the reader. She herself must philologically interpolate the chronicle; that is, she needs to contemplate the chronicler's contemplation of history to comprehend history's perfection in her own mind.

Analogously for "The New Melusine," Benjamin continues, such a repeated interpolation is necessary; Goethe has philologically interpolated the meaning of the old Melusine fairy tale, whose truth Benjamin could see and understand only once he himself read "The New Melusine" with philological interpolation. Through Goethe's words, he explains to Scholem, the perfect "content" (*Gehalt*) of the fairy tale can be contemplated, as can the preterminological aspects of this "content." This is the core aspect of the fairy tale Benjamin has in mind when he says the fairy tale "had seized me most deeply and inspired me to interpolation." "The New Melusine" can tempt the reader with the promise of disclosing a certain "connection" of otherwise "enigmatic phenomena." The tale's temptation and his subsequent philological interpolation cause Benjamin to write both the letter and "Notes on 'New Melusine,'" which were likely the nucleus of the *Märchenbuch*. These are unfortunately lost today. To understand what type of non-Kantian concepts "The New Melusine" disclosed to

Benjamin, it is necessary to look at a fragment in which he refers to these notes.

The letter and this fragment, which the *Gesammelte Schriften* edited together under the title "Language and Logic II" ("Sprache und Logik II"), suggest that Benjamin's interest in Goethe's fairy tale developed on two different but interrelated layers.[21] First, Benjamin saw its significance on the methodological layer with regard to theories of cognition and more specifically to theories of philology and literary hermeneutics, as the 1921 letter shows. Second, the literary layer itself interested him, the concrete preterminological phenomena, the "enigmatic phenomena" he mentions in the letter, that the tale offers for contemplation. The letter proposes that a theory of cognition is exemplified in "The New Melusine" by explaining that philological interpolation "simply reveals in its form the intention of the content [*Gehalt*]." The hermeneutic foundation of this method of philological interpolation is detailed more closely in "Language and Logic II" in the fragment that makes reference to "Notes on 'New Melusine.'" It offers an alternative for the concept of truth, "a harmonic concept of truth" that is supposed to originate from a respect for the intention of the object of study itself. In contrast, the old concept of truth originated from the side of the analyst and her intentionality, which equates truth with the state of having reached a certain density of comprehension. Yet, Benjamin explains, following this false intentionalist concept of truth will reveal nothing of the matter in question, because pressing it for a full comprehension will merely destroy whatever might be true within it. To demonstrate this false truth, Benjamin refers to the myth of the veiled image of Sais, whose unveiling would cause its destruction, as well as to his reading of "The New Melusine": "S[ee] a[lso] on the 'veiling power of knowledge' in the notes on 'New Melusine.'"

This clarifies the relation between truth, philology, and "The New Melusine" and suggests that Benjamin wanted to use his reading of Goethe's tale and the interpolation problem to write a theory of literary cognition that poses philology as the mode of literary scholarship that respects the intention of the work for comprehending any truth. This Melusinian theory of cognition is thus quite similar to the hermeneutic traditions of close reading proposed at the same time by such scholars as I. A. Richards and William Empson, who would later influence the New Criticism movement. Benjamin considered this cognition key and left explicit traces from the fragment at the heart of the "Epistemo-Critical Foreword" ("Erkenntniskritische Vorrede") of the *Trauerspielbuch*, which defines truth as "intentionless being": "The comportment appropriate to truth is therefore an entering and disappearing into it [*ein in sie Eingehen und Verschwinden*], not an intending in knowing [*nicht ein Meinen im Erkennen*]."[22] On the one hand, "entering and disappearing" has obviously turned into a proper concept in the Benjaminian theoretical framework that replaces "philological interpolation," but on the other hand, "entering and disappearing" is also a term that specifically relates to the content of "The New Melusine," reflecting what Benjamin comprehended on the literary layer of the fairy tale.

There can be no doubt that entering and disappearing are the preterminological concepts that reading "The New Melusine" according to his theory of philological cognition revealed to Benjamin. In Benjamin's idea of fairy tales as ahistorical, this meant that Goethe had already discovered these terms in the old Melusine tale and had interpolated them philologically when writing his renewed Melusine. He extracted the narrative schemata from the various Melusine versions, which are often partly legends and linked to history, as in the case of Jean d'Arras's chronicle of the House of Lusignan, and he could thus write not another legend but the Melusine story as a fairy tale. In the context of the *Elective Affinities* essay of 1922, Benjamin briefly mentions "The New Melusine" according to what he believed was Goethe's intention, stating that the sole aspect of Goethe's tale to present the notion of disappearing: "In the readiness for withdrawing and disappearing [*Entfernen und Verschwinden*], is it not bliss [*Seligkeit*] that is hinted at, bliss in small things [*Seligkeit im Kleinen*], which Goethe later made the sole motif of the 'New Melusine'?"[23]

Not only is Benjamin's theory of philological close reading active in the background of his interpretation, his reading of "The New Melusine" is responsible for his theory of philological close reading. Disappearing is more than some notion from the preterminological strata of the history of philosophical concepts that is brought forth by the story itself. It, along with entering (though to a lesser degree) are the key idioms for Benjamin's theory of philological cognition. Both arise immediately from reading the fairy tale; the disappearing of the Melusine woman into her dwarflike figure presents the disappearing of the philological truth of the fairy tale form. This interrelation between the two meanings of the concept of disappearing also, and necessarily, works in the opposite direction: only if the fairy tale disappears during philological cognition can the concept of disappearance be presented as the key for this process. For this fleeting character, the philological truth resembles the fragility of the veiled image of Sais.

"The New Melusine" not just poses a poetology of philological or aesthetic cognition; above all, it establishes that the specific quality of the fairy tale form is its ability to pose concepts through poetology. When Benjamin mentions "The New Melusine" over and over in his letters as the paradigm for his *Märchenbuch*, he underscores that since reading the Goethe story, the fairy tale form has acquired the quality of the container of a class of concepts — disappearing, entering, and so on — that are indispensable for philosophical understanding and not attainable in any other medium. This is Benjamin's philological proof that fairy tales exclusively allow philosophy and aesthetic theory to go beyond the threshold of Kantian terminology, a quality that Goethe already had recognized intuitively when rewriting the old Melusine. Benjamin's project of a *Märchenbuch* intended to pose conclusively essential philosophical theorems through analyses of fairy tales, suggesting — fairy tale by fairy tale, concept by concept — a groundwork for a set of pre-Kantian metaphysical notions of cognition. This claim can be supported by remarks on "The New Melusine" and on disappearing that are aimed at philology itself and by another explicit pairing of a fairy tale, Tieck's "The Fair-Haired Eckbert," and another concept: forgetting.

Forgetting

"The Fair-Haired Eckbert" — also called a *Kunstmärchen*, like Goethe's "The New Melusine" — turns up during the same years in Benjamin's letters and notes about the *Märchenbuch*. In 1925, Benjamin already mentions "an essay I plan to write on Tieck's 'The Fair-Haired Eckbert' for the next issue of their journal — it will probably be only a few pages long."[24] Again, no texts remain with this theme, even though they were significant enough that Benjamin still refers to a "Notes on 'Fair-Haired Eckbert'" in a section about memory contained in the earliest notebook for the *Arcades Project (Passagenarbeit)* from 1928. The short reflection reads, "The theory of not-yet-conscious knowing [*Lehre vom Noch nicht bewußten Wissen*] may be linked with the theory of forgetting [*Lehre vom Vergessen*] (notes on The Fair-Haired Eckbert) and applied to collectives in their various epochs."[25] Benjamin's discovery of the concept of forgetting in "The Fair-Haired Eckbert," parallels his discovery of the key notion of disappearing in "The New Melusine," and this pairing one fairy tale with one notion remained a programmatic choice still in effect years after initially establishing it. In a letter to Theodor W. Adorno from 1940, Benjamin still refers to these pairs as conceptual units: "It seems unavoidable to me that I will again be confronted with the question you raised in the course of my own work.... The first thing for me to do will be to return to the *locus classicus* of the theory of forgetting [*Theorie des Vergessens*], which, as you well know, is represented for me by [Tieck's] *The Fair-Haired Eckbert*."[26]

By calling the tale a "*locus classicus* of the theory of forgetting," Benjamin not only openly acknowledges that theoretical problems do in fact figure in fairy tales for him, but also reveals that Adorno is undoubtedly aware of these loci or topoi that he has developed since the early 1920s. Since then, they must have become a set of critical topoi that regulated both Benjamin's philosophy of cognition and his practice of reading and hence functioned as a tool set at the basis of his work from the mid-1920s to his death in 1940.

For its use of the locus of forgetting, there is one such application in Benjamin's Kafka essay that helps us understand his reading of Tieck and hence the quality of this fairy tale concept. In every known schema for his essay "Franz Kafka," Benjamin places "The Fair-Haired Eckbert" in a crucial position, confirming its quality as a true topos for his fundamental philosophy, that is, a notion with conceptual autonomy.[27] It is contained in the final version of the essay, where it exhibits how Benjamin's reading of Tieck's fairy tale equipped him with the concept of disappearing that was the precondition for understanding Kafka:

> Incidentally, Kafka is not the only writer for whom animals are the receptacles of the forgotten [*Behältnisse des Vergessenen*]. In Tieck's profound story *The Fair-Haired Eckbert*, the forgotten name of a little dog, Strohmian, stands for a mysterious guilt. One can understand, then, why Kafka never tired of hearing about the forgotten from animals [*den Tieren das Vergessene abzulauschen*]. They are not the purpose, to be sure, but one cannot do without them.[28]

Their ability to interact with animals, Benjamin argues, is what relates Kafka's protagonists to the old mythical forces. The resurfacing of this figuration of myth in Kafka becomes meaningful only because Tieck's fairy tale had shown that forgetting is the activity necessary in order to overcome myth. Even more so, since "The Fair-Haired Eckbert" is not directly concerned with rendering mythical forces completely forgotten, but instead poses oblivion as an overall virtue. Here is where Benjamin's philological interpolation of Tieck's tale allows him to compare it to Kafka's and implicitly to put Kafka in the genealogy of the fairy tale tradition. While in Tieck, forgetting only leaves the "cipher of an enigmatic guilt," Kafka specifically seeks out such ciphers to work against the forgetfulness of past, enigmatic relations between the human realm and that of myth. In their antihistoricity, fairy tales have therefore conserved identifiers of myth's grip on humanity that historical thought and historiography had masked and rendered inaccessible since the eighteenth century with the disappearance of the folklorist fairy tale. Whereas Kafka's story tries to reclaim the concept of forgetting as a virtue by writing literature, Benjamin remains on the side of theory. His *Märchenbuch* aimed to propose an exit from the constant rewriting of fairy tale notions and would have explained, for example, why forgetting and disappearing are among the crucial human strategies against myth.

Literary Form and Virtuality

Benjamin's reading of "The New Melusine" and "The Fair-Haired Eckbert," as well as his opposition between the erratic, ahistorical fairy tale and the historical *Sage*, make tangible that in his view, fairy tales propose an overcoming of the constraints of historical timeliness, historical forces, and historical ideas and philosophies. His continuous return to them and their omnipresence in literary history reveal fairy tales as an archive of concepts whose short narrative form excluded them from history. Their timeless and placeless form allowed them to contain and transport a subhistorical layer of historical concepts and to point to a different nature of things uncaptured by historical transfers and their discursive forces. This explains why Benjamin uses Tieck's fairy tale as a topos, for example, to contrast the world of Kafka's guilt-stricken protagonists with the fairy tale's different ontology. More generally, the fairy tale complex plays a crucial part in advancing Benjamin's works from the years around 1920 to 1922, during which he had already posed various critical concepts through literary readings, such as the problem of fate in Molière's *The Imaginary Invalid* in his essay "Fate and Character," or the problem of mythical force as contained in the legend of Niobe in his "Critique of Violence."[29] It is obvious that the *Märchenbuch* was supposed to continue this line of work in a more systematic manner, fulfilling the requirements necessary for further academic qualification. Benjamin makes the most thorough expression of this broad literary, political, and academic objective behind the fairy tale in a curriculum vitae he wrote in early 1928, not yet having fully given up on the idea of becoming a professor. At this point, he seemed to have developed the core thesis of his fairy tale project, which he provides in brief:

> At the center of my work plans for the coming years are two subjects that link up with my latest book [the *Trauerspielbuch*], albeit in different ways. First: having attempted to lay bare the philosophical, moral, and theological content of allegory, I would now like to perform the same task for the fairy tale as an equally fundamental and originary repository of certain traditional themes — namely, as the disenchantment of the sinister powers embodied in the legend [*als Entzauberung der finsteren Gewalten, die sich in der Sage verkörpern*].[30]

This thesis continues the *Märchen*-versus-*Sage*, ahistorical-versus-historical opposition, but is even more specific in that the *Sage* now becomes the bearer of mythical forces, whose philological remedy is contained in the fairy tale's narrative. The notion or "content" of a fairy tale contains its ability to undo the historical forces, including contemporary formations such as capitalism or fascism, by providing forms of narration that would reinsert ahistorical morals into a modern age striving to discard the nonhuman. Fairy tales offer recourse to all sorts of suppressed ontologies and related ways of cognition that have been suppressed by the Cartesian and Kantian methods and must be regained to understand truth in history, which would become a primary focus for the *Arcades Project* and the essay "On the Concept of History."

In terms of the theory of small prose narratives, the formalism of the fairy tale is a unique condition, one that Benjamin recognized to its full extent. For him, the fairy tale has registered another world's actuality, proven by the fact that children in their not-yet-human ontology can naturally and "sovereignly access the world conveyed through the fairy tale."[31] Benjamin's extensive studies of child reality and child cognition are no mere side topic; they were clearly meant to underwrite his fairy tale studies. Benjamin saw children's book illustrations, especially, as well as toys and games, as transmission structures of lost and inaccessible aspects of humanity. While this field of study reinforced the centrality of Benjamin's fairy tale project, philological and literary thought remained its cause and purpose and also was supplemented by studies of phenomenology, surrealism, and psychoanalysis. These all reinforce Benjamin's conviction that in a way, narrative strategy in fairy tales is based on a reversal of the processes of adult cognition. Fairy tales do not begin with the normal, realistic, adult state of things and then magnify it to understand it, as the modern Cartesian sciences would do, but rather start with the minimized state of things that is immediate, "guiltless,"[32] and "sovereignly" accessible to the child. A whole subsection of the fairy tale project is dedicated to how this minimized nature of things is then magnified to the adult normativity of the world, a world in which the fairy tale comprehension must be discarded and replaced by the enigmatic state of phenomena.[33] Fairy tales and children both know of another nature of things, he writes, which is the adult nature of things, but in its "state of disappearance." Melusine's disappearing is therefore both program and example of a philological "reduction," as Benjamin calls it at one point,[34] with a word echoing the Husserlian practice of "reducing" the phenomena of the lifeworld to their essence.[35] It is a form of philological-phenomenological "reduction" that the fairy-tale form achieves. The true, nonadult, nonmodern nature of things can be known only by experiencing the other, parahuman form of life that emerges from fairy tales.

Against Myth: The Archive of the Homo narrans

However one assesses Benjamin's theory of the fairy tale, it is a general indicator of the specific and unique agency it finds and reclaims in this short narrative form. Benjamin recognized the formal potential of the fairy tale in order to employ it as a catalyst for a nonrealist, non-Kantian cognition of the world. In this, he was not alone in the 1920s because this particular literary genre also was selected by others for its formalist potential. Most famously, Propp published his *Morphology of the Folktale* at the same time as Benjamin worked on his

Märchenbuch, and Benjamin's friend Bloch also turned to the fairy tale in the late 1920s. For all of them, the fairy tale became the genre that had been symptomatically overlooked by modernity until its crises posed a set of problems that the ahistorical, nonsubjective narratives of the fairy tale promised to solve on an immediate, noncritical level. Fairy tales do not propose a theory. Rather, they teach a formalist mode of seeing the world that promises to reorganize perception and cognition around the essential deep structures of humanity, instead of following intentionalities or teleologies. The progressive quality of the fairy tale is in essence a metaphysical reduction in the sense posed by "The New Melusine," a Husserlian interruption or *epoché* of the present that posits abstract and not necessarily dialectical solutions for concrete historical problems. Fairy tales cannot be adapted to match specific states of a culture, but offer a genealogy of relations among agents of society, whether they are inanimate or animate, human or nonhuman.

In the opening chapter of his *Morphology of the Folktale*, Propp, like Benjamin, suggests this kind of deep structure of reality, which he also relates to Goethe's morphological thought.[36] But whereas Propp refers explicitly to the fairy tale classifications undertaken by Antti Aarne around 1910, Benjamin does not seem to be aware of such comparisons of source material. Both agree that the potential of the fairy tale form must be developed if it is to show its autonomous functional value in opposition to a mere application as children's literature. To name one other example, in his 1930 "The Fairy Tale Moves on Its Own Time" ("Das Märchen geht selber in der Zeit"), Bloch does not go beyond a differentiation between *Sage* and fairy tale in order to arrive at a theory of the fairy tale, yet he still recognizes the critical potential of the fairy tale for cultural philosophy.[37] Compared with Bloch's allusions to the continuation of fairy tales in Jules Verne's novels and Disney's movies, Benjamin's demarcation of the nonrealist value of the fairy tale and of the value of short narrative forms in general have a much longer reach. For him, fairy tales allow us to understand the force of literature and to demonstrate how such literary understanding can help to instruct modernity about the principal forces that have been active in societies for millennia.

In Benjamin's "The Storyteller" essay, the theory of the fairy tale reveals itself as what it has been all along: a theory concerned with narrative itself: fairy tales present the human as *Homo narrans*, and it is for this reason that children have natural access to them; that is, they represent a state of humanity prior to its maturity.[38] In an argument that aligns with Vico's idea of a precritical "topica sensibile" that collects and transmits prehistorical human knowledge through the millennia, Benjamin argues that before the forces and narratives of mythical power came to exist among peoples, narration brought equilibrium between them:

> The fairy tale, which remains the child's first advisor because it was once mankind's first adviser, secretly lives on in the story [*Erzählung*]. The first true storyteller was and remains the teller of fairy tales. When good counsel was rare, the fairy tale could offer it, and when need was urgent, the fairy tale's help was closest to hand. The need was the need brought by myth. The fairy tale teaches us about the first measures mankind took to shake off the weight of the nightmare myth had placed on its chest. . . . Fairy tales have long taught mankind and still teach children today that it's best to confront the powers of the mythical world with cunning and audacity [*List und Übermut*]. . . . The fairy tale's liberating spell does not make use of nature in a mythical way, but signals its complicity with liberated mankind. Adults notice this complicity only occasionally, that is, when they are happy; but children first discover it in fairy tales and it makes them happy.[39]

At this point, Benjamin finds nothing short of a social ethics of the *Homo narrans* codified in the fairy tale archive. The *Homo narrans* can bear and interact with the world only by means of short narrative forms. They are the archives of generations, telling about their practices of defending the freedom to decontextualize and recontextualize one reality with another. This archive of short forms is therefore also directed against the concentration of power through the unifying force of myths and its narratives, whether about nations, cultures, or other lineages. Of this archive, Benjamin gives a number of examples in the "Storyteller" essay that can be structured according to his *Märchenbuch* plan of reading fairy tales as containers of fundamental concepts of cognition. Each fairy tale presents one such concept by providing it with a "figure":

> In (1) the figure of the fool [*Gestalt des Dummen*], [the fairy tale] shows us how mankind "plays dumb" to protect itself from myths; in (2) the figure of the youngest brother, it shows us how mankind's chances increase as it leaves the prehistorical era of myth behind; in (3) the figure of the man who set out to learn what fear is [*Gestalt dessen, der auszog das Fürchten zu lernen*], it shows us that we can see through our fears; in (4) the figure of the clever wag [*Gestalt des Klugen*], it shows us that the questions posed by myths are as simple as the Sphinx's riddle; through (5) animal figures [*Gestalt der Tiere*] that come to children's aid, it shows us that nature is not beholden to myth, but prefers to gather around mankind.[40]

As with the functions of disappearing and forgetting, the concepts — or, better, virtues — posed by these five "figures" [*Gestalten*] that Benjamin lists could be, for example: (1) *figure of the fool* — dissimulation; (2) *figure of the youngest brother* — patience; (3) *figure of the man who set out to learn what fear is* — serenity; (4) *figure of the clever wag* — wittiness; (5) *animal figures* — animism. Like disappearing and forgetting, these are mental defenses evoked during hermeneutic processes, especially that of reading. Fairy tales can summon them because fairy tales have been told in order to elicit "philological interpolation" in all kinds of life situations for hundreds of years and have not lost this cultural capability in modernity.

Benjamin's rediscovery therefore sets up the fairy tale as an archive of the ahistorical *Homo narrans* at a time when such an archive must have appeared more valuable than ever during the transformations of institutions, statehood, and society. This archive of verbal acts represents a counterforce nearly untouched by modernity and allows Benjamin to defend the mode of "philological interpolation" as one that has shaped humanity forever against the pressure of adapting to the contemporary. He shows that fairy tales, counterintuitively, are not the opposite of reality, but rather access the underlying structure of reality. Directed against full envelopment in the lifeworld, fairy tales exercise the ability to distinguish between schematic reduction and lived reality. Switching between the two is an ability in danger of extinction in a world shaped by the absolutism of the present and the contemporary.[41] Benjamin uses fairy tales as a training ground to shape the phenomenological ability to understand the world.

After literary speech devalued schematic models of narration in the eighteenth century, the significance of reclaiming the fairy tale proved to be a heuristic tool for adapting both literary theory and cognitive theory to a formalism that had almost been forgotten. Only once it is brought into the light of theory can the fairy tale be understood as what it is, that is, a specific, modern form of litera-ture. To the high modernism of Benjamin and Propp, it unveils the many shortcomings of modernity's antiformalist understanding of reality and of literature. Fairy tales propose a cognition that is nei-ther empirical nor speculative, neither realistic nor fantastical, but formal, with its formalism located between realism and fantasy. Its narrative form is highly adaptive and relational because it can enter and modulate a large variety of human contexts. Fairy tales can alter motif histories (the Melusine fairy tale versus the legendary Melusine tradition), reformulate questions of genre (the fairy tale versus the *Sage*), modify mental activity (truthful cognition versus intentional-ity), and even guide quotidian behavior (respecting the fleetingness of a desired moment or person). In each example, only the contextu-alization of the fairy tale leads to new insights of both the ahistorical continuity of the fairy tale and the necessary implication for a spe-cific context. Taking the place left vacant by the *ars topica*, the fairy tale brings forth specific correspondences, arguments, and insights in situations and discourses that would have otherwise remained unseen. In regard of its agency, the fairy tale is therefore likely the most effective short narrative form and bears a specific metaliter-ary virtue. It makes visible and unmasks, it reduces and magnifies, it reformulates and declares, and thus is active as a virtual reality wherever retold or transmitted. The unique quality of Benjamin's theory of the fairy tale affirms this agency by proving the omnipresence of fairy tales through the need for the concepts they first formulated — disappearing, forgetting, and so forth — even if their retelling has been temporarily neglected.

CHAPTER SIX

Epiphanies, Enacted Stories,

and the Praxeology of Short Forms

The Short Form is its own necessity and suffices in itself

—Roland Barthes, *The Preparation of the Novel*

This chapter explores two sites of the emergence of short narrative forms in the twentieth century: Joyce's sudden new coining of such a form around 1903, his so-called "epiphanies," and the theoretical concept of the "enacted story," which was coined by Arendt in her book *The Human Condition* in 1958.

The epiphany distinguishes itself from the earlier cases of fairy tale, proverb, and novella by uniting the features characteristic of each separately—the ability to change perception, the posing of arguments, and a unique form—and thus will require briefly revisiting earlier arguments about the afterlife of *ars topica*. The appearance of the epiphany as a new genre shows that around 1900, the afterlife of the *ars topica* had contributed to the conditions for the possibility of forming new short narrative forms with a topical function almost out of nowhere; that is, the topical function could now fully express itself within the forms of modern literary discourse.

Arendt's theorem of the enacted story not only confirms the active features of short narrative forms, but requires her to return to the origins of the *ars topica* between Socratic discourse and Aristotelian dialectics, to the concept that in Chapter 1 I called the "embodied effectiveness" of a topos. Arendt's proposition that stories can become enacted or even act themselves thus traverses the whole arc of the topical function up to its appearance in the domain of modern literature, and it also shows its relevance for understanding the political and social aspects at work in literary discourse. I will therefore outline how short narrative forms can actively take part in social communication and quotidian practice in what is the culmination of this study: a final proposal for a praxeology of short forms.

Epiphany, Perception, Argumentation, Agency

There are few examples of genres that result equally from the practice of literature and the practice of life. One such genre, the Joycean epiphany, best demonstrates how, based on an epistemology of the small narrative form, narration and life intertwine until they merge into a gesture or an action that is still a literary form but already part of life. A minute genre, the Joycean epiphany is hard to define: part observation, part prose poem, part micronarrative. Of Joyce's original seventy or so epiphanies, only forty exist today and survive only in notebooks. Not one was meant to be published. Judging from the notebooks, these writings, which could easily be dismissed as ephemeral exercises, were elevated by Joyce to a genre with a pragmatic function and a precise definition. In a passage in the *Stephen Hero* manuscript, he defines the epiphany as follows:

> Stephen as he passed on his quest heard the following fragment of colloquy out of which he received an impression keen enough to afflict his sensitiveness very severely.
>
> The Young Lady — (drawling discreetly) . . . O, yes . . . I was . . . at the . . . cha . . . pel . . .
>
> The Young Gentleman — (inaudibly) . . . I . . . (again inaudibly) . . . I . . .
>
> The Young Lady — (softly) . . . O . . . but you're . . . ve . . . . . . ry . . . wick . . . ed . . .
>
> This triviality made him think of collecting many such moments together in a book of epiphanies. By an epiphany he meant a sudden spiritual manifestation, whether in the vulgarity of speech or of gesture or in a memorable phase of the mind itself. He believed that it was for the man of letters to record these

epiphanies with extreme care, seeing that they themselves are the most deli-
cate and evanescent of moments. He told Cranly that the clock of the Ballast
Office was capable of an epiphany.[1]

This frequently quoted passage contains both the theory of the
epiphany and one of its examples. Epiphanies are defined as triviali-
ties, that is, vulgar, irrelevant, or even meaningless occurrences that
suddenly manifest a spiritual cognition. What is important in the
quoted definition is that both the spiritual cognition and the worldly
cause for its occurrence can be recorded in writing.

However, the recording process is not merely a hasty jotting
down, but an operation to be executed "with extreme care," as the
novel cautions. Joycean epiphanies are thus results of a procedure
that is directly opposed to the almost mechanical modernist writing techniques such as the surrealists' *écriture automatique* that are
designed to capture elusive thoughts or observations as quickly as
possible. In contrast to their apprehension of an otherwise inaccessible, fleeting reality, the Joycean spiritual cognition is always present in the epiphany and thus only intensifies the more that rewriting
and correcting is done to it. The epiphany fully embraces the procedure of writing to bring out the delicacy and evanescence of those
moments. This is why only the "[woman and] man of letters" can
have epiphanies, as the text cautions, because the phenomenological
structure of the epiphany is above all a full result of the epistemological qualities of literary speech around 1900.

Joyce implies that for people of letters, occurrences in the world
can become phenomena only through a long, intensive procedure of
writing. It is this scriptural contemplation, rather than a mere accurate recording, that guarantees that the epiphanic moment will also
recur on reading the final epiphany. Epiphanies are not read to recall
the worldly occurrence, but reading an epiphany *is* the true epiphanic
experience that is the raison d'être of the whole genre. Epiphanies
are thus always already literary in their ontology, even before they
are written. They exist on the condition that the phenomenological

structure of reality is identical with the semantic structure of literary speech, or at least on the supposition that there is no epistemological priority of perceiving the world over writing it. As will be laid out in more detail below, epiphanies break up reality into nonlinear literary speech that approximates reading to perception.

Understanding them from this perspective — as the performance of contemplative writing procedures that fuse literary language with lived reality — also dismisses the long-standing claims of Joyce scholars that the epiphanies give specific spiritual and definable transcendent insights.[2] The literary ontology of the epiphanic experience, in other words, cannot be had by other means or media. Epiphanies are therefore a paradigmatic example of a short narrative form that is half knowledge of the world, half literary practice. Its invention by a single author around 1903 shows that at that point, the topical function had fully emerged as the epistemological condition for short narrative forms.

To record the full range of observations, descriptions, and dialogue fragments as in the example from *Stephen Hero*, the epiphanies do not follow canonical genre categories of lyric, epic, and drama but are transgeneric. At the same time, they have a strong form, a beginning and an end, a prosody, as well as a visual and punctuational composition. Some of the means Joyce uses in them stem from dramatic texts, such as bracketed stage directions; others are from modernist poetry, such as the dotted space between letters. Yet they are all organized around the principle of creating the epiphany for later recurrence within the full tool set of the "man of letters." Unlike Charles Baudelaire's "petit poème en prose" or Benjamin's "dialectical image," the text of the epiphany that Joyce structures recreates the dissolved structure of life in the modern everyday world that they were meant to represent. This radical performativity of writing shatters and almost disregards the unity of words and thoughts. As Umberto Eco has noted, "Epiphany is a way of discovering reality and, at the same time, a way of defining reality through discourse."[3] Their function is to translate "an actual experience into a linguistic equivalent of reality."[4]

While Eco therefore characterizes Joyce as the "last inheritor of the romantic tradition,"[5] this definition appears too focused on the epiphany's programmatic quality of recollecting the spiritual side of experience and leaves out that the factual core of the epiphany is the procedural act of writing. Joyce's epiphanies employ writing as a dysfunctional, fragmentary, and necessarily incomplete medium that has lost touch with earlier forms of spiritual scripture or romantic rendering. The art of the epiphany is not to translate or to capture, but formulaically to assign a single letter, sign, word, or syntagm to each corresponding item, gesture, act, or sensation in reality. Instead of a romanticism or a realism, which both rely on semantic literary representation, the epiphany proposes a different analogy between life and literature. Between the scene of life and the epiphanic moment, the writer places the page of paper, like a screen, on which the epiphanic form must be conjured like a puzzle. He must assign a written item on the page to an item in life, inventing a new assemblagelike mode for the interrupted nineteenth-century mediation of realistic depiction via meaning. Joyce's is a formalistic, diagrammatic procedure of notation that moves two-dimensionally on the page and proceeds in gestural emendations item by item, more like a collagist. See, for example, this two-dimensional use of the page in the surviving manuscript of epiphany no. 12, made by Joyce's brother:[6]

As the single surviving manuscript with Joyce's scrupulous cor-
rections also shows, the writer fills in and adjusts the scriptural elements on the page like parts of a visual riddle that requires contemplation and reordering until a fragmentary image can finally be read
and notation can again return to its literary purpose of narrating a
scene. This painstaking procedure successfully circumvents the sev-
ered immediacy of realist descriptions, but it can do so only because
the short narrative form has provided it with an epistemological form
and capability. Without the afterlife of the *ars topica*, there would be
no Joycean epiphany. While it resembles a prose poem, this formalist
bricolage of semantic items creates a completely new type of literary language, which allows it to achieve a much more overwhelm-
ing epiphanic effect for the reader, disclosing in fragmentary, anti-
mimetic, and topical semantics an image of the fragmented life.

These scriptural mechanics behind the epiphany foreshadow Joyce's
later self-fragmenting, hypertextual style in *Ulysses* and *Finnegans
Wake*. Around 1903, they are still phenomena parallel to the symbolic
realism of Walter Pater, Schnitzler, or the early Mann, from which
the epiphanies still retain the closure and formalism that will be over-
shadowed in Joyce's later novels because of their virtual endlessness.
Compared with the novel, the epiphany is a device within the symbolic
everyday, not its total simulation. Barthes called this their "instantly
meaningful event" because epiphanies do not require interpretation,
and even consciously evade it. By opposing them to the omnipresence
of the strictly seventeen-syllabic Haiku in Japanese culture, Barthes
identified the epiphanies and their quotidian blandness as a type of
short form that was usually not recognized as important and suppressed in the West because it contradicts the common rule that short
forms such as the maxim and the aphorism must be erudite or acute
to compensate for their brevity. "In the West," Barthes explains, "we
are overwhelmingly conditioned to furnish every reported fact with
an interpretation: culture of Priests; we interpret, we're incapable
of tolerating *short* forms of language."[7] His reading of the epiphanies
does not directly mention his earlier studies of the *ars topica* traced in

Chapter 1 but still continues that line of thought, namely, the problematic hermeneutical requirements of modern literary forms and the attempts to replace this hermeneutical demand with a semantics of form that does not need interpretation and speaks directly to the present. Joyce, in other words, invents a short form that can address the here and now and thus compensates for the modern Western tradition's lack of short literary forms specifically able to capture the present. The pragmatist features of the epiphany show that this new, post-topical quality of literary speech had fully developed, confirming in practice what Lessing, Hölderlin, and Kleist could only identify as a theoretical lack via their attempt to regain the fable for modern use. The epiphanies are certainly not the only such type of writing attempted since around 1900, but their existence proves in general that short narrative forms increasingly combined the qualities of topical discourse: to speak pragmatically to a present in order to provide arguments, to alter perception, and to provide life and discourse with a specific form.

Epiphanies perform a modulation of perception by suggesting that, similar to fairy tales, their use of literary speech can compete and even supplant sensitive perception, as Benjamin, Propp, and Bloch recognized a few years after Joyce. Whereas Benjamin identified fundamental mental operations such as dissimulation and patience in the parareality of the fairy tales, Joyce's epiphanies encode similar human operations but disguise this through their hyperrealism, which result in the effect that the reader is not reading, but rather having an epiphany of reality that requires reading. In this way, the following epiphany, no. 9, presents a character sketched through a series of isolated, truncated, and almost generic speech gestures. As a whole, they convey no full character, as in a novel, but rather a formal attitude of how one can behave banally against the world. The Tobin persona this epiphany evokes hence seems to be a "figure of the fool" whose banality Benjamin had praised as presenting one of the modes transmitted in fairy tales that humans use to defend against the destructive cultural qualities conveyed by myth:

[Mullingar: a Sunday in July:
noon]

Tobin — (*walking noisily with thick boots and*
tapping the road with his stick) . . . . O
there's nothing like marriage for
making a fellow steady. Before I came
here to the *Examiner* I used to knock about
with fellows and boose . . . Now I've a
good home and . . . . I go home in the
evening and if I want a drink . . . .
well, I can have it . . . . My advice to
every young fellow that can afford it
is: marry young.[8]

The Portrait of the Artist as a Young Man and its earlier, unfinished version, *Stephen Hero*, already contain adaptations of the epiphanies, sometimes even more than once, and decades later, this would continue in
Ulysses and *Finnegans Wake*. In all these cases, the epiphanies are slightly
modified and then inserted into the narrative as occurrences that are
in themselves not meaningful, but will become significant in relation
to the rest of an episode. Epiphany no. 9 is embedded at the very end
of the *Stephen Hero* manuscript, adapted into an episode in the city of
Mullingar where Joyce had presumably written it.

In the novel, the epiphany helps Joyce paint a dismissive picture of
the banal petit-bourgeoisie, small-town milieu, with its intellectual
and journalistic shortcomings. He turns the Tobin figure into Mr.
Garvey, a journalist at a newspaper, also called the *Examiner*, whom
the protagonist Stephen Dedalus is supposed to meet at his office, but
finds instead at a bar flirting with the barmaid. At the bar, Garvey
gives Stephen unsolicited advice on how to improve his writing and
about the quality of marriage, finally inviting Stephen, naively, to visit
him again soon. The argument about the banality of life that Joyce had
captured only negatively and implicitly through the bland, generic,
and hence formal speech gestures of the stand-alone epiphany — "O

there's nothing like marriage for making a fellow steady," "I go home in the evening and if I want a drink . . . . well, I can have it," and so on — is then made contextually explicit and is expressed directly in the novel. Embedding the epiphany's hyperrealist capturing of banality into the context of the novel makes it appear as if it were a natural, everyday reaction: "Stephen mumbled his thanks and decided that he would endure severe bodily pain rather than visit Mr. Garvey."[9] As in the case of the proverb in Keller's *Clothes Make the Man*, this intradiegetic function of the epiphany within the novel's events is then also repeated on the extradiegetic level of the formal relation between epiphany and novel. Mr. Garvey's intradiegetic instructions for improving Stephen's writing skills are an extradiegetic contradiction. Since Joyce's original epiphany had allowed Tobin to be part of the novel in the first place in the figure of Mr Garvey, Garvey's offer to improve Stephen's writing skills means endangering his own existence in the novel. Garvey's instructions about writing are thus not only banal, but always already secondary and inferior to Stephen's because Garvey is a result of Joyce's writing, and not the other way around. That Joyce wrote the epiphany independently from the novel, specifically to capture formalistically an "epiphanic" everyday moment, means that while it may now be part of the diegetic action in the novel, the epiphany retains its formalistic agency also beyond the novel. One could even conclude that Joyce decided to write this segment of the novel around the core of the epiphany not because he intended to "make use of" what he had written years earlier on the existing Tobin figure and its stupidity on the content level. Rather, Joyce wanted to contain the formulaic banality he had uniquely encoded in the epiphany to intensify the events of the novel while proving at the same time that the short form of the epiphany transgresses the novel. Morris Beja has listed all such evident adaptations of the forty surviving epiphanies that Joyce made in his four novels, yet many more actual or supposed adaptations can be found, or at least inferred, which demonstrates even to the philologist the intradiagetic and extradiegetic semantic potential of the form that Joyce chose for the epiphanies.[10]

The epiphany is hence no rendering or representation of reality. Lived reality is not immediately translated into a depiction consisting of words, syntagms, or sentences. Instead, in the procedure of writing, scriptural signs recreate a different reality that is not a mimetic imitation of lived reality. Epiphanies do not simulate lived reality; they dissimulate it. To do so, the epiphanies use a structural, diagrammatic approach to notate on a page the life that surrounds us. Their author is a formalist who understands writing as a strictly rule-based process without immediate access to the world, in opposition to an artist who, in the tradition of the aesthetics of genius, uses writing as a tool to imitate or express the world.

As we have seen, epiphany no. 9 achieves such a formalist creation of a reality both for Stephen Dedalus in the novel and for Joyce, who might be better called the "organizer" or the "assembler" of the epiphany.[11] But unlike forms of writing that create an alternative reality, the epiphany is a formal continuation of the structure of the everyday lifeworld and can let the reader return to it, better prepared to act in it. The epiphany in no. 9, for example, captures the stupidity of city life, but also points to a helpful aspect of knowing how to use this stupidity, which is quite reminiscent of the entries in Flaubert's *Sottisier* and *Dictionary* and the argumentative quality they carried. The banality of the petit-bourgeoisie is no longer the same after reading the epiphany, whether one has read it by itself or in its later embeddedness in a novel, because the epiphany has revealed Tobin's stupidity as being a formal gesture informing everyday behavior, that is, it captures in writing a formalistic form of life that can exist outside the novel. After all, lived reality is also where Joyce had originally experienced and captured it. Because of its autonomous structure, the epiphany outperforms the novel in its ability to enter the reader's everyday world and so is able to convey banality as a formal gesture that may be performed or taken up by the reader.

Joyce thus delivers an original and new narrative form conveying what, according to Benjamin, the fairy tale had already condensed into a formulaic story over generations. "In the figure of the fool," writes

Benjamin in "The Storyteller"'s typology of figures, the fairy tale "shows us how mankind 'plays dumb' to protect itself from myths."[12] Being struck by this insight into the formal power of Tobin's "playing dumb" creates reactions that interrupt and transgress the continuous everyday — like Stephen's "bodily pain" in the novel — which we also might experience when reading an epiphany. What the epiphany achieves by causing this vertical interruption of the horizontal continuity of lived reality is to reveal the formal character of Tobin's banality while modeling at the same time how it can be used. In sum, this being struck by the epiphany reveals to Stephen and also to the reader how an unresolvable issue, a problem arising out of the lived continuity of reality that he or she encounters, can be transgressed by an interrupting formal gesture, for example that of banality or stupidity. The epiphany does not instruct the reader on the level of content, that is, not by suggesting the reader respond by evoking how everything is banal, but instead by suggesting the reader respond to their own unresolvable situations by formulaically behaving banally or stupidly. The epiphany's literary phenomenology of the world thus instructs us to see the "topical" formalism and universality inherent in many allegedly "individual" situations of lived reality. Rather than creating mimetic simulations of reality that sharpen or augment the actual lived reality, epiphanies are devices that propose a reduced and estranged reality as an alternative to that reality[13] and that at the same time provide ways to engage with it accordingly.

Seen in this light of the afterlife of *ars topica*, epiphanies exhibit all three qualities discussed in the prior chapters. Like novellas, they have a form that allows them to enter lived reality and formally restructure it; like proverbs, they are micronarratives that contain arguments to be used in lived reality by the reader; and like fairy tales, they change our perception of lived moments and offer entry points as to how we can respond differently in such lived moments. As a consequence, epiphanies also demonstrate how codependent the three qualities of form, argumentation, and perception really are in manifesting the agency of short narrative forms.

Thus, for example, when reading the epiphany no. 9 by itself, its formal agency interrupts my ongoing lifeworld. Having been struck by the bland banality of the fool figure Tobin, I am trying to relate what I read back to my surrounding lifeworld by finding a formal relation between the epiphany and my lived moment. This attempt at relating results in my looking for an argument encoded in its micro-narrative—here, how banality or stupidity is a formal gesture that can be used—which I then take back to my ongoing lived reality as a kind of formula of advice; for example "When faced with an unresolvable situation of malign intent, play dumb!" I then carry the epiphany's agency with me as an option to behave in my lifeworld as a remedy for the next encounter where, feeling like a fool, I realize that my behavior or my answers fail me. The epiphany's initial agency that originally interrupted me stays with me through this chain of my interactions with the world and the epiphany. For this simplicity of behavior, the epiphany is a remarkable example for how the after-life of the *ars topica* had arrived in various short narrative forms by the late nineteenth century. This manifestation exhibits how short narrative forms had fully acquired the *ars topica*'s formal agency in the reader's daily life.

Short Forms as Actors

Another instance in which the narrating of stories has reemerged as a form of agency is Arendt's theory of politically effective speech. Arendt tried to renew ideas of embodied speech by connecting modernity with the function of speaking and arguing in the Greek polis. In her theory of action in the public space, Arendt describes the twentieth-century yearning and need for a form of speech conscious of the body of the speaker and of the presence surrounding her. In the political anthropology in her book *The Human Condition*, this form of embodied speech becomes possible again in a life form she calls the *"vita activa."* The *vita activa* is opposed to the alternation between contemplation and labor, the dichotomy of idea and implementation, that has shaped life in most of the West. To emphasize that a life of action—a life that is neither mere contemplation nor mere labor — becomes possible again, Arendt argues that humans need to signal their condition of being humans among humans by uniting their bodies and minds through their speech. More specifically, this can be achieved through a form of narrating or storytelling that she terms the "enacted story"; a person fully takes part in society only when his or her actions, opinions, and words appear to others as a united whole.[14] Without such enacted stories, she writes shortly after the end of World War II, modern society remains under threat.

To reclaim this unity of acting and speaking in modernity and to argue against the separation of theory and practice, Arendt provides a rereading of the Socratic method that goes against the traditional understanding of it since Aristotle. The dichotomy of theory and praxis, of philosophy and politics, she argues, was not merely an opinion proposed by Plato's rendition of Socrates, but was a direct consequence of Socrates' failure at his own trial. When his method failed Socrates after he tried to defend himself, the Socratic unity of speech and action also failed. As a consequence, Arendt continues, Plato changed the principle of embodied discourse so important to Socrates. With his conviction began the split between rhetoric and dialectic that Aristotle later fully separated into a theory of speech and a theory of thought. For Arendt, this sealed the loss of the *vita activa* in the Greek polis and permitted Aristotle systematically to separate rhetoric and dialectic. Her intention to regain in the twentieth century part of the Socratic mode of using discourse led Arendt to come up with the term "enacted story" in which knowledge, persuasion, fiction, and the speaker's corporeal here and now appear united. She writes:

> In the process of reasoning out the implications of Socrates' trial, Plato arrived both at his concept of truth as the very opposite of opinion and at his notion of a specifically philosophical form of speech, *dialegesthai*, as the opposite of persuasion and rhetoric. Aristotle takes these distinctions and oppositions as a matter of course when he begins his *Rhetoric*, which belongs

to his political writings no less than his *Ethics*, with the statement: *he rhetorike estin antistrophos tes dialektike* (the art of persuasion [and therefore the political art of speech] is the counterpart of the art of dialectic [the art of philosophical speech]). The chief distinction between persuasion and dialectic is that the former always addresses a multitude (*peithein ta plethe*) whereas dialectic is possible only as a dialogue between two.[15]

Arendt's theory of the enacted story is the resurfacing of the afterlife of the *ars topica* in the discourse of short-form storytelling in the twentieth century, with the *ars topica* seen as a continuation of the original Socratic method against the grain of Plato's and Aristotle's differentiations between word and thought. It is not surprising that this is the point in Arendt's argument at which literary narration as an agent appears, although Arendt acknowledges this role of literature only indirectly, by reminding modernity about the way we truly approach one another in the public realm, that is, by asking each other to tell our story:

> Action and speech are so closely related because the primordial and specifically human act must at the same time contain the answer to the question asked of every newcomer: "Who are you?".... This disclosure of "who" in contradistinction to "what" somebody is—his qualities, gifts, talents, and shortcomings, which he may display or hide—is implicit in everything somebody says and does.[16]

We judge or rather experience another person as a holistic unity of the story they tell about themselves. It is here that Arendt coins the term "enacted story" when describing the presence of a speaker speaking their views in the public realm.[17] "However, the specific revelatory quality of action and speech, the implicit manifestation of the agent and speaker, is . . . indissolubly tied to the living flux of acting and speaking."[18] This means that such stories turn into a practice that comprises speaker, story, and audience. In Arendt's view, such stories act on their own behalf and are not fully controllable by the storyteller, but rather become part of him or her: "What the

storyteller narrates must necessarily be hidden from the actor himself, at least as long as he is in the act or caught in its consequences,
because to him the meaningfulness of his act is not in the story that
follows. Even though stories are the inevitable results of action, it
is not the actor but the storyteller who perceives and 'makes' the
story."[19]

Short prose narratives therefore pose as humans telling a story and
provide a model of active speech in post-topical modernity. Arendt's
political philosophy is based on the fact that there exists a form of
storytelling in the post-topical tradition since 1800. This form of storytelling is not only the cornerstone of social communication in her
theory of the *vita activa*, but is also an undercurrent that has formed
the modes of short literary speech after 1800. Perhaps their relation is
even inverted. The existence of short literary forms, which Arendt
deemed essential given the work she dedicated to those of Kafka, Hermann Broch, and W. H. Auden, is the condition of the possibility for
Arendt's model of uniting thought and word in the *vita activa*.[20] Without short forms, there would be no enacted story. Within the fields
of social, political, and narrative philosophy, Seyla Benhabib,[21] Judith
Butler,[22] and Allen Speight[23] have identified this strong concept of narrative on which Arendt's political theory rests, yet literary theory has
largely overlooked this undercurrent of her thought. Arendt's attempts
to reestablish the relationship between public speech and storytelling
in the enacted story confirm that the afterlife of *ars topica* is active in
all modern types of short narrative forms.

Finally, the qualities of the enacted story enlighten the epistemological quality of short forms in general. For that purpose, Arendt's
description of the enacted story's rootedness in lived presence can
serve as model. This would mean posing the question "Who are you?"
not to the enactor of the story, but to the story itself. In this anthro-
pomorphic model for a hermeneutics of the short form, the "disclosure of 'who' " of the story would bring out more than its "what," that
is, more than features such as genre, type of narrator, plot, historical
placing, protagonists, and so forth. Instead, fully recognizing the

"revelatory quality of speech and action"[24] — seeing short forms as always already embedded in human actions — would bring out the capabilities that reveal the story's agency beyond what it is able to know about itself. This agent of the story's "speech and action" is the form of the story and can become visible only through "the disclosure of the agent in the act" in a praxeological model of literary hermeneutics. Without this disclosure of the story itself, Arendt continues, the "action" — the action of narrating or reading the story — "loses its specific character . . . . It is then indeed no less a means to an end than making is a means to produce an object. This happens whenever human togetherness is lost."[25]

Through the act of telling its story, whether by reading it or listening to it, the form of the story becomes the agent of this act of telling. A theory of the agency of short narrative forms has to recognize this quality of disclosing the form of the story. The enacted story speaks uniquely and distinctively to the reader, is always *in actu* and evokes the complete here and now of world and setting. It is precisely this condition of a literary form that Jolles had in mind in his observation that setting, protagonists, and time, for example, are secondary in a novella. In the end, "It all comes down to what happens."[26] Unlike a novel or a diary, a novella is capable of answering the question, "Who are you?" *as a short form* and specifically aims to do so. "The Short Form is its own necessity and suffices in itself," as Barthes defined it, which means that the drive to reveal itself as this self-necessary and self-sufficient form is its specific agency.[27] In so doing, the short form enters into a practical relationship with the reader's world and thus achieves a greater effect than the mere telling of a story.

For a Praxeology of Short Narrative Forms

Given this positioning of short forms between subject and world, the question that must be addressed, at least briefly, is the question of what agency the subject has when faced with short narrative forms. Who is the addressee of the epiphanies? For whom are they speaking, and to whom? In common hermeneutical models, an epiphany can be addressed only to the indivisible self, a self who is reading independently from the world. But this unidirectional reception aesthetics cannot account for the fact that the epiphany as such is *in* the world and available to anyone, like an autonomous entity. How individualistic and singular an act can the mere reading of a generally available cultural artifact such as a story, then, really be? Unidirectional models of reading cannot account for the autonomous position of short narrative forms in the world. For this reason, Arendt based her theory of enacted stories on the bidirectional model of the Socratic discourse, which also was the root of the *ars topica* as well as the pre-Aristotelian understanding of how fables work as *ainos*. This hypothesis contradicts the common narratological or rhetorical views that follow a causal chain according to which a narrator or speaker addresses a reader or a subject. What this book has been trying to show — that short narrative forms have their own agency that acts between reader and world — requires the suspension of the unidirectional account of causation that usually lies at the basis of representational models of literature.

To reflect the agency of short narrative forms, the common model of a linear unidirectionality:

narrative ⟶ reader (⟶ world)

must be replaced by a model of circular bidirectionality to account for the agency of the short narrative form:

Whereas the first model is limited to the reception of the short form by the reader and its possible application in the world, the second model displays the interaction between the reader, the world, and the short form as the interplay between three discrete entities as agents. It reflects the analyses proposed here according to which reading an epiphany or a novella is not a causal task with a telos, but a practice that necessarily includes the short narrative form as an autonomous agent. The epiphany can be read and will help the reader position herself in a particular way when facing the world. But the epiphany can also interfere in the reader's life and change her behavior toward the world. Whereas the unidirectional model is true for the novel, the bidirectional model accounts for the true agency of the short form. It shows that the epiphany is created as an agent by both the world *and* the reader, each of whom demand the application of the epiphany to the other. But the epiphany can also be applied to and subsequently interfere in both directions: the world equips the epiphany with a formalistic ability that the epiphany then applies to the reader, as we saw in the insight about the dissimulative effect of the banality in epiphany no. 9. But the reader can also use the epiphany as a device within the world and apply it in order to interfere in the world, for example by simulating stupidity to deflect against stupidity in the world.

This schematic theory of the agency of short narrative forms can also be reformulated more generally as a praxeology of literary forms. What literary theory has called "genre" — novella, epiphany, fairy tale, and so on — should therefore not be understood as a result of mere classificatory taxonomy, but rather as a name for a particular type of interaction or practice between the narrative form, the world, and the reader; a fairy tale changes perception, a proverb presents an argument or/and instructs how to argue, a novella singles out an incident from the world to extract a general meaning from it. As seen above, a Joycean epiphany can achieve all three of those ends. Novellas, fairy tales, and epiphanies can be conceptualized from the parallels of the rhetorical, logical, and advising intentions that they have retained from the *ars topica*. These stories are not genres; they are semantic configurations that take into account the text and its form but also the text's use as a cultural object in social practices. As seen in Chapter 2, for example, Blumenberg tries to remind philoso-phy of its fabulatory origin because the fable is a form of story that is specifically used in reflective, contemplative, and pensive prac-tices: the philosopher who likes to think reads fables and therefore practices philosophical activities, specifically, the pensiveness that Blumenberg deemed crucial. Short narrative forms are specific con-stitutions of practices that arise in the triangle linking the reader, the narrative, and the world.

"Practices," as they're understood here, are the actions of subjects and the tools they use as holistic routines beyond the subject-object dualism and not merely as rational decisions of a singular operator. That understanding derives from the analytic method of praxeol-ogy that has been increasingly studied and used in sociology and other social sciences. I am proposing that the role that short narrative forms play in modern life might best be described in terms of such practices. The discipline of praxeology rests on Pierre Bourdieu's, Foucault's, Bruno Latour's, and Butler's works, which understand a great many interactions of humans with things and cultural objects as such practices.[28] Foucault's idea of the "technologies" or "prac-tices of the self" is one origin of this theory. Another is the actor-network theory made famous by Latour, which has been understood as a praxeology because it describes research in natural sciences not as mere theory, but as an intricate network of repeated activities and routines carried out between scientists, data, and objects such as lab equipment.[29] The sociologist Andreas Reckwitz defines such social practices in the following way:

> A practice [*eine Praktik*] designates a routine of behavior that depends on implicit knowledge, but that at the same time is materially embedded in bod-ies and artefacts, as well as their specific arrangement. A practice — such as the practice of writing, for example — refers to a micro-unit, an everyday and cultural technique, which is, however, necessarily sustained by material units — e.g., in the example case of writing by the body specifically trained for writing, by writing tools, places of writing, etc. — which therefore enable, but also limit the practice.[30]

So far, such practice theories have been applied only to the production of literature, most famously in Barthes's concept of *écriture*[31] and subsequently as the core of a "scene of writing"[32] or the sociological process of authors[33] but not to the hermeneutic reception of literature. Karlheinz Stierle's book *Text as Action* (*Text als Handlung*, 1975) lays the groundwork for such a theory in the context of the reader reception studies of the Konstanz School, but his proposal of a "unified literary theory as a theory of speech action" has not been widely developed, nor has it turned into a praxeology of reading or a praxeology of the agency of literary forms, as I have proposed.[34] Another approach has been taken more recently by Caroline Levine and Terence Cave, among others, to describe the aesthetic and interactive potentialities literary formations offer to readers with the concept of "affordance" borrowed from psychology and design theory.[35] Being a "weak concept," as Cave acknowledges, affordance however primarily allows for a "redescription"[36] of literary agency with new terminology adapted from sociology and behavioral psychology. It thus operates on a different disciplinary track from this study, which attempts understanding the civic agency of literary formations from within genealogies of literary speech.

Foucault's description of the *lettre de cachet* as a form of literature at the center of a whole set of practices that involve not only social interaction, but specifically reading and interpretation, is perhaps the paradigmatic existing example of a literary praxeology. The above case studies of specific short narrative forms are therefore foundations for such a literary praxeology, which does not necessarily require social practices to be at work but can limit itself to hermeneutic practices that can remain within the boundaries of the literary work. A praxeology of literary forms brings out the social implication of the epistemological implications of this form. In this regard, to refer to just one other example, Benjamin's analysis of the pragmatic function of the novella, *The Marvelous Young Neighbors,* in Goethe's *Elective Affinities* is such a study of intradiegetic and extradiegetic practices.

As a 2013 collected volume suggests, something like "a knowledge of genres" exists. That is, literary genres not only can formalize the interactions between reader and world, but also can contain specific knowledge of the world, for example, knowledge of nature as such.[37] To possess this transcendental quality, literary forms must have an a priori active or practical quality. In the context of Rheinberger's epistemological theories of experimental systems, small narrative forms could then also be described as "epistemic things," that is, objects that contain knowledge of the world and bring it into a specific poetic formation that is involved in practices of reading and interpretation.[38] With reference to Blumenberg's theorem of the nonconceptuality of metaphors, Rheinberger has also argued that epistemic objects "act at a distance," a definition of their activity on the basis of indeterminacy, which Blumenberg's fable theory strongly enforces.[39]

This brief outline of a praxeology of short narrative forms must suffice here, but it affirms what has been argued about the inherent agency of short forms. With the Arendtian unity of action and speech in mind, literary forms could be described as *acting at a distance*, that is, as acting in the world by their configuration of epistemological condition and specific indeterminacy. Arendt's return to the Socratic origins of the *ars topica* to arrive at a demand for the disclosing of the self in storytelling thus summarizes the argument of this volume: the afterlife of the *ars topica* consists of practices in which short narrative forms act between self and world.

Civic Storytelling

and the Postliterary Image Life

Since the late twentieth century, the appeal of civic storytelling has extended beyond literary texts, assimilating the spread of the visual means of photography, video, film, animation, video games, virtual reality, and augmented reality. In addition, lived and personal storytelling has returned in such projects as *The Moth* and NPR's *Radio Diaries*. It seems fair to say that storytelling has left the realm of literature and has become omnipresent. The formerly specific term "storytelling" now covers a spectrum from the New Journalism of Tom Wolfe and Joan Didion in the 1970s, to the documentary films of Alexander Kluge and Werner Herzog, to business practices involving viral public-relations campaigns and product-marketing strategies. Yet only very few of these inflationary uses of the term "storytelling" warrant what we have called "civic storytelling," the recasting and reimagining of civic life through a certain kind of brief narrative that can radically modulate the ontology of human encounters. While expanded storytelling such as the New Journalism or public relations perhaps appear to draw on the novella's original proximity to the newspaper, in the sense of a story accentuating a novelty, this so-called storytelling glosses over its problems to make them disappear, resulting in the opposite of the narrativized accentuation of civic storytelling. Fact is approximated to fiction not to catalyze the understanding of specific problems, but to redirect the reader's or viewer's attention away from the problems at hand. This results in a breakdown of the separation of form and content, the differentiation for which a novella or a report must introduce arguments and to which it must guide attention.

Despite the exaggerated currency of storytelling, there is a strand of nonliterary and nontextual storytelling in the decades after Joyce and Arendt that truly acts with civic interest and brings the short narrative form into the postliterary realm. These narratives mix documentary and factual accounts of general knowledge with personal, subjective perspectives, reports, and experiences that turn an event or a problem into an experience, updating the novella, fairy tale, and epiphany forms. There may be no climate change, to give one example, unless a narrator tells the story of seeing it with their own eyes, narrating by social media post, smartphone-filmed video, or in conversations with relatives or friends the failure from one winter to the next of crops reliably grown for a century. Because they are personal, some of these exploratory stories have been called "essays," yet these are not the same things as the essays of Montaigne or Virginia Woolf, not true soliloquies of thought. Postliterary civic storytelling is essayistic in its experimental mixing of media genres, crossing the textual essay's conjectural initiation of thought with an exploration of various media genres. The term "essay" is also inaccurate because it omits the narrative core of these accounts. Instead, such storytelling "essays" stand in the tradition of short narrative forms and update genres such as the fable, the novella, because they perform a topical form of speech addressing the here and now. They present an event or a phenomenon, and not a mere idea, which is why postliterary short narrative forms that narrate civic stories can be videos, photo stories, or graphic novellas, but also mixed-media installations in art spaces or virtual-reality experiences. Before facts or information can be drawn from such short-form narratives, their form guides our attention to extraordinary occurrences within the everyday, bringing them and the underlying problems and questions into the world for the first time.

Stranger Than Fiction

The media artist Steyerl has pointedly caught the problem of story-telling today by arguing that the trend of mixing personal and documentary media in journalism or art is not just typical of the digital realm, but it is also symptomatic of a general cultural discontent with fiction. She detects this problem in the fact that "the mix of fact and fiction is one of the main tools of contemporary political manipulation." While the simultaneous increase of personal essayistic story-telling thus merely seems to remedy the larger trend in manipulation with its individualized version, in which one might see the effects of neoliberalism on the person, Steyerl is also witnessing an active "response" to this development: "There is a new lease on realism, to safeguard veracity, facts, reality, etc.," resulting in a complementary increase in the documentary, almost as a remedy to the omnipresent essayification and essayistic storytelling.[1]

The problematic consequence of the deepening opposition between essayism and realism, she continues, is that the middle ground between the two is no longer desired by narrators of either side. Fictional storytelling finds itself caught in a third space between speculative essay and realist documentation and is declared dangerous if it does not position itself clearly as an unhinged essayistic story or as quasi-documentary autofiction. Current novellas, epiphanies, and fables are required to justify the validity of their genuine mode — how and why their own values are different from the manipulative political fictions such as sensationalism, fake news, or conspiracies, on the one hand, and from the warranted, fact-based, personal, and witnessing narratives on the other. The ability of storytelling to introduce new problems into society, as Arendt had demanded, is thus already ontologically prohibited when fiction is exempt from civic discourse. The public is increasingly trained to pay more attention to how a narrative is framed, whether as proven fact or as unsubstantiated commentary, than to allow the story its own unpredictable and selective adaptation of reality and fiction.

With respect to her own work as a media artist, Steyerl formulates an emphatic advocacy of fictional storytelling: "It seems that one not only has to defend facts, but maybe fiction has to be defended equally rigorously. It is a fact that telling fictional stories does not necessarily equal lying. So, while the assault on facticity erodes civic life, trying to mitigate the situation by minimizing fiction erodes art."[2] Her defense of fiction does not obey the rules of the lie-or-fact polarization but seeks to reground art and fiction in the pre-essayistic mode where fact and fiction cohabit in narratives that seek to emphasize greater societal problems, as we saw, for example, in how Storm's story of Hauke Haien turned a dike into a body politic physically negotiating between nature and culture.

Elsewhere, Steyerl explains that the apparent lack of similar civic problems being identified in the postliterary era since the 1980s resulted from an increased tendency of real life to separate from its own fantasies. This led to the paradox that the imaginary threads always running through real life can no longer be fully imagined, since their transfer into actively fantasized or fictional modes is suppressed by the need to focus on facts. To approach this paradox as an aesthetic problem solved by fictional storytelling, Steyerl reoccupies the term "documentary," albeit only in quotation marks. What she desires to be "documentary" is thus the form of a genre, rather than a mode of representation: "My conviction is that, now more than ever, real life is much stranger than any fiction one could imagine. So somehow the forms of reporting have to become crazier and stranger, too. Otherwise they are not going to be 'documentary' enough, they are not going to live up to what's happening."[3]

Steyerl's undertaking is to work against the fact-or-fiction dichotomy by documenting the paradoxical and hence fictional ingredients of all that is falsely deemed purely factual. For postliterary storytelling, the underlying question we can extract from Steyerl's theory is hence primarily a formal one: How can reality or real life today be evoked, rendered, and addressed in its postliterary version? Steyerl implies the detachment of reality from textuality when she points out how much a representation of "real life" would have to take into account what she terms "image life," a concept signifying the mode of everyday life in current post-textual societies. We live with images, in images, and as images, that is, as both conscious and unconscious consumers, objects, and agents of images. "The thing formerly called real life," Steyerl summarizes, "has already become deeply imaged," and hence can no longer be grasped by "what we used to call representation."[4] Neither theories of representation nor representational artistic practices have been able to capture how our image life can be narrated.

In a world that is no longer a textual reality but increasingly an "imaged" reality, civic storytelling and short narrative forms must consist of an "imaged storytelling" that works beyond the mere and often disciplinary, institutional, and medium-specific distinctions that still determine that a certain problem be narrated only in a certain way. Such conventional pairing suggests that simple normative differentiations are still unquestionably applied when a story is told: Must it be a text, image, or film? Art, literature, or essay? Online, in the university, or the museum? Such categories restrict storytelling modes to certain media, genres, and institutions and over time have even helped cause increasingly polarized modes of thinking and framing content in either-or dichotomies. These increasingly irreconcilable categories fundamentally illustrate Steyerl's point about the decreasing ability of listeners, readers, and the public to engage with not easily categorizable narratives. An experimental and avant-gardist attitude such as that radiating from Joyce's epiphanies or Flaubert's *idées reçues* no longer creates interest in today's postliterary "real life," but does not receive the attention it demands and deserves simply because it falls into categories such as "text" and "literature" that no longer apply to early twenty-first-century real life in its fullest sense.

The modern and modernist rules of formatting narratives and stories have ceased to function today, and Steyerl's diagnosis that the divergence of fact and fiction has left open a large, uncovered area of fiction suggests that the problem must hence be solved by letting genres, institutions, and media fully overlap in the same way that our "real life" always overlaps with our "image life." Instead, however, even mixed-media formats often keep separate speculative and factual passages and do not allow the crossing of modes and their mutual intensification. Speculative novellas such as the magical novellas of César Aira, for example his 2002 *Varamo*, or speculative film legends such as the 2015 film *Il Solengo*, directed by Alessio Rigo de Righi and Matteo Zoppis, have tried to answer this misleading policing of modalities by consciously yet defensively suppressing clear genre definitions.

A more aggressive and effective approach is offered by Steyerl herself. In another 2016 interview, she is asked about her mixing of scientific articles and artistic videos and answers with an imperative to conflate media, genre, and institution to aim for new epistemologies of today's hybrid forms of life:

> There are certain rules of science that, on the one hand, are very helpful but, on the other, also constitute mental barriers. Pure speculation, however, or fabulation — means I am unscrupulously drawing on — are sometimes cutting open unforeseen breaches between one area and another — between different disciplines or traditions but also quite often between completely separate geographic regions. I believe that we have to think together what does not belong together because that's reality today. And that's where extended procedures [*erweiterte Verfahren*] are needed.[5]

One can sense here that Steyerl's theoretical analyses about the emboldened distinctions between fact and fiction are only preparing conclusions she draws for her own storytelling work in her films and also, to some extent, in her presentations. "Documenting" reality, in other words, is increasingly an act of creating active narrative forms by emphatically mixing genres so that they spill into each other without providing the reader or viewer with markers or warranties about the level of fictionality or facticity — all while capturing as closely as possible the lived realities of humans, which would be unnarratable by the means of nineteenth-century realism.

Figures 3–6.
Stills from Hito Steyerl, *How Not to Be Seen: A Fucking Didactic Educational .MOV File*, 2013, signed certificate sent via Fedex—10/11/2016, HD video, single screen in architectural environment, 15 minutes, 52 seconds. Image CC 4.0 Hito Steyerl. Images courtesy of the artist, Andrew Kreps Gallery, New York and Esther Schipper, Berlin.

Steyerl's 2013 work *How Not to Be Seen*, for example, an almost six-teen-minute video that has also been shown as installation, could be categorized as a short narrative fiction, perhaps as a novella or a fairy tale or even as a story bearing "the air of a fable," as a recent catalogue suggests.[6] Ascribing such genres to Steyerl's video work is not beside the point; it offers an exercise that is highly suited to gauge the sys-temic impact of short narrative forms in the postliterary realm. In fact, Steyerl provides her works, both videos and video installations, with a thoroughly narratological groundwork that understands the limits of the author in the postliterary. The works use the collective visuality of our "image lives" to tell us stories that are by definition collective, made up of analyses, examples, and fictional applications. Seen as a small narrative form, Steyerl's works are fairy tales accord-ing to Benjamin's theory. Both formally analyze malignant actors and structures in the world while at the same time narrating plots that encapsulate the overcoming of this evil, often in concluding utopian parables. The viewer is instructed how such an analysis of evil can be used to turn its mode of controlling the world on its head. In *How Not to Be Seen*, for example, a fundamental dialectic between visibil-ity and controllability is narrated through historical dispositives of optical sovereignty, from camera technology to gated communities, but is then turned topsy-turvy by a fantastical revenge fairy tale. The very people who were treated only as pixels by digital-observation machines hijack the same camera technology that subjected them to the digital realm and thus, by controlling their own visibility dis-positive, decide finally to live on as "happy pixels" in "low-resolution gif loops."[7]

With regard to her own theoretical takes on the possibility of "documentarism" today, Steyerl's work can be best summed up as escalations of the documentary in which realism becomes an agency against itself. Steyerl's narratives begin very much in the way novel-las, proverbs, and Joycean epiphanies begin, that is, as close to reality as possible. They then so overstretch their realist diegesis and its surfaces of the "image life" that they create glitches in what now no longer can be considered a reliable representation. Steyerl has described her extended procedures of storytelling as "ripping reality,"[8] an undertaking similar to Eyal Weizman's project of a "forensic architecture."[9] This points to a two-step process of narration to tear through reality's surface and then to "rip off," to appropriate reality by modeling it differently, a process that accurately explains the poetological structure of Steyerl's video works. In contrast to other critical media artists of the postliterary era such as Harun Farocki and Trevor Paglen, the critical theory produced by tearing through reality in Steyerl's works is only the debris of the videos. Their primary effect is to narrate an unrealistic short story with its "ripped" realistic means so that it can interfere with our everyday lives. In their fabulatory tales, they accentuate the shortcomings and blind spots of reality and offer them to political discourse.

As a consequence, Steyerl's diegeses underline that our twenty-first-century forms of image life are not (or not yet) comprehensible by rendering and synthesizing factual information but only by undoing its existing explanations by concentrating and intensifying them until they tip over into fairy tales and fables. For that reason, Steyerl has described her working method not as "creating evidence or doing any form of consciousness-raising" but instead as working toward "finding ways to improve situations."[10] Her verb "to improve" points to operations of semantic formatting such as emphasizing, intensifying, and accentuating, which by going back to her diagnosis about today's lives as being lived through paradoxically unavailable images underlines that real situations of the image life can be narrated only by "extended procedures." The diegesis of such storytelling procedures must disregard the mental barriers between heuristic fantasy, personal fiction, investigative reporting, and scientific theory and their respective media or institutions. Unsurprisingly, the phenomenon of "improving situations" through fabulistic stories echoes Blumenberg's interest in "inducing" "pensiveness" by the same type of stories, the unexpected opening of breaches and glitches in the lifeworld by interruption and disturbance. "We think about where we stand," writes Blumenberg in a definition applicable to Steyerl's videos, "because we were disturbed in not thinking about it. Pensiveness means: everything is not as obvious as it was."[11]

No Climate Change without Storytelling

When Steyerl opts to reintroduce fiction into the documentation of reality, she is in fact choosing to return to an earlier stage of short-form narration, that is, the eighteenth-century stage of protonovellas found in the *lettre de cachet* system and in similar case history collections. As discussed earlier, case studies and case histories have generally been read to contain a specific scientific knowledge relevant for fact-based epistemologies such as scientific observation, medicine, and law. Yet they reveal facts in such casuistic systems only because readers in such a system know what range of information they are looking for and already understand such stories as representations of a specific type of case. A doctor interested in studying epilepsy might collect a set of case histories of what are believed to be epilepsy patients but will overlook the linguistic, geographic, or even narratological knowledge also contained in them. The epistemic system in place prescribes what can possibly be found in such case stories, namely, by definition, nothing outside of the system that organizes them. What gets overlooked in such a system is the agency of the form of the story.

A case history narrates an event so that it appears to offer knowledge. The casuistic framing, however, makes the reader forget the short form's crucial part in the production of this knowledge. This means, in turn, that whenever short forms are considered to contain knowledge, an aspect of narratological form is at play in fictionally simulating such knowledge, in particular when short forms render scenes, events, or situations that are not yet easily sortable into casuistic systems. As seen particularly with the novella, short narrative forms narrate realities that involve unheard-of events or occurrences, which indicate that these events are unheard of because no collective or systematic effort exists to make them heard and to understand the causes and reasons for their happening.

The definition that unheard-of events must be told, however, is exactly what Steyerl demands today from the "documentation" of our "image life"; there must not be any compliance with the preexisting epistemic systems such as "reality" or "fabrication," and the "documentation" of unheard-of events must exhibit how our lived lives are indeed stranger than fabrication or reality. What is unheard of — a story depicting an "improbable veracity" (*unwahrscheinliche Wahrhaftigkeit*) — suffices to be told. Steyerl thus reactivates this Kleistian formulation, which as Rüdiger Campe has developed,[12] marks the narratological border case of creating reality through fictional prose, that is, narrating what is virtually real (true) but factually unrealistic or improbable. For Steyerl, however, such improbable veracities must be extended to improbably veracious formats and media, thereby making the story worth telling by extending its means. Scientific arguments, Steyerl argues, should occur side by side with highly speculative fabulations, purely fabricated characters, and realistic everyday settings, whether as narration or image. With her program, Steyerl lays out what short-form civic storytelling in our day must do to narrate occurrences of life again in such a way that they indeed continue the effectiveness of topical speech. They give form to everyday occurrences and hence change how realistically these occurrences are perceived so that they can be introduced into society as issues demanding attention, response, and reaction.

One such current area that has attracted much attention from storytellers in the recent two decades is the environment, in particular under the conditions of climate change. While the plots of stories about the environment and the climate all follow one and the same basic interest — to capture specific sensations and situations — there are primarily local and personal occasions and reasons to tell climate stories, particularly because the narrator can be the witness only of the environment and the climate they live in and have experienced.[13] While originally, climate change was conveyed and documented through secondary statistical data such as carbon dioxide levels in the atmosphere, by the early 2000s, geographers had begun to provide first-person accounts of climate change. One such study published in 2008 documents the stories told about a changing climate by the First People Iñupiat members of the small community of Point Hope, Alaska, the northwesternmost settlement in the Western Hemisphere. The cultural geographer Chie Sakakibara, who studied their narrative culture from 2005 to 2007, concluded that "contemporary storytelling among the Iñupiat of Point Hope seeks to cope with an unpredictable future":

> Arctic climate change impacts human lifeways on a cultural level by threatening their homeland, their sense of place, and their kinship with the environment.... Such change is culturally processed through the tradition of storytelling, and storytelling serves as a way of maintaining connectivity to a disappearing place. The types of stories and modes of telling them reveal people's uncertainty about the future based on knowledge of the immediate past....The Iñupiat memory stays alive with their home, and the drowning home is to be remembered as the storytelling practice keeps the human kinship with the land visible and tangible as a cultural form of communication.[14]

Sakakibara presents climate storytelling among the Iñupiat as the continuation of a folk practice already in place. It follows no preframed epistemological system, like Western empiricist casuistry, but arises from within a community dealing primarily with the practical challenges of a rising sea level and melting tundra. Academic and journalistic categorizations of fact, fiction, and fabrication, of science, story, and subjectivity, cannot be applied to the storytelling she describes among the Iñupiat. Their practices are not caused by climate change, but rather assimilate the occurrences, uncertainties, and preparations resulting from a warming Arctic Circle into their existing storytelling routines and frameworks.

In light of this and other examples of how indigenous people adapt life practices to the Anthropocene, the global efforts to explore, track, and exhibit climate change through storytelling can be understood as a relearning of older techniques of the *Homo narrans*.[15] As seen in the calls for a recognition of such practices by Benjamin,

Propp, and Bloch, Western modernity has systematically concealed the communicative and political potential of collective storytelling, especially as fairy tales or folk tales. Understanding the regional and larger environment via sense experience and direct communication has been devalued, as well, since the arrival of science-based disciplines of environment monitoring. That short-form storytelling, however, always has been the most capable way of processing environmental and climatic situations for the individual was foreshadowed by Locke's seventeenth-century example of how a personal commonplace anecdote about the weather creates a better situational understanding than syllogistic or systematic knowledge could. John Durham Peters has recently pointed to the deeply modern yet phenomenologically impoverished predisposition at stake here when he argues that the twenty-first century must "open again the relationship of media to nature" on a fundamental level, which, according to him, should lead to a new "a philosophy of elemental media."[16] Short-form storytelling is perhaps one of the few human practices that has such openness to the media-nature relationship deeply inscribed in it. The Iñupiat of Point Hope, in other words, model for Western civilization the epistemological practices and qualities of storytelling that were lost since Locke's hopeless attempt to defend a country gentlewoman's anecdotal reasoning against modern science. In a reversal of the catastrophic Western dismissal of Indigenous practices in the last centuries, the temporalities of who needs to catch up to whom have now been flipped. While the Iñupiat and others will likely retain their storytelling practice during the ongoing climate catastrophe and following the resulting changes, the question is rather whether the West and the Westernized can roll back to a pre-Lockian state of the *Homo narrans* in time to adapt their lives to their storytelling.

A range of projects already exists that aim to reawaken such storytelling about the climate for nonindigenous and nonfolkloristic people and communities. Storytelling, however, is primarily considered a journalistic and documentary work that communicates facts about climate change in multiple modes and media. A recently funded UK-based initiative of documentary filmmakers called the Climate Story Lab, for example, promotes existing films about the climate and provides a "tool box" for "both storytellers and cultural organizers — from museum curators to college professors to festival programmers — to facilitate necessary climate narrative conversations."[17] The global political conversation about climate change is accurately framed as a "narrative" because it includes a large non-factual, fictional, but nonetheless effective component. Their goal is not to extend science, but to aim to initiate the telling of stories about the minute effects of climate change around the world, ideally reaching "a biodiversity of stories as diverse as the ecosystem we seek to save." Similar to the casuistic case history projects of the seventeenth and eighteenth centuries, the multitude of stories that such large-scale storytelling projects aim to promote serve primarily a particular predefined cause. In each story, climate change is supposed to be identified. In contrast to the criminalistic *lettres de cachet*, or the psychological *Erfahrungsseelenkunde*, there isn't a single ideal addressee, such as a king, a judge, or a doctor, who needs to be persuaded according to preexisting norms and rules. Climate-change storytelling addresses a multitude of audiences across the world — the *Homo narrans* as its desired universal audience — and each will read such stories about climate change with different preconceptions, expectations, or even biases. The openness of such projects makes them less scientific and more discursively aimed at an open public. Hence, they compare to oral histories, which have been perhaps the most politically effective form of collective storytelling projects in the twentieth century. Revealingly, both collective oral history and collective climate change storytelling have a common goal beyond merely spreading experiences. They capture and record lived realities that are in danger of being overlooked, forgotten, and mistreated exactly because they are not necessarily available as empirical data, but as anecdotes, situations, and unheard-of events.

The Belarusian author Svetlana Alexievich has compiled

numerous such storytelling projects, most famously those of survivors of the 1986 Chernobyl nuclear disaster, in her 1997 book *Voices
from Chernobyl: The Oral History of a Nuclear Disaster.*[18] In her epilogue,
Alexievich confronts the opposition between factual reporting and
fictional storytelling that is at stake in the ongoing renewal of this
form of civic interaction. While she set out to write an "oral history,"
as the subtitle of the book acknowledges, Alexievich is convinced
that "the simple fact . . . is no closer to the truth than a vague feeling."
It was thus not overlooked scientific data, but a relentless "spilling of
these feelings past the facts" on the side of the Chernobyl survivors
that caused her to collect these stories. Her anthology sets out to
reach beyond factual history to a deeper history made of emotions
exclusively transferable through the plots of stories. Comparing her
own interest in storytelling to Russian literature, Alexievich argues
that oral histories must go beyond the facts in a way that only literary
narration can. "Why repeat the facts — they cover up our feelings,"
she writes, summarizing the threat and thereby justifying, at least
implicitly, how she has freely montaged and adapted the interviews
she conducted over several years in Belarus for her book. Plot formations and their dramaturgy also lead Alexievich to focus on the
everywoman and everyman who experienced Chernobyl because it
was they who "were . . . answering the most important questions,"
not academies or politicians.[19]

Alexievich's self-assessment underlines that the literary techniques
of editing, narrativizing, and montaging are essential to produce collective storytelling whose formal structure attracts the attention
needed to compete with purely factual, nonliterary discourses such as
science and journalism. As seen in the context of the *lettres de cachet*,
the most irrelevant person in society can make their story heard at the
top or the center of society only by short-form storytelling resembling
the novella, the epiphany, or the fairy tale to create genuine attention
from the bottom up. For this reason, Foucault had likened these *lettres*
to the novella, and this bottom-up urge of storytelling continues in
Alexievich's single-handed montage of individuals.

The 2010s were a time when purely bottom-up storytelling could be seen to return in the context of climate change in nonindigenous, largely science-driven mass-information societies. A 2017–18 project by the American journalist Meera Subramanian reported a reemergence of storytelling in a series of nine articles titled "Finding Middle Ground: Conversations across America" that she wrote for *InsideClimateNews.com*. Moving from shellfish harvesters on the Texas coast to Georgia peach farmers and dogsledders in Wisconsin, Subramanian traces how the facts of a changing environment — warmer winters, more rain, flooding, heavier storms, rising sea levels, and overfishing, to name just a few — look from the bottom to those relying economically on its day-to-day stability. Finding such signs and instantiations of climate change on an immediate, direct level of economic dependance ensures the genuine emergence of a story from an individual's lifeworld. But Subramanian is not just looking for working-class authenticity. Without bias, she depicts the opposing stories constructed by those working on the ground to make sense of the change they are witnessing around them. Her work is thus journalistic only on the surface, resembling instead the work of the cultural geographer Sakakibara, who depicted the Iñupiat in Alaska, the difference being that through Subramanian, we see that climate storytelling has now suddenly reemerged among nonindigenous cultures suddenly faced with unexpected changes. "Human beings are natural storytellers," Subramanian recounts, describing what she found in her series, "and there are two narratives being told in America today about how to make sense of extreme weather events." She offers the following explanation for these fundamentally different narratives:

> One narrative comes from scientists and large international organizations with unwieldy names like the Intergovernmental Panel on Climate Change (IPCC), who offer a lot of numbers and complicated science about a warming planet.... The other narrative turns to a single book filled with parables of good versus evil and drama far more compelling than what the IPCC reports

offer. The Bible explains tragedy and human suffering and redemption as being part of God's plan, giving meaning to natural disasters.[20]

As applicable as Subramanian's opposition between science and religion might be, especially where she encounters climate change skepticism from Evangelical Christians, it seems clear that the difference between science and the Bible stems from their opposing implications for narratology and storytelling. While there are not always specifically and literally biblical oppositions to the top-down narrative of science, the centuries-long success of the Bible lies in its narrative composition. Hundreds of parables and episodes are offered for interpretation, and the Bible's resistance to science and, for that matter, the resistance of other religious books to science, is more reflective of the human condition as storytellers than of the internal failures of science. In fact, the Bible's descent from a vast tradition of apocryphal storytelling was disguised only after its canonization from a growing story anthology to a single completed book in late antiquity and the early Middle Ages. Almost all scriptural religions are results of prior mythological, parabolic, fantastical, legendary, and other short-form storytelling collections, pointing to the anthropological consistency of making sense of changing worlds by adapting existing plots and narratological devices to new events and environments.[21] Subramanian even discloses that she did not mention climate change when collecting the stories of her interlocutors, but instead let them tell their own version of what we have generally come to call "climate change." For any anticlimate-change project that relies on individuals acting out of their own conviction, this means that such apocryphal storytelling is necessary to make sense collectively before collective action can begin.

A Georgia peach grower's family, for example, whose farm dates back to 1897, tells Subramanian how their well-established peach varieties no longer receive the required amounts of "cold hours" below forty-five degrees Fahrenheit each winter. This prevents the peach buds in their orchards from fully developing and results in a devastating crop loss that occurred in two-thirds of the most recent years prior to 2017. In the way that the peach farmer Robert Dickey tells the story about this development to Subramanian, we can hear a novella emerging about the worrisome days early in the year, when cold was expected but did not arrive.

> But warm winters are especially vexing. When crops are lost to freezes and hail storms, the damage is immediate and obvious. The effects of a low-chill year vary wildly among varieties of peaches, between micro-climates within a single orchard, even from the base of the branch to its tip. "It was very unusual," says Robert, recalling how baffled he was by his orchards this spring. "We did not know what some of the peaches on the tree would do."

While the Dickeys emphatically avoid the term "climate change," these vexing events and the tense weeks in early spring still lead them to adapt their own bottom-up story, all the way to imagining how the next fateful winter could once again lead to a positive yield.

> "I was very skeptical two years ago," Mr. Bob's son Robert says. "But with two warm winters I'm beginning to pay a lot more notice to it." I ask how many consecutive winters he'd have to experience before he started planting varieties that could handle warmer weather. He laughs, then says, "Maybe one more." . . . But the past, they insist, does not predict the future. The Dickeys use the word "optimistic." They use the word "hope." Quietly, they are adapting, innovating, recovering and hedging their bets. They are planting test plots of low-chill peaches and watching them closely.

All of Subramanian's nine articles tell about turning points in individuals' lives that are merely a casuistic experience of climate change but that occur regardless of these individuals' abiding by the scientific, top-down climate-change narrative. A devastating flood in West Virginia leads some members of a small, heavily Republican community to rebuild their houses on higher ground while praying in the hope that what they call "the weather" will improve. Conservative farmers in North Dakota decide to reduce their cattle herds in response to unforeseeable hardships brought by flash droughts, arguing that they "love Mother Earth." Young Christian students introduce the collective human effect into the usual Evangelical climate-change narrative of an almighty God by labeling climate change a "structural sin."

What Subramanian reports from her travels across the United States is narratologically interesting because it exhibits that competing apocryphal climate change narratives are increasingly coalescing and merging, especially where they are generated and told close to turbulent environmental conditions. This status quo of climate storytelling in the United States manifests the opposite of the top-down-induced landscape of scientific truths that are mapped onto single incidents according to scientific accounts of these changes, leaving aside as irrelevant the locals' views and cognitions. Subramanian presents a form of storytelling that is a "citizen storytelling," the sister of "citizen science," where everyone must speak up about how they observe the weather extremes in comparison with their own historical weather memory and related experiences. Again, Locke's 1690s observation that looking at the weather, "a country gentlewoman will . . . clearly see the probable connexion of all these [factors] . . . without tying them together in those artificial and cumbersome fetters of several syllogisms" reminds us of the long-overlooked epistemic quality of topical short-form narratives for the environment and shows that communal action demanded by twenty-first-century climate change must begin with civic storytelling.

Since 2010, several online aggregator platforms have formed that invite often subjective accounts, stories, and observations from interested citizens across the world. Such "citizen storytelling" projects function within a more organized framework than common social media posts using hashtags, whose effect on Twitter or Instagram is visible only during truly catastrophic climate events such as a tsunami or extensive wildfires. A relatively early, but constantly growing platform is *ISeeChange.com*, a website that invites individual "sightings" such as the date of first snow, the sighting of blossoms, and the flooding of streets. *ISeeChange*, which was founded 2012, also publishes coordinated "stories" from individual "sightings," curating the collections of incidents and inviting individuals to participate. This includes a call to "volunteer to map urban heat in New Orleans" and an edited correlation of separate "sightings" into larger contexts that associate them with more in-depth scientific and journalistic reports, including, among others, a "story" about the increasing numbers of people displaced by natural disasters.

The need for such technological implementation of collective storytelling is summarized by the environmental humanist Rob Nixon, who argues that such low-threshold and media storytelling, whether done by a journalist such as Subramanian or on a platform such as *ISeeChange*, has finally superseded the activism of the specialist author. "'Writer' has become a more demotic designation," writes Nixon, "less grand, less glamorous, less distinctively vocational, and more likely to involve mongrel blends of word, image, and video. *Écriture engagée* will never again be a specialist calling à la Sartre — or even à la [the Nigerian environmental activist] Ken Saro-Wiwa — now that we have entered what one might call the age of the writer-hacktivist."[22]

It is no longer the very strong unity of theory and fiction, as combined in the figure of the singular author, that can problematize the environment or climate through a plot. The story has now become a device of collective intelligence, told from within coalitions and communal experiences so that their telling as short forms can again incite new experiences. Such coordinated efforts actualize the power of the short form as an independent agency in the world that can — and in the case of climate change, *must* — act on its own behalf.

Known Practices of Storytelling and Unknown Forms of Life

As different as amateur online climate storytelling projects such as *ISeeChange* might seem from Steyerl's elaborate videos and installations, they are two examples of a shift from the textual form of the short narrative to forms with heightened social impact in the postliterary. Since the last decades of the twentieth century, short forms have been entering our "image life" by hijacking it, mixing text, voice, photographs, films, TV excerpts, video games, and virtual reality into stories that continue the topical function of narratives in everyday life. Besides Steyerl's artworks and the crowd-based climate stories, there are numerous fictional stories that have extended their narrative diegesis beyond textuality and into images.

The reach of the postliterary short form results in two new functions. On the one hand, there is, as in Steyerl's case, the short form's function to "document" as yet unknown ways of life deemed too strange even for established fictional genres. On the other hand, there is the short narrative form's translation of life forms such as the current "image life" or life in the climate crisis into phenomena, providing them with the agency to take place and realize themselves in reality and society. These two aspects — to "document" by fiction and to become a phenomenon's agency — compose the short form's anthropological practice within political society. They interfere into known factualities and systematized lives with unheard-of events and life forms that recall the *Homo narrans* in us and leave us with the only possible practice: to follow the story and adapt our world to it.

The experimental extent of the current adaptations of the short narrative form for the postliterary imaginations of the present can be best illustrated with a brief list of further examples, which at the same time gives an outlook on how seemingly stable human realities in the image life have been, and will be, interrupted by such postliterary storytelling.

Rainer Werner Fassbinder's contribution to the 1977 anthology film *Germany in Autumn (Deutschland im Herbst)* is an autofictional story about a distressed director and his boyfriend during the proceedings against the members of the Red Army Faction. The real-time realism of this thirty-minute episode is intensified by Fassbinder's playing himself, caught between consuming alcohol and drugs and the newspaper's, telephone's, radio's, and television's reporting of distressing news. It presents to us, in a few minutes, how a familiar lifeworld is suddenly transformed by the mediascape of a looming state of emergency and amplifies all emotional, psychological, addictive, and other previously existing tensions. No viewer of the episode can return to their prior reality without tension after watching Fassbinder succumbing to this experiment, whatever the viewer's current mediascape and political situation may be.

In 1980, the French author and photographer Hervé Guibert published a story called "Suzanne et Louise" consisting of single-paragraph vignettes and photographs that show and describe his two aunts, Suzanne and Louise, exhibiting them in their private rooms and during encounters—real, dreamed, and fictional—that Guibert has had with them. This story culminates in a final photograph in which Guibert places himself in his own story, sitting between his aunts, to signal, finally, that its author can no longer be indifferent to the story, or rather, that the agency of the short form finally had entered his own life during its conception.

In 1988, the Polish director Krzysztof Kieślowski released ten one-hour films, each telling a separate, self-contained story about an ethical dilemma involving citizens living in a housing project in 1980s Poland. Resembling a novella cycle such as the *Decameron*, these films, called *Dekalog*, are based on the biblical Ten Commandments and take place in the same neighborhood. They are double-sided narrative investigations that test, via fictional narrative, how these kinds of archaic rules can possibly be followed in late twentieth-century societies while at the same time experimenting, via the form of the film novella, with how following a rule can be told from within the postliterary image life.

In 2016, the book *Franckushima* was published, a 256-page "graphic essay" retelling the 2011 Fukushima nuclear catastrophe like a disaster novella, only spilled over into a graphic novel about the failed evacuation of the area and the aftereffects of radioactivity and then into a scientific essay on the prevailing nuclear risks in France and elsewhere. The book was cocreated by a Japanese-French team of artists, scientists, and lawyers under the coordination of the illustrator

Géraud Bournet. It applies graphic storytelling to a varying set of genres that shift between documentary illustration, visual literature, and possibilitarian heuristics to induce political, legal, and activist actions to prevent further disasters of the same kind.

In 2020, the architect Samaneh Moafi and her team of collaborators at the collective Forensic Architecture published an eleven-minute video titled *The Beirut Port Explosion*, renarrating the devastating fires and explosions in a warehouse at the Beirut harbor in August 2020. Using governmental documents and publicly available video and photo footage and its metadata, the video reconstructs a 3-D model of the fires, smoke-plume shapes, and their location in the warehouse during the minutes before the enormous detonation that would devastate a large part of the city of Beirut and throw the Lebanese government into turmoil. What is at first purely speculative storytelling is applied here to condense possibilities and a plurality of media into realistic likelihoods. This transforms the heretofore unexplored disaster from an unheard-of phenomenon in the media into a realistic scenario of malfeasance that must provoke future investigations into the parties and actors responsible for the negligence. Upon release, this multimedia narrative was marked as "ongoing," and all relevant 3-D models and files were made openly available via GitHub.

Such short narrative forms continue the tradition of topical storytelling for a postliterary and less textual public sphere. While today's academic disciplines seem to have clearly defined what history is, what literature is, what journalism is, what an investigation is, and what art is, these stories disregard such definitions and such separations. Steyerl's works, climate-change storytelling projects, and the examples above all demonstrate that the theoretical and practical transgressions of genre, media, and epistemological borders are symptomatic of a larger shift in the tradition of topical speech away from textuality and its seemingly stable formats. Instead, the Aristotelian and Arendtian rule of topical speech as the medium of appearance in the political space has begun to undergo subtle, but far-reaching transformations in the twenty-first century. The loss of literature's monopoly on short narrative forms that we are experiencing since the rise of visual mass media in the twentieth century is thus no crisis of storytelling. It should rather be understood as just another stage in the morphology of how storytelling implements and modulates human encounters in society. In fact, the situation at the beginning of the twenty-first century should perhaps be compared to the situation in the mid-eighteenth century, when between Baumgarten's last poetical *ars topica* and Schlegel's first pragmatic novella theory, new modes of storytelling were rising to the surface while the existing determinators of the early modern lifeworld — statehood, personhood, citizenship, politics, religion, to name just a few — were undergoing radical transformations.

The deepest interest of this study is therefore to invite readers to think through the problem of topical storytelling in our time and to identify undiscovered strands of short narrative forms of fiction that apply topical speech to everyday problems in order to introduce them, as originally and necessarily fictional problems, into discourses of events. Given the agency of the short narrative form, Arendt's argument that enacted storytelling is required to open the space of politics now can be linked back to the short form in new ways; wherever short narrative forms insert unheard of events and perceptions into the public sphere, these events and perceptions necessarily have become a matter of the political. As evident in the context of the *lettres de cachet*, the fairy tale, and climate-change storytelling, such new storytelling modes and genres arise mostly between people and in situations that are not on the radar of academic discourses and other allegedly close observers of culture. The invitation to seek out topical storytelling in interdisciplinary and nonacademic fields is hence also an invitation to extend the academic concepts and ideas of what literary, essayistic, or multimodal storytelling might be into the necessarily nonacademic, not yet analyzed and theorized realm. We can keep all historical layers of short narrative forms relevant for both humanistic study and society only by knowing what storytelling and topical speech is today. Interacting with short narrative forms as readers, viewers, and participants changes not just *what* we know about the world and society, but also *how* we know what world and society are. To discover what civic storytelling is at any given time — as heuristic practice, as media format, as epistemological interference — varies the very makeup of the human world.

Acknowledgments

I started this book at the Yale German Department, and it would not exist without the rare atmosphere of encouragement, dedication, openness, and community I encountered there. I am thankful especially to Carol Jacobs and Kirk Wetters, but most of all to Rüdiger Campe, who has been the most enchanting, curious, and tireless interlocutor anyone could possibly have. I am also immensely grateful for the inspiring and energizing discussions I have shared over the years between Stanford, New Haven, Princeton, and Berlin, especially with Robert Pogue Harrison and Christopher Wood, but also with Anselm Haverkamp, Hans Jürgen Scheuer, Paul Fleming, Daniel Heller-Roazen, Juliet Fleming, Björn Quiring, Anita Traninger, and Julika Griem. There are many, many others that remind me how being a humanist has to be a human endeavor; among them are Dorothea, Cliff, Josh, Ulrich, Christophe, Maren, Regina, Wolfgang, Florian, Hanna, Karen, and Eileen. The editors and the team at Zone Books deserve special thanks, most importantly Meighan Gale and Jonathan Crary for making this project happen during difficult pandemic years. I am particularly grateful to Bud Bynack because working through his attentive queries and edits generated real constructive joy. The person who has offered me not only his thoughts, ideas, and questions, but above all his friendship to make this project worthwhile is my friend Steffen. Unfathomable and impossible to ever thank for are finally the endless days, months, and years that

Christy has spent with me to make this happen, one day after the other. I dedicate this work to my parents because none of it would exist without them.

Notes

Wherever possible, I have quoted English translations; slight modifications are marked in the notes. Otherwise, all translations are my own.

INTRODUCTION

1. Wlad Godzich and Jeffrey Kittay, *The Emergence of Prose: An Essay in Prosaics* (Minneapolis: University of Minnesota Press, 1987); Svetlana Efimova and Michael Gamper, eds., *Prosa: Geschichte, Poetik, Theorie* (Berlin: De Gruyter, 2021).

2. Michel Foucault, "Language to Infinity," trans. Donald F. Bouchard and Sherry Simon, in *The Essential Works of Foucault, Volume 2, Aesthetics, Method, and Epistemology*, ed. James D. Faubion (New York: New Press, 1998), pp. 92–93.

3. Hans Blumenberg, "The Concept of Reality and the Possibility of the Novel," in *History, Metaphors, Fables: A Hans Blumenberg Reader*, ed. and trans. Hannes Bajohr, Florian Fuchs, and Joe Paul Kroll (Ithaca, NY: Cornell University Press, 2020), p. 515, Blumenberg's emphasis in original.

4. Hito Steyerl, "Ripping Reality," in *Duty Free Art: Art in the Age of Planetary Civil War* (New York: Verso, 2017), pp. 191–205.

5. Walter Benjamin, "The Storyteller," in *The Storyteller Essays*, ed. Samuel Titan, trans. Tess Lewis (New York: NYRB Classics, 2019), pp. 66–67. Walter Benjamin, "Der Erzähler," in *Gesammelte Schriften*, ed. Rolf Tiedemann and Hermann Schweppenhäuser, 7 vols. in 14 (Frankfurt am Main: Suhrkamp, 1972–1999), vol. 2.1, pp. 457–58.

CHAPTER ONE: THE *ARS TOPICA*,
ITS DISAPPEARANCE, AND ITS AFTERLIFE

1. A recording of the conversation can be found at "Panel and Launch Event / Clipping, Copying, and Thinking, with Ann Blair and Kenneth Goldsmith," *Cabinet Magazine*, March 18, 2011, http://www.cabinetmagazine.org/events/cp_launch.php.

2. Throughout this study *"ars topica"* will denominate the practice and the theory of dealing with topoi to avoid confusion with the other English term "topics," which will be used exclusively for Aristotle's work of the same name.

3. Ernst Robert Curtius, *European Literature and Latin Middle Ages*, trans. Willard R. Trask (Princeton, NJ: Princeton University Press, 2013); Ernst Robert Curtius, *Europäische Literatur und lateinisches Mittelalter* (Bern: Francke, 1948). His work lacks a definition of what this continuity of semantic topoi such as the "puer senex" or "old boy" might suggest in terms of being a remainder of the *ars topica* or of other topoi, and it also falls short of discussing their effect on literary form.

4. For a discussion of Curtius's approach to topoi, see Stefan Goldmann, "Zur Herkunft des Topos-Begriffs von Ernst Robert Curtius," *Euphorion* 90 (1996), pp. 134–49; for Curtius's general intent, see Hinrich C. Seeba, "Ernst Robert Curtius: Zur Kulturkritik eines Klassikers in der Wissenschaftsgeschichte," *Monatshefte* 95.4 (2003), pp. 531–40.

5. *Toposforschung* is also the title of two different volumes that are part overviews of the discussion since Curtius, part critical commentary on the intentions and gains of Curtius's project. Peter Jehn, ed., *Toposforschung. Eine Dokumentation* (Frankfurt am Main: Athenäum, 1972), and Max L. Baeumer, ed., *Toposforschung* (Darmstadt: Wissenschaftliche Buchgesellschaft, 1973).

6. Chaïm Perelman and Lucie Olbrechts-Tyteca, *The New Rhetoric: A Treatise on Argumentation*, trans. John Wilkinson and Purcell Weaver (Notre Dame: University of Notre Dame Press, 1969). Perelman and Olbrechts-Tyteca include the use of loci as crucial part their rhetoric of argumentation while not emphasizing them explicitly. The first to do so explicitly, to my knowledge, perhaps the first time since Vico and Baumgarten, is Theodor Viehweg, who calls for an *ars topica* to be again a part of legal studies, citing Perelman as inspiration: Theodor Viehweg, *Topik und Jurisprudenz* (Munich: Beck, 1969). Exemplary for linguistics is the work of J. C. Anscombre, especially "Topique or not topique: Formes topiques intrinsèques et forms topiques extrinsèques," *Journal of Pragmatics* 24.1–2 (1995), pp. 115–41. For the field of discursive studies see the approach of Ruth Amossy, who extends Perelman's concept of topical argumentation beyond the use

for mere agreement, suggesting that an *ars topica* also addresses ways of thinking, seeing, and feeling: Ruth Amossy, *L'argumentation dans le discours* (Paris: Nathan, 2000), as well as Amossy, "Publikum und Topik," in *Die neue Rhetorik: Studien zu Chaïm Perelman,* ed. Josef Kopperschmidt (Munich: Fink, 2006), pp. 307–32. In communication studies, one work uses the classical *ars topica* as a theoretical concept, partly indebted to Curtius, to understand discursivity in educated societies to be generally topical: Lothar Bornscheuer, *Topik: Zur Struktur der gesellschaftlichen Einbildungskraft* (Frankfurt am Main: Suhrkamp, 1976). A more recent work is more specifically indebted to communication studies and intends to update the *ars topica* for current training in communicative situations: Sara Rubinelli, *Ars Topica: The Classical Technique of Constructing Arguments from Aristotle to Cicero* (Dordrecht: Springer, 2009). For a general overview across these areas, see Dieter Breuer and Helmut Schanze, eds., *Topik: Beiträge zur interdisziplinären Diskussion* (Munich: Fink, 1981), and *Topik und Rhetorik: Ein interdisziplinäres Symposium,* eds. Gert Ueding and Thomas Schirren (Tübingen: Niemeyer, 2000). Both volumes leave an open, almost uncommented gap between the historical *ars topica* from antiquity to 1750 and its theoretical application after 1950, a systematic problem in the history of *ars topica* that this study tries to address.

7. Gerhart von Graevenitz, *Mythos: Zur Geschichte einer Denkgewohnheit* (Stuttgart: Metzler, 1987); see especially the chapter "Die *topische* Überlieferung. Die Mythologie der Mythographen," pp. 45–119.

8. Uwe Hebekus, "Topik/Inventio," in *Einführung in die Literaturwissenschaft,* eds. Miltos Pechlivanos, Stefan Rieger, Wolfgang Struck, and Michael Weitz (Stuttgart: Metzler, 1995), pp. 82–96.

9. Wilhelm Schmidt-Biggemann, *Topica Universalis: Eine Modellgeschichte humanistischer und barocker Wissenschaft* (Hamburg: Meiner, 1983).

10. Peter von Moos, *Geschichte als Topik: Das rhetorische Exemplum von der Antike zur Neuzeit und die historiae im "Policraticus" Johanns von Salisbury* (Hildesheim: Olms, 1988). See also Eugene Vance, *From Topic to Tale: Logic and Narrativity in the Middle Ages* (Minneapolis: University of Minnesota Press, 1987) for a similar medieval take on the problem between topoi and narratives.

11. Walter Haug, "Kritik der topischen Vernunft. Zugleich keine Leseanleitug zu *Geschichte als Topik* von Peter von Moos," *Beiträge zur Geschichte der deutschen Sprache und Literatur* 114.1 (1992), pp. 47–56.

12. Frauke Berndt, "Poetische Topik," in *Handbuch Literarische Rhetorik,* ed. Rüdiger Zymner (Berlin: De Gruyter, 2015), pp. 433–60.

13. The encyclopedia articles on the concept of *ars topica* are the most comprehensive and important secondary sources of the problem that provide the backdrop of the historical lineages behind this chapter. Most importantly and most recently, see Tim Wagner, s.v. "Topik," in *Historisches Wörterbuch der Rhetorik*, ed. Gert Ueding (Tübingen: Niemeyer, 2009). See also Stefan Goldmann, Christoph Kann, and Oliver Primavesi, s.v. "Topik; Topos," in *Historisches Wörterbuch der Philosophie*, eds. Joachim Ritter, Karlfried Gründer, Gottfried Gabriel, 12 vols. (Basel: Schwabe, 1998); Wilhelm Kühlmann and Wilhelm Schmidt-Biggemann, s.v. "Topik," in *Reallexikon der deutschen Literaturwissenschaft*, ed. Jan-Dirk Müller (Berlin: De Gruyter, 2003); Petter Hess, s.v. "Topos," in ibid.

14. *Oxford Dictionary of English*, s.v. "Topic," https://www.lexico.com/definition/topic.

15. Teaching students of rhetoric and dialectic to have ready-made arguments and pieces of discourse, however, is already present in earlier treatises by Isocrates, Gorgias, and others, as Cicero also notes. See Wagner, s.v. "Topik," in *Historisches Wörterbuch der Rhetorik*. A synchronous history of metaphorization from location to subject matter can also be traced for "theme," which is derived from ancient Greek verb *tithenai*, "to put" but also meant "area in which something is put up." Like its relative "thesis," "theme," however, retained the connotation of the act of claiming or proposing something as "something that is claimed" and therefore has appeared similar to "topic" only since early modernity, not interfering with the history of *ars topica* or topos. See Bernhard Asmuth, s.v. "Thema," in *Historisches Wörterbuch der Rhetorik* (Tübingen: Niemeyer, 2009), vol. 9, pp. 528–41, and Albrecht Berger, s.v. "Theme," in *Brill's New Pauly*, http://dx.doi.org/10.1163/1574-9347_bnp_e1217380.

16. The theoretical lineage of the mnemotechnical function of topoi is very extensive, running parallel and underneath the history of the *ars topica* itself, however in a very multifaceted way that ranges from the training of the mind to variations on syntax, visual practices, and didacts and would thus require its own chapter. For an overview of the topoi of memoria, see the canonical studies by Francis Yates, *The Art of Memory* (London: Routledge, 1966) and Mary Carruthers, *The Book of Memory: A Study of Memory in Medieval Culture* (Cambridge: Cambridge University Press, 1990). With special regard to the connection between *ars topica* and *ars memorativa*, see Christoph Kann, "Der Ort der Argumente: Eigentliche und uneigentliche Verwendung des mittelalterlichen *locus*-Begriffs," in *Raum und Raumvorstellungen im Mittelalter*, eds. Jan A. Aertsen and Andreas Speer (Berlin: De Gruyter, 1998), pp. 402–18.

17. The radical attempt to conceive of the whole of a discussion as a topical system

suggests that a network theory of discourses *avant la lettre* is the basis of Aristotle's *Topics*, a view that neither Michel Foucault, Niklas Luhmann, nor Friedrich Kittler have even hinted at in their work. Luhmann, for instance, evokes the question of *ars topica* only in the limited sense of "common place" and "storehouse" when assessing the print medium's effect on the storage of knowledge in the fifteenth century; Niklas Luhmann, *Theory of Society*, trans. Rhodes Barrett, 2 vols. (Stanford, CA: Stanford University Press, 2012); especially volume 1, chapter 9, "Symbolically Generalized Communication Media, 1: Function," pp. 190–99.

18. Roland Barthes, "The Old Rhetoric: An Aide-Mémoire" (1970), in *The Semiotic Challenge*, trans. Richard Howard (New York: Hill and Wang, 1988), p. 65.

19. Roland Barthes, "L'ancienne rhétorique: Aide-mémoire," *Communications* 16 (1970), p. 206.

20. Aristotle, *Topica*, ed. and trans. E. S. Forster. Loeb Classical Library 391 (Cambridge, MA: Harvard University Press, 1960), 100a18, p. 273.

21. Today's remainders of this topical tradition are known, for example, as the "5 Ws," that is, the basic questions to be answered in every journalistic work.

22. Barthes, "The Old Rhetoric," pp. 66–67.

23. See the specific contexts for Aristotle's *Rhetoric* and Cicero's *De oratore* in Lucia Calboli Montefusco, s.v. "Topics," in *Brill's New Pauly*.

24. Barthes, "The Old Rhetoric," p. 66.

25. Ernst Robert Curtius, *European Literature and Latin Middle Ages*, trans. Willard R. Trask (Princeton, NJ: Princeton University Press, 2013), §10.6, "The Pleasance," pp. 195–200.

26. Aristotle, *Metaphysics*, trans. Hugh Tredennick, Loeb Classical Library 271 (Cambridge, MA: Harvard University Press, 1933), 4.2.1004b, p. 157.

27. Here I do not follow Forster's translation of the *Topics*, but the more literal renderings by Robin Smith in Aristotle, *Topics, Books I and VII with Excerpts from Related Texts*, trans. and commentary Robin Smith (Oxford: Oxford University Press, 1997), 101a30, p. 2; see also Smith's commentary on the sentence, pp. 51–52. In accordance with Smith's translation is Wagner and Rapp's German translation in Aristotle, *Topik*, trans. and commentary Tim Wagner and Christoph Rapp (Stuttgart: Reclam, 2004), p. 47.

28. See Aristotle, *Topics, Books I and VII*, p. 51.

29. Ibid., 101a30, p. 2. See also Wagner and Rapp in Aristotle's *Topik*, p. 47: "Für die Begegnungen (mit der Menge) aber, weil wir uns, nachdem wir die Meinungen der Leute gesichtet haben, mit ihnen nicht aufgrund fremder, sondern aufgrund ihrer eigenen Ansichten auseinandersetzen werden und dabei das zurechtrücken, was sie uns nicht

richtig zu sagen scheinen."

30. Aristotle, *Topics, Books I and VII*, 100a30, p. 1.

31. Aristotle, *Topica*, 114b31, p. 373.

32. Cicero, *Topica*, trans. H. M. Hubbell, Loeb Classical Library 386 (Cambridge, MA: Harvard University Press, 1949), pp. 382–83.

33. Ibid., pp. 386–87, translation slightly altered.

34. See Manfred Fuhrmann, "Die zivilrechtlichen Beispiele in Ciceros Topik," in *Topik und Rhetorik*, pp. 51–66.

35. See Eleonore Stump's summary of the complicated reception history of Aristotle's *Topics* in her introduction to Boethius, *De differentiis topicis*, trans. Eleonore Stump (Ithaca, NY: Cornell University Press, 1978), pp. 20–24.

36. Boethius, *De differentiis topicis*, p. 29.

37. Ibid., pp. 29–30.

38. Goldmann, Kann, and Primavesi, s.v. "Topik; Topos," in *Historisches Wörterbuch der Philosophie*.

39. Petrus Hispanus, "De locis," in *Language in Dispute: An English Translation of Peter of Spain's Tractatus, Called Afterwards Summulae logicales*, ed. and trans. Francis P. Dinneen (Philadelphia: John Benjamins, 1990), p. 49.

40. Walter J. Ong, *Ramus: Method, and the Decay of Dialogue* (Chicago: University of Chicago Press, 2004), p. 65.

41. Rudolph Agricola, *De inventione dialectica libri tres*, ed. and trans. Lothar Mundt (Tübingen: Niemeyer, 1992), p. 18.

42. See, for example, Thomas Murner, *Logica memorativa Chartiludiu logice, sive totius dialectice memoria; & novus Petri hyspani textus emendatus* (Strasbourg: Gruninger, 1509), excerpted in Figure 1. On Murner's extensive work in the diagrammatic didactics of logic and law, see Badische Landesbibliothek Karlsruhe and Bibliothèque nationale et universitaire de Strasbourg, *Thomas Murner (1475–1537): Elsässischer Theologe und Humanist* (Karlsruhe: Badische Landesbibliothek Karlsruhe, 1987). On Murner's relation to Petrus Hispanus and Agricola, see: Ong, *Ramus*, pp. 85–91.

43. On Fuchsberger's dialectics, see Michael Giesecke, *Der Buchdruck in der Frühen Neuzeit: Eine historische Fallstudie über die Durchsetzung neuer Informations- und Kommunikationstechnologien* (Frankfurt am Main: Suhrkamp, 1991), pp. 630–35.

44. "Welche mit kurtzen worten den bloossen handel fürlegt, der nachmals von der Rhetorica mit meererem anhang zierlicher Rede haerfür gebracht." Ortolf Fuchsberger,

Ein gründlicher klarer anfang der natürlichen und rechten kunst der waaren Dialectica (Zürich: Geßner, 1556), p. 4.

45. "Leert nit finden, was man reden oder schreyben woell, sonder wie das, so zuovor erdacht und erfunden, gefoermbt, und mit was ordnung der woerter es soelle beschriben und geredt werden." Ibid.

46. "Auß welchem bauren gespraech eigentlich vernummen, die dise kunst der natur so gar anhangt, daß sy nichts anders dann natur ist. Dann dise baure habend kein kunst nie gelernet, un gebend doch der kunst ein exempel. Der erst ersuocht und erfindt ursach, was er zuo bekrefftigug irs fürschlags anziehen woelle. Aber der ander bringt die selben erfundne außzüg in ein argumentliche form oder schlußred, welche resoluiert oder in besseren augenscheyn gelegt, also moecht lauten: Alle ding, so der menschen hertzen von Gott ziehend, sind zuo meyde: verdrossen predigt thuond solliches, darum sind die selbigen zuo meyden." Ibid., pp. 204–205.

47. Peter Mack, *Renaissance Argument: Valla and Agricola in the Traditions of Rhetoric and Dialectic* (Leiden: Brill, 1993), p. 363.

48. Agricola's sketch is an early version of a later widely read and rewritten type of treatise, instructions for studying, or *ratio studii*, which combined the quotidian conduct of life with the scholarly conduct of the mind and of writing, a programming of the scholarly form of life that received its canonical rendering in Erasmus's *De ratione studii* (1511).

49. Rudolph Agricola, Letter to Jacob Barbireau, June 7, 1484, in *Letters*, ed. Adrie van der Laan and Fokke Akkerman (Assen: Royal van Gorcum, 2002), p. 211, printed throughout the sixteenth century as *De formando studio*.

50. In Aristotle's model, the acquisition of knowledge had not been a condition for dialectics because members of a dialectical setting were members of the same academy or polis and thus shared narrow conventions of expertise and everyday experience. When during the Renaissance the source of material that could be discussed extremely expanded, the gathering of material itself required a formalized method to create a reliable background of common knowledge among discussants before any subject be raised for conversation.

51. The scene of writing, as prescribed by Agricola, is the catalyst for the change in topical conditions. See Rüdiger Campe, "Die Schreibszene," in *Paradoxien, Dissonanzen, Zusammenbrüche: Situationen offener Epistemologie*, eds. Hans Ulrich Gumbrecht and K. Ludwig Pfeiffer (Frankfurt am Main: Suhrkamp, 1991), pp. 759–72.

52. For an overview of the rhetorical, compilatory, and didactic functions for which such books were used, see Joan Marie Lechner, *Renaissance Concepts of the Commonplaces*

(New York: Pageant Press, 1962).

53. Ann M. Blair, *Too Much to Know: Managing Scholarly Information before the Modern Age* (New Haven, CT: Yale University Press, 2010).

54. Francis Bacon, *The Advancement of Learning*, ed. Michael Kiernan (Oxford: Oxford University Press: 2000), p. 118: "But this is true, that of the *Methodes* of *Commonplaces*, that I haue seen, there is none of any sufficient woorth, all of them carying meerely the face of a *Schoole*, and not of a *World*, and referring to vulgar matters, and Pedanticall Diuisions without all life, or respect to Action."

55. For the development, rise, and end of the scientific, epistemological idea of a *topica universalis* between Ramus and Bacon, see Schmidt-Biggeman's extensive detailed study, *Topica Universalis*, which unfortunately relies too much on the historical development and less of the role of the topics in it.

56. "Domini enim quaestionum sumus, rerum non item." ("For we are Commanders of Questions, not so of things.") Francis Bacon, "De Augmentis Scientiarum," in *The Works of Francis Bacon*, ed. James Spedding, 15 vols. (Boston: Houghton Mifflin. 1858), vol. 2, pp. 73–498, book 5, chapter 3.3: "Topica Particularis, sive Articuli Inquistionis de Gravi at Levi," pp. 389–94, p. 394. Translation quoted from Francis Bacon, *Of the Advancement and Proficience of Learning; or, The Partitions of Sciences*, trans. Gilbert Watts (Oxford: Lichfield, 1640), pp. 240–44, "*A Particular Topique*, or the Articles of Enquiry de Gravi & Levi."

57. "Lorsqu'on a un sujet à traiter, il est tres-dangereux d'avoir recours à ces lieux communs, parceque tant de diferentes choses, et ce grand nombre de divers sentimens confondent l'esprit, et l'empéchent [et l'occupent tellement qu'il n'est pas libre pour consulter attentivement la verité, et] se former une image nette de ce qu'il doit dire. Ne vous laissez point ébloüir par ces beaux titres de Theatre de la vie humaine, de Poliantée, de Parterre des Orateurs." Bernard Lamy, *Entretiens sur les sciences, dans lesquels on apprend comme l'on doit étudier les sciences, et s'en servir pour se faire l'esprit juste, et le coeur droit*, ed. François Girbal and Pierre Clair (Paris: Presses Universitaires de France, 1966), quoted in Ann Moss, *Commonplace-Books and the Structuring of Renaissance Thought* (Oxford: Clarendon Press of Oxford University Press, 1996), p. 277, with a phrase inserted by Moss that was omitted in later editions. In a footnote, Moss comments on the list of titles Lamy refers to: "The *Theatre de la vie humaine* is Zwinger's *Theatrum* and/or its subsequent reworkings. The *Poliantée* is Lang's compilation, to which Janus Gruterus had added two supplementary volumes in 1624. The *Parterre des Orateurs* is probably *Le Parterre de la rhétorique françoise*, *entaillé de toutes les plus belles fleurs d'éloquence qui se montrent dans les œuvres des orateurs*

tant anciens que modernes, ensemble le verger de poesie . . . (Lyons, 1659, repr. there in 1665). Its title is redolent with the history of the commonplace-book. Nevertheless, it is not in fact a commonplace-book, but a simplified and prettified traditional Rhetoric, in the main a collection of rhetorical formulae and made-up examples of figures of thought." Ibid.

58. On Locke's commonplace books see Richard Yeo, "John Locke's 'New Method' of Commonplacing: Managing Memory and Information," *Eighteenth Century Thought* 2 (2004), pp. 1–38; Lucia Dacome, "Noting the Mind: Commonplace Books and the Pursuit of the Self in the Eighteenth Century," *Journal of the History of Ideas*, 65.4 (2004), pp. 603–25; more recently, Michael Stolberg, "John Locke's 'New Method of Making Common-Place-Books': Tradition, Innovation and Epistemic Effects," *Early Science and Medicine* 19 (2014), pp. 448–70.

59. See G. G. Meynell, "John Locke's Method of Common-Placing as Seen in His Drafts and his Medical Notebooks, Bodleian MSS Locke d. 9, f. 21 and f. 23," *Seventeenth Century* 8.2 (1993), pp. 245–67.

60. John Locke, "A New Method of a Common-Place-Book," in *Literary and Historical Writings*, ed. J. R. Milton (Oxford: Oxford University Press, 2019), pp. 281–306.

61. Isaac Watts, *Logick; Or, The Right Use of Reason in the Enquiry after Truth*, 2nd ed. (London: Clark and Hett, 1726), p. 74.

62. Locke, "A New Method of a Common-Place-Book," pp. 4–5. The full instruction regarding headings reads: "If I would put any thing in my Common-Place-Book, I find out a head to which I may refer it. Each head ought to be some important and essential word to the matter in hand, and in that word regard is to be had to the first letter, and the vowel that follows it; for upon these two letters depends all the use of the index."

63. This essay is spread in pieces throughout Locke's journal of 1677; see John Locke, "Of Study," in *The Educational Writing of John Locke*, ed. James L. Axtell (Cambridge: Cambridge University Press, 1968), pp. 405–22. Axtell's commentary is on pp. 405–406.

64. On this essay, see Richard Yeo, "John Locke's 'Of Study' (1677): Interpreting an Unpublished Essay," *Locke Studies* 3 (2003), pp. 147–65.

65. Locke, "Of Study," p. 418.

66. Ibid.

67. Ibid.

68. John Locke, *An Essay Concerning Human Understanding*, ed. Roger Woolhouse (London: Penguin Books, 1997), p. 591.

69. Ibid., p. 596.

70. Ibid., p. 593.

71. Ibid., p. 594

72. See ibid., p. 601.

73. See Rosalie Colie, "The Essayist in his Essay," in *John Locke: Problems and Perspectives*, ed. John Yolton (Cambridge: Cambridge University Press, 1969), pp. 234–61.

74. For the genetic questions of the *Essay*, see Locke's early draft and selected notes from his commonplace books in John Locke, *An Early Draft of Locke's Essay: Together with Excerpts from His Journals*, ed. R. I. Aaron and Jocelyn Gibb (Oxford: Clarendon Press of Oxford University Press, 1936), as well as the new edition, without the notes, in John Locke, *Drafts for the Essay Concerning Human Understanding, and Other Philosophical Writings*, Vol. 1, *Drafts A and B*, ed. Peter H. Nidditch and G. A. J. Rogers (Oxford: Clarendon Press of Oxford University Press, 1990). Other entries from Locke's commonplace books related to the *Essay* have been published as well by The Digital Locke Project, http://www.digitallockeproject.nl..

75. This paradox might possibly be related to the modern return of the concept of "common sense" happening at the same time, which would imply that "commonplace" is what everyone needs to obtain subjectively—a subjective topos from the common world—before they can all have a "sense of the common," which would be the objective "average" of all such perception data of such subjective "places." Descartes's notion of "bon sens" might be closer to this hypothesis. See Florian Neumann, s.v. "Sensus communis," in *Historisches Wörterbuch der Rhetorik*.

76. See *Oxford English Dictionary*, s.v. "Commonplace," https://www.oed.com.

77. "Ich werde mich einer andern Lehrart bedienen, dabey sich die Sache sehr in Kurze bringen läßt. Denn was die Lehren der Alten so weitläufig machte, das waren die sogenannten Loca, oder Classen, oder Fächer der Beweisgründe, darauf sie ihre Schüler verwiesen, wenn sie gute Beweise finden wollten. Die Anzahl derselben war entsetzlich groß. . . . Nach den heutigen Arten der Reden aber . . . können wir uns leicht ohne die Topik der Alten behelfen. . . . Wir haben dergleichen Reden nicht mehr, und weder in unsern Lobreden, noch Lehrreden, noch Complimenten können uns die topischen Fächer was helfen. Folglich müssen wir einen andern Weg gehen, wenn wir von den Beweisgründen Regeln geben wollen." Johann Christoph Gottsched, *Ausführliche Redekunst*, 1st ed. (Leipzig: Breitkopf, 1736), p. 107

78. "Der Redner muß nemlich die Sachen selbst wohl inne haben, davon er reden will. . . . Hier sieht nun ein jeder, daß man ohne alle topischen Erfindungsfächer, gar leicht wird Beweisgründe finden können." Ibid., p. 109.

79. Giambattista Vico, *On the Study Methods of Our Time*, trans. Elio Gianturco (Ithaca, NY: Cornell University Press, 1990).

80. Ibid., p. 14.

81. Ibid.

82. Ibid., p. 17.

83. Antoine Arnauld and Pierre Nicole, *Logic or the Art of Thinking*, trans. Jill Vance Buroker (Cambridge: Cambridge University Press, 1996), p. 182.

84. Giambattista Vico, *The New Science*, trans. Thomas Goddard Bergin and Max Harold Fisch (Ithaca, NY: Cornell University Press, 1948), p. 150.

85. Vico, *The New Science*, p. 149.

86. Alexander Gottlieb Baumgarten, *Aesthetica*, trans. Dagmar Mirbach (Hamburg: Meiner, 2007), §131, pp. 108–109.

87. "Wir möchten eine weitere Regel der ästhetischen Topik hinzufügen.... Wer... Psychologe ist, was ich aus vielen Gründen für besonders notwendig erachte, der überfliegt sein Thema, wenn ich so sagen darf, im voraus urteilend, indem er es nach irgendeinem genügend vollständigen Katalog der sinnlichen Vermögen der Seele untersucht, etwa mit den Fragen: Habe ich ein gegebenes Thema oft empfunden? Vieles in ihm? Genügend Würdiges? Wahrscheinliches? In einem Licht, so daß ich es genügend lebhaft hinzustellen vermag? Usw." Ibid., §140, pp. 116–19.

88. "Wann ich z. B. meinen eigenen Lebenslauf, auch nur zu meiner eigenen Belustigung aufsetzen wollte, so würde ich mich zuerst fragen: wie reich ist er wohl, wie groß ist die Verwandtschaft, was für Veränderungen werden darin vorkommen, ferner wie wichtig sind sie, was für Wahrheit, was für Wahrscheinlichkeit, was für Lebhaftigkeit ist da? Wo muß ich das volle Licht hinsetzen? Wo soll ich rühren? Dies ist die besondere Topik, die wir bei den ersten Übungen vorschlagen." Anonymous, "Nachschrift eines Ästhetik-Kollegs Baumgartens," in *Alexander Gottlieb Baumgarten: Seine Bedeutung und Stellung in der Leibniz-Wolffischen Philosophie und seine Beziehungen zu Kant: Nebst Veröffentlichung einer bisher unbekannten Handschrift der Ästhetik Baumgartens*, ed. Bernhard Poppe (Leipzig: Noske, 1907), §139, p. 140.

89. Gottsched, *Ausführliche Redekunst*, p. 110.

90. This apocryphal expression does not appear anywhere in Warburg's publications, but has long been circulated through Ernst Gombrich's Warburg biography and recently also has been found at the Warburg Institute in the papers of a seminar Warburg gave at the University of Hamburg in 1925. See Christopher D. Johnson, *Memory, Metaphor, and Aby*

Warburg's Atlas of Images (Ithaca, NY: Cornell University Press, 2012), p. 45.

91. "We too have minute perceptions of which we are not aware in our present state. We could in fact become thoroughly aware of them and reflect on them, if we were not distracted by their multiplicity, which scatters the mind, and if bigger ones did not obliterate them or rather put them in the shade." Gottfried Wilhelm Leibniz, *New Essays on Human Understanding*, ed. and trans. Peter Remnant and Jonathan Bennet (Cambridge: Cambridge University Press, 1996), p. 134. For "petites perceptiones" see Aby Warburg, *Fragmente zur Ausdruckskunde*, ed. Ulrich Pfisterer and Hans Christian Hönes (Berlin: Akademie, 2015).

92. William S. Heckscher, "*Petites perceptions*: an account of sortes *Warburgianæ*," in *Art and Literature: Studies in Relationship*, ed. Egon Verheyen (Durham, NC: Duke University Press, 1985), pp. 435–80.

93. William S. Heckscher, "The Genesis of Iconology," in ibid., pp. 253–79, esp. pp. 245–49. On Heckscher's own methods, see Charlotte Schoell-Glass and Elizabeth Sears, *Verzetteln als Methode: Der humanistische Ikonologe William S. Heckscher (1904–1999)* (Berlin: Akademie, 2008).

94. James Joyce, "Epiphanies," in *The Workshop of Daedalus: James Joyce and the Raw Materials for A Portrait of the Artist as a Young Man*, ed. Robert Scholes (Evanston, IL: Northwestern University Press, 1965), pp. 3–52.

95. "Ein Kompendium, eine Enzyclopädie des ganzen geistigen Lebens eines genialischen Individuums." Friedrich Schlegel, *Kritische Fragmente*, Fragment 78, in *Kritische Friedrich-Schlegel-Ausgabe*, ed. Ernst Behler et al., 26 vols. (Munich: Schöningh, 1958–), vol. 2, p. 156.

96. Walter Benjamin, "The Storyteller," in *The Storyteller Essays*, ed. Samuel Titan, trans. Tess Lewis (New York: NYRB Classics, 2019), p. 63. Walter Benjamin, "Der Erzähler," in *Gesammelte Schriften*, ed. Rolf Tiedemann and Hermann Schweppenhäuser, 7 vols. in 14 (Frankfurt am Main: Suhrkamp, 1972–1999), vol. 2.1, p. 454.

97. Benjamin, "The Storyteller," p. 64; "Der Erzähler," p. 455.

98. Roland Barthes, *The Preparation of the Novel: Lecture Courses and Seminars at the Collège de France, 1978–79 and 1979–80*, trans. Kate Briggs (New York: Columbia University Press, 2011), p. 100.

99. Ibid., p. 102.

100. André Jolles, *Einfache Formen* (Tübingen: Niemeyer, 1968), translated as André Jolles, *Simple Forms: Legend, Saga, Myth, Riddle, Saying, Case, Memorabile, Fairy Tale, Joke*, trans. Peter J. Schwartz (New York: Verso, 2017). Jolles's genealogical method stands out for two

reasons. While its approach is a product of the author's larger interest in historical genealogies, it appears to be equally fueled by a totalitarian determination to reduce cultural
artifacts such as literary genres or artworks to primal, that is, decisive evolutionary traits of
cultures and humans in a competitive struggle for the survival of civilizations. While not all
of Jolles's arguments show clear signs of such literary-sociological Darwinism, the work is
based on a general value hierarchy between cultural artifacts, which aligns it with such projects as Oswald Spengler's *The Decline of the West* (1919) and fittingly falls in line with Jolles's
openly racist and National Socialist views in the 1920s and 1930s. See Walter Thys, ed., *André
Jolles (1874–1946): "Gebildeter Vagant"* (Amsterdam: Amsterdam University Press, 2000).

101. A selective overview of the literary scholarship of the small form in modernity:
Elmar Locher ed., *Die kleinen Formen in der Moderne* (Bozen: Edition Sturzflüge, 2001);
Claudia Öhlschläger, "Poetik und Ethik der kleinen Form: Franz Kafka, Robert Musil,
Heiner Müller, Michael Kohlmeier," *Zeitschrift für deutsche Philologie*, 128.2 (2009), pp. 261–
79; Alexander Košenina and Carsten Zelle, eds., *Kleine anthropologische Prosaformen der
Goethezeit (1750–1830)* (Hannover: Wehrhahn, 2011); Tim Killick, *British Short Fiction in the
Early Nineteenth Century: The Rise of the Tale* (London: Routledge, 2008); Florence Goyet,
The Classic Short Story, 1870–1925: Theory of a Genre (Cambridge: Open Book, 2014); Andeas
Huyssen, *Miniature Metropolis: Literature in the Age of Photography and Film* (Cambridge, MA:
Harvard University Press, 2015); Ben Grant, *The Aphorism and Other Short Forms* (London:
Routledge, 2016); Pierre Alféri, *Brefs* (Paris: P.O.L., 2016); John H. Muse, *Microdramas: Cru-
cibles for Theater and Time* (Ann Arbor: University of Michigan Press, 2017); Leslie Adelson,
Cosmic Miniatures and the Future Sense (Berlin: De Gruyter, 2017); Andrew Hui, *A Theory of
the Aphorism: From Confucius to Twitter* (Princeton, NJ: Princeton University Press, 2019);
Irina Dumitrescu and Bruce Holsinger, eds., "In Brief," special issue, *New Literary History*
50.3 (2019); Maren Jäger, Ethel Matala de Mazza, and Joseph Vogl, eds., *Verkleinerung: Epistemologie und Literaturgeschichte kleiner Formen* (Berlin: De Gruyter, 2021).

102. Reinhart Koselleck, "Historia Magistra Vitae: The Dissolution of the Topos into
the Perspective of a Modernized Historical Process," in *Futures Past: On the Semantics of
Historical Time*, trans. Keith Tribe (New York: Columbia University Press. 2004), pp. 26–42.

103. The modern lifeworld, following Baumgarten's *topica aesthetica*, has been considered a "topical lifeworld," that is, as the enveloping of the subject in nothing but potential
topoi of itself that lack any common function. See Peter L. Oesterreicher, "Verstehen heisst
Verbindenkönnen: Die Erfindung des Selbst in der topischen Lebenswelt," in *Die Formel
und das Unverwechselbare: Interdisziplinäre Beiträge zu Topik, Rhetorik und Individualität*, ed.

Iris Denneler (Frankfurt am Main: Peter Lang, 1999), pp. 15–25.

104. Locke's scribal routine of commonplacing thus was to become paradigmatic: commonplace projects of literary writers since 1800, such as the *Zibaldone* (1817–1832) of Giacomo Leopardi, Paul Valéry's *Cahiers* (1895–1945), Edith Wharton's *Commonplace Book* (ca. 1890–1909), and W. H. Auden's *A Certain World* (1970) reflect this.

CHAPTER TWO: AFTER THE *ARS TOPICA*

1. G. W. F. Hegel, *Aesthetics: Lectures on Fine Art*, trans. T. M. Knox, 2 vols. (Oxford: Clarendon Press of Oxford University Press, 1975), vol. 1, p. 387, "The Fable." It continues: "In this situation Aesop does not regard animals and nature in general, as the Indians and Egyptians do, as something lofty and divine on their own account; he treats them, on the contrary, with prosaic eyes as something where circumstances serve only to picture human action and suffering. But yet his notions are only witty, without any energy of spirit or depth of insight and substantive vision, without poetry and philosophy. His views and doctrines prove indeed to be ingenious and clever, but there remains only, as it were, a subtle investigation of trifles. Instead of creating free shapes out of a free spirit, this investigation only sees some other applicable side in purely given and available materials, the specific instincts and impulses of animals, petty daily events; this is because Aesop does not dare to recite his doctrines openly but can only make them understood hidden as it were in a riddle which at the same time is always being solved. In the slave, prose begins, and so this entire species is prosaic too."

2. Leslie Kurke, *Aesopic Conversations: Popular Tradition, Cultural Dialogue, and the Invention of Greek Prose* (Princeton, NJ: Princeton University Press, 2011), p. 242.

3. See Hans Jürgen Scheuer, s.v. "Ainos" in *Historisches Wörterbuch der Rhetorik*, ed. Gert Ueding (Tübingen: Niemeyer, 1992), vol. 1, pp. 295–98.

4. See the examples in Eduard Fraenkel, "Zur Form der AINOI," *Rheinisches Museum für Philologie* 73 (1924), pp. 366–70.

5. Friedrich Hölderlin, Letter to Casimir Ulrich Böhlendorff, November 1802, in *Selected Poems and Letters*, trans. Christopher Middleton (Amsterdam: The Last Books, 2019), pp. 182–84; and in Friedrich Hölderlin, *Sämtliche Werke und Briefe*, ed. Michael Knaupp, 3 vols. (Munich: Hanser, 1992), vol. 2, p. 922.

6. *O Kind, dem an des pontischen Wilds Haut*
    Des felsenliebenden, am meisten das Gemüth
    Hängt, allen Städten geselle dich,

Das gegenwärtige lobend

Gutwillig,

Und anderes denk in anderer Zeit.

Friedrich Hölderlin, "Unfaithfulness of Wisdom," in *Poems and Fragments*, trans. Michael Hamburger, 4th ed. (London: Carcanet, 2004), p. 705, and Friedrich Hölderlin, "Untreue der Weisheit," in *Sämtliche Werke und Briefe*, vol. 2, p. 379.

7. For example, "O son, make your mind most like the skin of the rocky sea creature in all the cities you visit." Pindar, "Fragment 43," in *Nemean Odes. Isthmian Odes. Fragments*, ed. and trans. William H. Race, Loeb Classical Library 485 (Cambridge, MA: Harvard University Press, 1997), pp. 244–45.

8. Hölderlin, "Unfaithfulness of Wisdom," p. 705; "Untreue der Weisheit," p. 379.

9. Ibid.

10. Pindar, "Fragment 43," p. 244.

11. Ibid., pp. 244–45.

12. Pindar, "Fragment 43," in *Carminum poetarum novem, lyricae poeseos principum, fragmenta* (Geneva: Estienne, 1560), pp. 356–57, p. 357.

13. *A Greek-English Lexicon*, s.v. "Epaineō," eds. Henry George Liddell and Robert Scott (Oxford: Oxford University Press, 1996).

14. See Karl Meuli, "Herkunft und Wesen der Fabel," in Thomas Gelze, ed., *Gesammelte Schriften* (Basel: Schwabe, 1975), pp. 731–56. Scheuer, s.v. "Ainos." See also the observations made without reference to the concept of *ainos* by Klaus Grubmüller, "Zur Pragmatik der Fabel: Der Situationsbezug als Gattungsmerkmal," in Vorstand der Vereinigung der deutschen Hochschulgermanisten, ed., *Textsorten und literarische Gattungen: Dokumentation des Germanistentages in Hamburg vom 1. bis 4. April 1979* (Berlin: Erich Schmidt, 1983), pp. 473–88. A wide overview is provided by Gert-Jan van Dijk, *Ainoi, Logoi, Mythoi: Fables in Archaic, Classical, and Hellenistic Greek Literature* (Leiden: Brill, 1997).

15. Gregory Nagy, "Early Greek Views of Poetry and Prose," in *The Cambridge History of Literary Criticism, Volume 1: Classical Criticism*, ed. George A. Kennedy (Cambridge: Cambridge University Press, 1990), pp. 11–12. See as well Gregory Nagy, "Mythe et Prose en Grèce Archaïque: L'Aînos," in *Métamorphoses du Mythe en Grèce Antiqu*, ed. Claude Calame (Geneva: Labor et Fides, 1988), pp. 229–42.

16. Hom. Od. 14.508; Homer, *Odyssey*, trans. A. T. Murray, 2 vols., Loeb Classical Library 105 (Cambridge, MA: Harvard University Press, 1919), vol. 2, bks 13–24, pp. 72–73.

17. Aristotle, *Art of Rhetoric*, trans. J. H. Freese, Loeb Classical Library 193 (Cambridge,

MA: Harvard University Press, 1926), 1393a30, pp. 272–73.

18. This separation of the genre from its use is a fallacy. That this systematization cannot fully describe or represent the function of the fable "in action" becomes evident when Aristotle inevitably needs to provide examples of cases in which fables historically have had the effect he meant to put forth. Paradoxically, this amounts to a reference to the fable's living function, its here and now as an *ainos*, effectively undoing the conceptualizing interest of the *Rhetoric*. The reader of the *Rhetoric* has not fully understood the effect of an exemplary use of a fable until an example of this use is provided, which practically leaves an instance of the *ainos* concept *après la lettre* in the *Rhetoric*.

19. Quintilian, *The Orator's Education, Volume 2: Books 3–5*, ed. and trans. Donald A. Russell, Loeb Classical Library 125 (Cambridge, MA: Harvard University Press, 2002), 5.9.19, pp. 440–41.

20. Friedrich Hölderlin, "On the Fable of the Ancients," in *Essays and Letters*, trans. Jeremy Adler (London: Penguin Books, 2009), p. 333. Hölderlin, "Von der Fabel der Alten," in *Sämtliche Werke und Briefe*, vol. 1, p. 115.

21. Johannes. Christus. Diesen möcht'

Ich singen, gleich dem Herkules, oder

Der Insel, welche vestgehalten und gerettet . . .

. . .

Das geht aber

Nicht. Anders ists ein Schiksaal. Wundervoller.

Reicher, zu singen. Unabsehlich

Seit jenem die Fabel. . . .

Friedrich Hölderlin, "Patmos: Fragments of the Later Version," in *Poems and Fragments*, trans. Michael Hamburger, 4th ed. (London: Carcanet, 2004), p. 571; Hölderlin, "Patmos," 3rd version, 5.53–60, in *Sämtliche Werke und Briefe*, vol. 2, p. 462.

22. See Bennholdt-Thomsen and Guzzoni's comments on that stanza of Patmos: Anke Bennholdt-Thomsen and Alfredo Guzzoni, "Die Träume," in *Analecta Hölderliniana III: Hesperische Verheißungen* (Würzburg: Königshausen und Neumann, 2007), pp. 141–77; regarding the "Fabel," see especially pp. 144–45.

23. Jean de la Fontaine, preface to *The Fables of La Fontaine* (London: Hachette, 1886), pp. liv–lxiii.

24. Johann Gottfried Herder, "Von der Aesopischen Fabel," in *Zerstreute Blätter* (Gotha: Ettinger, 1787), p. 140. Lessing equally points out the incongruity between taxonomy and explanation in Aristotle: "The overall classification is not correct; I would however

require a commentator to deliver us the reason for subdividing the fictional examples and teach us why there were only two kinds of it and no more. He would easily be able to abstract this reason, as I have done above, from the very examples Aristotle had provided." Gotthold Ephraim Lessing, "Abhandlungen über die Fabel," in *Werke und Briefe in zwölf Bänden*, vol. 4 of *Werke 1758–1759*, ed. Gunter E. Grimm (Frankfurt am Main: Deutscher Klassiker Verlag, 1990), p. 374.

25. For the basic challengers of exemplarity in post-topical literature, with a focus on the novel and the *roman à thèse* specifically, see Susan Suleiman, *Authoritative Fictions: The Ideological Novel as a Literary Genre* (Princeton, NJ: Princeton University Press, 1993); esp. chapter 1, " 'Exemplary' Narratives."

26. Lessing, "Abhandlungen über die Fabel," p. 375.

27. Ethel Matala de Mazza, "Offene Magazine für Erfahrungswissen. Sprichwörter, Fabeln, Exempel," in Michael Bies, Michael Gamper, and Ingrid Kleeberg, eds., *Gattungs-Wissen: Wissenspoetologie und literarische Form* (Göttingen: Wallstein, 2013), p. 273.

28. Herder, "Von der Aesopischen Fabel," p. 173.

29. Lessing, "Abhandlungen über die Fabel," pp. 401–402" "The general applause that La Fontaine received for his spirited way of narrating [*muntern Art zu erzählen*] caused the Aesopic fable gradually to be viewed in a completely different way from how the ancients had regarded it. For the ancients, the fable belonged to the area of philosophy, from which the teachers of rhetoric imported it. Aristotle did not treat it in his *Poetics*, but in his *Rhetoric*; and what Aphthonius and Theon say about it they also say in preliminary exercises of rhetoric. In the case of the moderns, too, what one wants to know about Aesop's fable must be sought in rhetoric up to the time of La Fontaine. He succeeded in turning the fable into a graceful poetical plaything [*einem anmutigen poetischen Spielwerke*]; he enchanted; he got many imitators who found no better way to maintain the name of a poet than by expanding and diluting the fables with amusing verses. The teachers of poetics seized on it. The teachers of rhetoric allowed the seizure to happen and stopped praising the fable as a reliable means of vivid persuasion. In return, the teachers of poetics began to regard it as a game for children [*Kinderspiel*] that they had to teach us to spruce up as much as possible. — This is where we still are!!"

30. Heinrich von Kleist, "On the Gradual Production of Thoughts whilst Speaking," in *Selected Writings*, ed. and trans. David Constantine (London: J. M. Dent, 1997), pp. 405–409, title spelling "Americanized" in the text. Heinrich von Kleist, "Über die allmählige Verfertigung der Gedanken beim Reden," in *Sämtliche Werke und Briefe in vier Bänden*,

ed. Ilse-Marie Barth and Klaus Müller-Salget (Frankfurt am Main: Deutscher Klassiker Verlag, 1990), vol. 3, p. 536.

31. Kleist, "On the Gradual Production of Thoughts whilst Speaking," p. 406, punctuation and capitalization adapted to match Kleist's original.

32. See the commentary in Kleist, "Allmähige Verfertigung," p. 1122.

33. Kleist, "On the Gradual Production of Thoughts whilst Speaking," pp. 407–408, punctuation, capitalization, and translation adapted to match Kleist's original.

34. Francisco Rodríguez Adrados, "Terminology of the Ancient Fable," in *History of the Graeco-Latin Fable* (Leiden: Brill, 1999), p. 6.

35. Kleist, "On the Gradual Production of Thoughts whilst Speaking," p. 408; Kleist, "Über die allmähige Verfertigung der Gedanken beim Reden," p. 540.

36. Reinhart Koselleck, "Historia Magistra Vitae: The Dissolution of the Topos into the Perspective of a Modernized Historical Process," in *Futures Past: On the Semantics of Historical Time*, trans. Keith Tribe (New York: Columbia University Press. 2004), pp. 26–42.

37. As Rüdiger Campe observes about Kleist's variation of the commonplace "l'appétit vient en mangeant" while also speaking to my concerns: "The *ars topica* is the site in one's own speech where others speak." Rüdiger Campe, "Verfahren: Kleists Allmähliche Verfertigung der Gedanken beim Reden," *Sprache und Literatur* 43.2 (2012), pp. 2–21.

38. Hans Blumenberg, "Der Sturz des Protophilosophen: Zur Komik der reinen Theorie, anhand einer Rezeptionsgeschichte der Thales-Anekdote," in *Das Komische*, eds. Wolfgang Preisendanz and Rainer Warning (Munich: Fink, 1976), p. 17. Aesop translation quoted from *Aesop without Morals: The Famous Fables and a Life of Aesop*, trans. Lloyd W. Daly (New York: Yoseloff, 1961), p. 110.

39. Blumenberg, "Der Sturz des Protophilosophen," p. 17.

40. "The Humor of Pure Theory" is the subtitle of the 1974 piece.

41. Hans Blumenberg, *Paradigms for a Metaphorology*, trans. Robert Savage (Ithaca, NY: Cornell University Press, 2010), p. 5.

42. Compared with the learned erudition presented in his books, this other format of publication should perhaps be seen as the one he favored over the book for putting forth new philosophical paradigms. While his late books are themselves mostly compilations of shorter texts on one problem or anecdote, the particular selection of texts makes these books read like treatises. With regard to his idea of metaphorology, one could say that those books appear as the solidified surface of his philosophy, whereas the liquid substratum of his antidefinitional thought and style is much more palpable in the over hundreds

of short pieces on anecdotes and fables he published after 1980.

43. Hans Blumenberg, "Unknown Aesopica: From Newly Found Fables," in *History, Metaphors, Fables: A Hans Blumenberg Reader*, ed. and trans. Hannes Bajohr, Florian Fuchs, and Joe Paul Kroll (Ithaca, NY: Cornell University Press, 2020), p. 567.

44. Ibid.

45. Unfortunately, the relation between fable and anecdote in Blumenberg has been almost completely overlooked, recently, for example, by Rüdiger Zill, s.v. "Anekdote," in *Blumenberg lesen: Ein Glossar*, eds. Robert Buch and Daniel Weidner (Berlin: Suhrkamp, 2014).

46. While Blumenberg did not argue for a "fabulatory world philosophy," he had still criticized Husserl for focusing only on the European traditions. At the same time, folklore studies and non-Western philosophical genealogies, for example Confucianism, show a much stronger awareness that their beginnings lie in a kind of fabulatory philosophy.

47. Hans Blumenberg, "Das Lebensweltmißverständnis," in *Lebenszeit und Weltzeit* (Frankfurt am Main: Suhrkamp, 1986), pp. 7–68.

48. See Blumenberg's similar depiction of the Cartesian ideal in *Paradigms for a Metaphorology*, which again shows how the fabulatory philosophy picks up the central concerns of the earlier project: "In its terminal state, philosophical language would be purely and strictly 'conceptual': everything can be defined, therefore everything must be defined; there is no longer anything logically 'provisional,' just as there is no longer any *morale provisoire*. From this vantage point, all forms and elements of figurative speech, in the broadest sense of the term, prove to have been makeshifts destined to be superseded by logic" (pp. 1–2).

49. Hans Blumenberg, "Pensiveness," in *History, Metaphors, Fables*, pp. 525–30.

50. For a slightly different take on this question with a focus on the anecdote, see Paul Fleming, "On the Edge of Non-Contingency," *Telos* 158 (Spring 2012), pp. 21–35.

51. Blumenberg, "Pensiveness," p. 528.

52. Ibid., p. 529.

53. Hans Blumenberg, "Of Nonunderstanding: Glosses on Three Fables," in *History, Metaphors, Fables*, pp. 562–65.

54. Blumenberg, "Pensiveness," in *History, Metaphors, Fables*, p. 527.

55. Ibid., p. 528

56. "Disturbance" (*Störung*) is a key term for Blumenberg that for reasons of space cannot be further developed here. See his explanation in the "Theorie der Lebenswelt": "The

disturbance [*Störung*] of carrying out one's life remains the incitement of philosophy. To understand the emergence of philosophical thinking from the lifeworld, one has to look at the kind of thinking that occurs in the lifeworld. It is something that we call the arrival of pensiveness." Hans Blumenberg, "Theorie der Lebenswelt," in *Theorie der Lebenswelt*, ed. Manfred Sommer (Berlin: Suhrkamp, 2010), p. 61.

57. Blumenberg, "Unknown Aesopica," *History, Metaphors, Fables*, pp. 569–70.

58. Hölderlin, "Notes on Oedipus," in *Essays and Letters*, p. 318. Hölderlin, "Anmerkungen zum Oedipus," in *Sämtliche Werke und Briefe*, vol. 2, p. 310.

59. Hans Blumenberg, "An Anthropological Approach to the Contemporary Significance of Rhetoric," in *History, Metaphors, Fables*, p. 193.

60. See Philipp Stoellger, "Geschichten zum 'Begriff': Genese der Nachdenklichkeit aus dem Zögern," in *Metapher und Lebenswelt: Hans Blumenbergs Metaphorologie als Lebenswelthermeneutik und ihr religionsphänomenologischer Horizont* (Tübingen: Mohr, 2000), pp. 334–39.

CHAPTER THREE: FORM

1. Erasmus already canonizes and comments on "Clothes make the man" as "Vestis virum facit" in his sixteenth-century proverb collection *Adages* (3.1.60). Erasmus, *Adagiorum chiliades*, in *Ausgewählte Schriften: Ausgabe in acht Bänden, Lateinisch und Deutsch*, ed. Werner Welzig (Darmstadt: Wissenschaftliche Buchgesellschaft, 1972), vol. 7, p. 546.

2. André Jolles, "Einleitung," in Giovanni di Boccaccio, *Das Dekameron* (Leipzig: Insel, 1921), pp. lxxvii–lxxviii.

3. Hans Blumenberg, "The Concept of Reality and the Possibility of the Novel," in *History, Metaphors, Fables: A Hans Blumenberg Reader*, ed. and trans. Hannes Bajohr, Florian Fuchs, and Joe Paul Kroll (Ithaca, NY: Cornell University Press, 2020), p. 500.

4. J. L. Austin's concept of "speech act" has been most coherently developed for literary studies by Karlheinz Stierle, along with other pragmatic aspects of formalist, structuralist, and linguistic literary theories, including those of André Jolles, Karl Bühler, and John R. Searle, in Karlheinz Stierle, *Text als Handlung: Grundlegung einer systematischen Literaturwissenschaft* (Munich: Fink, 2012). For a brief overview, see Stierle's dispute with Carsten Dutt: Karlheinz Stierle and Carsten Dutt, "Was heißt und zu welchem Ende studiert man literaturwissenschaftliche Pragmatik," *German Quarterly* 87.1 (Winter 2014), pp. 1–16.

5. Florian Klinger, "Thatness in Kleist," *Deutsche Vierteljahrsschrift für Literaturwissenschaft und Geistesgeschichte* 82.4 (2013), p. 616.

6. Walter Benjamin, "Goethe's Elective Affinities," trans. Stanley Corngold, in *Selected Writings, Volume 1, 1913–1936,* ed. Marcus Bullock and Michael W. Jennings (Cambridge, MA: Belknap Press of Harvard University Press, 1996), p. 331; Walter Benjamin, "Goethes *Wahlverwandtschaften*" (1922), in *Gesammelte Schriften*, ed. Rolf Tiedemann and Hermann Schweppenhäuser, 7 vols. in 14 (Frankfurt am Main: Suhrkamp, 1972–1999), vol.1.1, p. 169.

7. Andreas Gailus, "Form and Chance: The German Novella," in *The Novel*, ed. Franco Moretti, 2 vols. (Princeton, NJ: Princeton University Press, 2006), vol. 2, p. 774.

8. Ibid., pp. 774–75, emphasis in the original.

9. Benjamin, "Goethe's Elective Affinities," p. 331; Benjamin, "Goethes *Wahlverwandtschaften*," p. 169.

10. On this complex of transgression of the text, see "The Problem of Plot" in chapter 8, "The Composition of the Verbal Work of Art," in Jurij Lotman, *The Structure of the Artistic Text*, trans. Ronald Vroon (Ann Arbor: University of Michigan Press, 1977), pp. 231–38.

11. See the invaluable collection with a focus on German novellas, Karl Konrad Polheim, ed., *Theorie und Kritik der deutschen Novelle von Wieland bis Musil* (Tübingen: Niemeyer, 1970).

12. Michail A. Petrovsky, "Composition in Maupassant" (1921), *Essays in Poetics* 12 (1987), pp. 1–21, and Petrovsky, "Morphology of the Novella" (1927), ibid., pp. 22–50. Aleksandr A. Reformatsky, "An Essay on the Analysis of Composition of the Novella" (1922), in *Russian Formalism*, eds. Stephen Bann and John E. Bowlt (Edinburgh: Chatto and Windus, 1973), pp. 85–101. See also the overview provided in Matthias Aumüller, "Die russische Kompositionstheorie," in *Slawische Erzähltheorie,* ed. Wolf Schmid (Berlin: De Gruyter, 2009), pp. 91–140.

13. See Viktor Shklovsky, *Literature and Cinematography*, trans. Irina Masinovsky (Champaign, IL: Dalkey Archive Press, 2008).

14. György Lukács, "Bürgerlichkeit und l'art pour l'art: Theodor Storm" (1909), in *Die Seele und die Formen* (Neuwied: Luchterhand, 1970), pp. 82–116; Erich Auerbach, *Zur Technik der Frührenaissancenovelle in Italien und Frankreich* (Heidelberg: Winter, 1921).

15. Gilles Deleuze and Felix Guattari, *A Thousand Plateaus*, trans. Brian Massumi (Minneapolis: University of Minnesota Press, 1987), p. 194.

16. Gailus, "Form and Chance."

17. Winfried Menninghaus, "*Das Meretlein*: Eine Novelle im Roman: Strukturen poetischer Reflexion," in *Artistische Schrift* (Frankfurt am Main: Suhrkamp, 1982), pp. 61–90; Hannelore Schlaffer, *Poetik der Novelle* (Stuttgart: Metzler, 1993); Gerhard Neumann, "Wunderliche Nachbarskinder: Zur Instanzierung von Erzählen und Wissen in Goethes

Wahlverwandtschaften," in *Erzählen und Wissen,* ed. Gabriele Brandstetter (Freiburg: Rombach, 2003), pp. 15–40.

18. Bianca Theisen, "Strange News: Kleist's Novellas," in *A Companion to the Works of Heinrich von Kleist,* ed. Bernd Fischer (Rochester, NY: Camden House, 2003), pp. 81–102; Niels Werber, "Paullinis Gespenster: Zur Entstehung der Novelle," in *Gespenster,* ed. Moritz Baßler (Würzburg: Königshausen & Neumann 2005), pp. 215–27.

19. Nicola Gretz, "Von 'hässlichen Tazzelwürmern' und 'heiteren Blumenketten': Adalbert Stifters *Abdias* und Gottfried Kellers *Ursula* im Spannungsfeld von Fallgeschichte und Novelle," in *Fall–Fallgeschichte–Fallstudie,* eds. Susanne Düwell and Nicolas Pethes (Frankfurt am Main: Campus, 2014), pp. 274–92.

20. Chenxi Tang, "The Transformation of the Law of Nations and the Reinvention of the Novella: Legal History and Literary Innovation from Boccaccio's *Decameron* to Goethe's *Unterhaltungen deutscher Ausgewanderten,*" *Goethe-Yearbook* 19 (2012), pp. 67–92.

21. Michel Foucault, "Lives of Infamous Men," in *Essential Works of Foucault, 1954–1988,* ed. Paul Rabinow, 4 vols. (New York: New Press, 2000), vol. 3, p. 160; Michel Foucault, "La vie des hommes infâmes," in *Dits et Écrits: 1954–1988,* eds. Daniel Defert with François Ewald, 4 vols. (Paris: Gallimard, 1994), vol. 3, pp. 237–53.

22. The terms is *"nouvelles"* in the French original, pp. 237 and 253; the English translation loses this explicit reference to the genre of the novella by translating the occurrences of the word first as "news" (p. 157) and then as "short stories" (p. 174).

23. Foucault, "Lives of Infamous Men," p. 157.

24. Ibid., p. 161.

25. Only two noteworthy texts exist that are interested in Foucault's work on the *lettres de cachet,* and neither of them notices, or understands the literary formalism that provides the basis for Foucault's arguments. The first is a sociohistorical article dealing with historiographical decisions: Leon Antonio Rocha, " 'That Dazzling, Momentary Wake' of the *lettre de cachet*: The Problem of Experience in Foucault's Practice of History," in *Foucault, Family, and Politics,* eds. Robbie Duschinsky and Leon Antonio Rocha (New York: Palgrave Macmillan, 2012), pp. 189–219. The second is a book by a literary scholar who is mostly interested in the relation between language and power, revisiting the Foucauldian work from the side of literature: Achim Geisenhanslüke, *Sprachen der Infamie: Literatur und Ehrlosigkeit* (Munich: Fink, 2014). Still and surprisingly, the book avoids (or overlooks) the function of the novella form for Foucault. Not even a general theory of the novella form is provided, which is even more astonishing because the book contains a whole chapter on novellas by

Schiller, Kleist, and Kafka.

26. Foucault, "Lives of Infamous Men," p. 158.

27. Ibid., p. 157.

28. That is the literal meaning of the Greek word *pará-deigma* of which Quintilian reminds his readers before replacing it with the latin *exemplum*; Inst. Rhet. 5.11.1; Quintilian, *The Orator's Education, Volume 2: Books 3–5*, ed. and trans. Donald A. Russell, Loeb Classical Library 125 (Cambridge, MA: Harvard University Press, 2002), pp. 430–31.

29. The change from exemplum to novella leads to the involvement of the reader's faculty of judgment: "For the reader or listener, this complication means the he can no longer simply agree with a pregiven solution and be content with it, but on the contrary, that he is being disturbed and called upon to consider and ponder an unresolved problem himself." See Hans Jörg Neuschäfer, "Der Typische Fall und der einmalige Fall: Die Komplizierung traditioneller Handlungsschemata durch 'besondere Umstände' (Novelle im Vergleich mit Vida und Exemplum)," in *Boccaccio und der Beginn der Novelle: Strukturen der Kurzerzählung auf der Schwelle zwischen Mittelalter und Neuzeit* (Munich: Fink, 1969) p. 42.

30. Foucault, "Lives of Infamous Men," p. 157.

31. Ibid., p. 159.

32. Ibid., p. 162.

33. Ibid., p. 241.

34. Ibid., p. 162.

35. Ibid.

36. Ibid., p. 171.

37. Ibid., p. 174.

38. Ibid., p. 173.

39. Ibid., p. 174.

40. Ibid.

41. Ibid.

42. Gailus, "Form and Chance," p. 775.

43. Arlette Farge and Michel Foucault, eds., *Disorderly Families: Infamous Letters from the Bastille Archives*, ed. Nancy Luxon, trans. Thomas Scott-Railton (Minneapolis: University of Minnesota Press, 2016); Arlette Farge and Michel Foucault, eds., *Le désordre de familles: Lettres de cachet des Archives de la Bastille au XVIIIe siècle* (Paris: Gallimard, 2014).

44. Quoted in Farge and Foucault, *Disorderly Families*, p. 201; Farge and Foucault, *Le désordre de familles*, pp. 325–26. Sequence numbers added.

45. Farge and Foucault, *Disorderly Families*, p. 202.

46. Foucault, "Lives of Infamous Men," p. 157.

47. Farge and Foucault, *Disorderly Families*, p. 257.

48. See A. Grözinger, s.v. "Bittrede," in *Historisches Wörterbuch der Rhetorik*, ed. Gert Ueding (Tübingen: Niemeyer, 1994).

49. Farge and Foucault, *Disorderly Families*, p. 256; Farge and Foucault, *Le désordre de familles*, p. 421.

50. Farge and Foucault, *Disorderly Families*, p. 257; Farge and Foucault, *Le désordre de familles*, p. 423.

51. Nicolas Pethes, "Epistemische Schreibweisen: Zur Konvergenz und Differenz naturwissenschaftlicher und literarischer Erzählformen in Fallberichten," in *Der ärztliche Fallbericht: Epistemische Grundlagen und textuelle Strukturen dargesteller Beobachtung*, eds. Rudolf Behrens and Carsten Zelle (Wiesbaden: Harrassowitz, 2012), p. 19.

52. See Hugo Aust, *Novelle*, 5th ed. (Stuttgart: Metzler, 2012), pp. 30–31.

53. Friedrich Schlegel, "Nachricht von den poetischen Werken des Johannes Boccaccio," (1801), in *Kritische Friedrich-Schlegel-Ausgabe*, ed. Ernst Behler et al., 36 vols. (Munich: Schöningh, 1958–), pp. 373–96, vol. 2, p. 395. Hereafter *KFSA*.

54. Ibid.

55. Friedrich Schlegel, "Fragmente zur Poesie und Literatur," in *KFSA*, vol. 16, p. 187.

56. Ibid., p. 287.

57. Ibid., p. 288.

58. Schlegel, "Nachricht von den poetischen Werken des Johannes Boccaccio," p. 394.

59. Friedrich Schlegel, "Critical Fragments," in *Philosophical Fragments*, ed. Rodolphe Gasché, trans. Peter Firchow (Minneapolis: University of Minnesota Press, 1991), p. 6; Friedrich Schlegel, "Lyceums-Fragmente," 48th Lyceum's-Fragment, in *KFSA*, vol. 2, p. 153.

60. Schlegel, "Critical Fragments," p. 13; Schlegel, "Lyceums-Fragmente," 108th Lyceum's-Fragment, in *KFSA*, vol. 2, p. 160.

61. Schlegel, "Fragmente zur Poesie und Literatur," p. 288, emphasis in the original.

62. Ibid., p. 266.

63. Schlegel, "Nachricht von den poetischen Werken des Johannes Boccaccio," p. 396.

64. Ibid., p. 393.

65. Ibid.

66. Schlegel, "Fragmente zur Poesie und Literatur," p. 301.

67. Ibid., p. 158.

68. Ibid., p. 159.

69. Ibid., p. 188.

70. "Only individual stories can be taken to be stand-alone novellas [*bloße Novellen*], not those that are only beautiful within a system." Schlegel, "Fragmente zur Poesie und Literatur," p. 296.

71. Ibid., p. 297.

72. Friedrich Schlegel, "Athenaeum Fragments," in *Philosophical Fragments*, p. 78; Friedrich Schlegel, "Athenäums-Fragmente," Fragment 383, in *KFSA* vol. 2, p. 236.

73. Friedrich Schlegel, "Dialogue on Poetry," in *Dialogue on Poetry and Literary Aphorisms*, ed. and trans. Ernst Behler and Roman Struc (University Park: University of Pennsylvania Press, 1968), p. 102; Friedrich Schlegel, "Gespräch über die Poesie," in *KFSA* vol. 2, p. 337.

74. See the definition of epideictic oratory: "Epideictic eloquence is a particular quality of rhetorical practice, namely, to present oneself as speaker when presenting a subject matter." Stefan Matuschek, s.v. "Epideiktische Beredsamkeit," in *Historisches Wörterbuch der Rhetorik*.

75. Gert Mattenklott, "Der Sehnsucht eine Form: Zum Ursprung des Romans bei Friedrich Schlegel; erläutert an der *Lucinde*," in *Literaturwissenschaft und Sozialwissenschaften*, vol. 8 of *Zur Modernität der Romantik*, ed. Dieter Bänsch (Stuttgart: Metzler, 1977), p. 153.

76. Theodor Storm, "Eine zurückgezogene Vorrede aus dem Jahre 1881," in *Theorie und Kritik der deutschen Novelle von Wieland bis Musil*, ed. Karl Konrad Polheim (Tübingen: Niemeyer, 1970), p. 119.

77. Ibid.

78. Ibid.

79. György Lukács, "The Bourgeois Way of Life and Art for Art's Sake," in *Soul and Form*, trans. Anna Bostock (New York: Columbia University Press, 2010), p. 92, translation modified. Lukács, "Bürgerlichkeit und l'art pour l'art," pp. 108–109.

80. Lukács, "The Bourgeois Way of Life and Art for Art's Sake," p. 93, translation modified; Lukács, "Bürgerlichkeit und l'art pour l'art," p. 110.

81. Gailus, "Form and Chance," pp. 774–75.

82. Theodor Storm, *The Rider on the White Horse*, in *The Rider on the White Horse and Selected Stories*, trans. James Wright (New York: NYRB Classics, 2009), p. 268; Theodor Storm, *Der Schimmelreiter: Text der Buchausgabe von 1888*, in *Der Schimmelreiter: Novelle von*

Theodor Storm: Historisch-kritische Edition, ed. Gerd Eversberg (Husum: Erich Schmidt, 2014), p. 80. The translation is at times somewhat inaccurate, despite the accuracy demanded by Storm's prose. Here, for example, it reads "body of the old structure" instead of "the body of the dike." I've corrected it wherever required and marked this in the notes.

83. Storm, *The Rider on the White Horse*, p. 255; Storm, *Der Schimmelreiter*, p. 70.

84. "Das wird ihn vom Euklid curiren," says his father. Storm, *The Rider on the White Horse*, p. 189; Storm, *Der Schimmelreiter*, p. 18.

85. Storm, *The Rider on the White Horse*, p. 189; Storm, *Der Schimmelreiter*, p. 18.

86. Storm, *The Rider on the White Horse*, p. 190; Storm, *Der Schimmelreiter*, p. 19.

87. Ibid.

88. Storm, *The Rider on the White Horse*, p. 195, translation modified; Storm, *Der Schimmelreiter*, p. 23.

89. Lukács, "The Bourgeois Way of Life and Art for Art's Sake," p. 92; Lukács, "Bürgerlichkeit und l'art pour l'art," p. 108.

90. Theodor Storm to Paul Heyse, August 29, 1886, in Storm, *Der Schimmelreiter*, p. 555.

91. Theodor Storm to Elwin Paetel, March 7, 1888, in ibid., p. 560.

92. Jolles, "Einleitung," p. lxxvii.

93. The only article in Storm scholarship that alludes to the formal congruence of dike and novella, without unfolding it, is Philipp Theison, "Gespenstisches Erzählen," in *Theodor Storm: Novellen: Interpretationen*, ed. Christoph Deupmann (Stuttgart: Reclam, 2008), pp. 104–25.

94. Lukács, "The Bourgeois Way of Life and Art for Art's Sake," p. 92; Lukács, "Bürgerlichkeit und l'art pour l'art," p. 108.

95. See Michael Masanetz, "Vom Leben und Sterben des Königskindes: *Effi Briest* oder der Familienroman als analytisches Drama," *Fontane Blätter* 72 (2001), pp. 42–93.

96. Storm, "Eine zurückgezogene Vorrede aus dem Jahre 1881," p. 119.

CHAPTER FOUR: ARGUMENTATION

1. This problem of relating "Wissenspoetik" (poetics of knowledge) and "Gattungs-wissen" (knowledge conveyed through genres) has been recently addressed by Michael Bies, Michael Gamper, and Ingrid Kleeberg, eds., *Gattungs-Wissen: Wissenspoetologie und literarische Form* (Göttingen: Wallstein, 2013). Especially important in regard of the "topical" quality of the proverb is Ethel Matala de Mazza's contribution, "Offene Magazine für Erfahrungswissen. Sprichwörter, Fabeln, Exempel," pp. 265–84 in the same volume.

2. Friedrich Schlegel, *Kritische Fragmente*, Fragment 78, in *Kritische Friedrich-Schlegel-Ausgabe*, ed. Ernst Behler et al., 26 vols. (Munich: Schöningh, 1958–), p. 156.

3. Uwe Hebekus, "Topik/Inventio," in *Einführung in die Literaturwissenschaft*, eds. Miltos Pechlivanos, Stefan Rieger, Wolfgang Struck, and Michael Weitz (Stuttgart: Metzler, 1995), p. 95.

4. For the new concept of reality, see Hans Blumenberg, "The Concept of Reality and the Possibility of the Novel," in *History, Metaphors, Fables: A Hans Blumenberg Reader*, ed. and trans. Hannes Bajohr, Florian Fuchs, and Joe Paul Kroll (Ithaca, NY: Cornell University Press, 2020), pp. 499–524. For a possible, if very loosely argued relation between reality, lifeworld, and topoi, see Peter L. Oesterreicher, "Verstehen heisst Verbindenkönnen: Die Erfindung des Selbst in der topischen Lebenswelt," in *Die Formel und das Unverwechselbare: Interdisziplinäre Beiträge zu Topik, Rhetorik und Individualität*, ed. Iris Denneler (Frankfurt am Main: Peter Lang, 1999), pp. 15–25.

5. Immanuel Kant, *Anthropology from a Pragmatic Point of View*, trans. Robert B. Louden, in *Anthropology, History, and Education*, ed. Günter Zöllner and Robert B. Louden (Cambridge: Cambridge University Press, 2007), p. 327. This definition can be located in Kant's general dichotomy between *Dummheit* and *Witz*; see the chapter "Dummheit und Witz bei Kant," in Achim Geisenhanslüke, *Dummheit und Witz: Poetologie des Nichtwissens* (Munich: Fink, 2011), pp. 19–49.

6. Kant, *Anthropology from a Pragmatic Point of View*, p. 327.

7. That the proverb is a container of commonsense knowledge or folkloric wisdom is the general belief held by anthropologists even today. See, for example, Clifford Geertz, "Common Sense as a Cultural System," *Antioch Review* 33.1 (1975), pp. 5–26. Geertz even mentions the example of narrative agency: "Silone says somewhere that southern Italian peasants pass their lives exchanging proverbs with one another like so many precious gifts," but he still defines the proverb as a commonsense tool of knowledge, not of self-fashioning, as implicated in social roles, or as having wider implications for the pursuit of daily life: "Commonsense wisdom is shamelessly and unapologetically ad hoc. It comes in epigrams, proverbs, obiter dicta, jokes, anecdotes, *contes morals*—a clatter of gnomic utterances—not in formal doctrines, axiomized theories, or architectonic dogmas." Ibid., p. 23.

8. See Manfred Eikelmann, s.v. "Sprichwort," in *Reallexikon der deutschen Literaturwissenschaft*, eds. Georg Braungart et al. (Berlin: De Gruyter, 2003).

9. See as a paradigmatic study of such a term and its implications, Georg Stanitzek,

Blödigkeit: Beschreibungen des Individuums im 18. Jahrhundert (Tübingen: Niemeyer, 1989).

10. The *Oxford English Dictionary* lists around twenty new compositions of "fool" between 1600 and 1850, such as "foolation," "fooldom," and "foolocracy," all turning the didactic (e.g., Nicolaus of Cusa's *Idiotus*, or Galilei's *Simplicio*) or the humorous (jester) concept of the fool into a dismissive characterization of a person with lack of knowledge and intelligence.

11. See Werner van Treeck, *Dummheit: Eine unendliche Geschichte* (Stuttgart: Reclam, 2015), p. 106.

12. See Gianfranco Marrone, "Le sottisier comme genre discursif," *Protée* 22.2 (Spring 1994), pp. 80–85.

13. The specific meaning of *sottise* in Flaubert's title is very much opposed to Voltaire's *Sottisier*, where the pejorative aspect of *sottise* still refers only to the book's experimental, unorganized character, similar to how Lichtenberg dismissed the quality of his notebooks by using the verb *sudeln*, "to scrawl," for the title *Sudelbücher*.

14. Gustave Flaubert, *Dictionary of Accepted Ideas*, in *Bouvard and Pécuchet*, trans. Mark Polizzotti (Normal, IL: Dalkey Archive Press, 2005), pp. 283–326.

15. Gustave Flaubert to Louis Bouilhet, November 14, 1850, in *The Letters of Gustave Flaubert*, ed. Francis Steegmuller, 2 vols. (Cambridge, MA: Belknap Press of Harvard University Press, 1980), vol 1, p. 127.

16. Gustave Flaubert to Louise Colet, December 16, 1852, ibid., p. 176.

17. See Anne Herschberg-Pierrot, s.v. "Gemeinplatz," in *Arsen bis Zucker: Flaubert Wörterbuch*, eds. Barbara Vinken and Cornelia Wild (Berlin: Merve, 2010).

18. See. Rüdiger Campe, "Die Schreibszene," in *Paradoxien, Dissonanzen, Zusammenbrüche: Situationen offener Epistemologie*, eds. Hans Ulrich Gumbrecht and K. Ludwig Pfeiffer (Frankfurt am Main: Suhrkamp, 1991), pp. 759–72.

19. Avital Ronell, *Stupidity* (Urbana: University of Illinois Press, 2002), p. 69.

20. Al-Muhtār Ibn-al-Hasan Ibn-Butlān, *Schachtafelen der Gesuntheyt, Vormals nye gesehen, dem Gemeynen nutz zu verstand*, trans. Hans Weiditz and Michael Herr (1533), p. xxi.

21. Anonymous, *La comédie de proverbes: Pièce comique d'apres l'édition princeps de 1633*, ed. Michael Kramer (Geneva: Droz, 2003).

22. Georg Philipp Harsdörffer, *Das Schauspiel Teutscher Sprichwörter: Auß dem Französischen übersetzet durch den Spielenden*, in *Frauenzimmer Gesprächspiel: Anderer Theil* (Nürnberg: Endres, 1642), pp. 265–356.

23. See, for example, H. Carrington Lancaster, "Molière's Borrowings from the

Comédie des Proverbes," *Modern Language Notes* 33.4 (1918), pp. 208–11.

24. Martin Luther, *Luthers Sprichwortsammlung*, ed. Ernst Thiele (Weimar: Böhlau, 1900). The book contains a transcription of Luther's notebook of 489 German Proverbs; Mss. Add. A. 92, Oxford Bodleian Libraries.

25. Harsdörffer, "Von der Sprichwörter Eigenschaften, Unterscheid und Dolmetschung," in *Das Schauspiel Teutscher Sprichwörter*, pp. 269–70.

26. Erasmus, "Nosce Teipsum" / "Erkenne dich selbst," *Adagiorum chiliades*, in *Ausgewählte Schriften: Ausgabe in acht Bänden, Lateinisch and Deutsch*, ed. Werner Welzig (Darmstadt: Wissenschaftliche Buchgesellschaft, 1972), vol. 7, pp. 416–21.

27. Harsdörffer, "Von der Sprichwörter Eigenschaften, Unterscheid und Dolmetschung," p. 272.

28. Ibid., p. 280.

29. An example of the dialogue reads like this:

> PHILIPPIN: Feurio! Feurio! Die Dieb sind da! wartet nur ihr Nachtvögel wir wollen euch Füß machen: Helfft, helfft ihr ehrlichen Nachbarn! Die rechten natürlichen Dieb stehlen unser Jungfrau, helfft, helfft weil es noch Zeit ist!
>
> ALLÄGRE: Geld, oder Blut!
>
> PHILIPPIN: O! Ich bin des Todts, wenn ihr mich umb das Leben bringt.
>
> ALLÄGRE: Ha, ha, du schreist wie ein Zahnbrecher, schweig, oder ich will dich schweigen machen.
>
> FLORINDA: Ach helfft, helfft, ihr lieben Leut, oder man trägt mich darvon wie ein Heilthumb.
>
> LIDIA: Gestolen Wasser ist Malvasier. Nun fort, fort die Vögel sind außgenommen, last uns aus dem Staub machen. (Ibid., p. 289)

> PHILIPPIN: Fire! Fire! The thieves are here! just wait you night birds, we will make you get a move on: Help, help, you honest neighbors! The fairly natural thieves are stealing our virgin, help, help because there still is time!
>
> ALLÄGRE: Money or blood!
>
> PHILIPPIN: Oh! I'm doomed to die if you cut me out of life.
>
> ALLÄGRE: Ha, ha, you're screaming like a tooth puller, be quiet, or I will make you.
>
> FLORINDA: Oh help, help, you good people, or I am being carried away like a relic.

LIDIA: Stolen water is Malvasier. Now begone, begone, the birds are gutted, let's fly the coop.

30. Gottfried Keller, *Der Grüne Heinrich*, in *Sämtliche Werke in sieben Bänden*, Thomas Böning et. al., eds. (Frankfurt am Main: Deutscher Klassiker Verlag, 1985–1996), vol. 2, pp. 849–52.

31. Walter Benjamin, "Gottfried Keller," trans. Rodney Livingstone, in *Selected Writings, Volume 2, 1927–1934*, ed. Michael W. Jennings, Howard Eiland, and Gary Smith (Cambridge, MA: Belknap Press of Harvard University Press, 1996–2003), p. 59.

32. Ibid.

33. See the overview of Keller's earliest plans for the cycle: Gottfried Keller, *Die Leute von Seldwyla*, in *Sämtliche Werke in sieben Bänden*, vol. 4, pp. 608–11.

34. Ibid., p. 11.

35. Ibid., p. 240

36. Ibid.

37. See the convincing narratological taxonomy by Stefan Manns, *Grenzen des Erzählens: Konzeption und Struktur des Erzählens in Georg Philipp Harsdörffers "Schauplätzen"* (Berlin: De Gruyter, 2013), especially chapter 6.3 "Das Sprichwort in den *Schauplätzen*," pp. 200–13.

38. Gottfried Keller, *Clothes Make the Man*, trans. Harry Steinhauer, in *Stories*, ed. Frank G. Ryder (New York: Continuum, 1982), p. 166. Gottfried Keller, *Kleider machen Leute*, in *Sämtliche Werke in sieben Bänden*, vol. 4, p. 303.

39. Keller, *Clothes Make the Man*, p. 166; Keller, *Kleider machen Leute*, pp. 303–304

40. Ibid., p. 167; p. 304.

41. Ibid.

42. Klaus Jeziorkowski, *Gottfried Keller: Kleider machen Leute: Text, Materialien, Kommentar* (Munich: Hanser, 1984), pp. 91–100.

43. The only work that actively brings together Keller's use of proverbs in his novellas doesn't recognize this structural relationship, merely noting that his interest in the proverb is not pedagogical, but artistic (*künstlerischer*). Wolfgang Mieder, "Das Sprichwort in Gottfried Kellers *Die Leute von Seldwyla*," in *Das Sprichwort in der deutschen Prosaliteratur des neunzehnten Jahrhunderts* (Munich: Fink, 1972), pp. 152–67.

44. Keller, *Clothes Make the Man*, pp 154, 155, 157; Keller, *Kleider machen Leute*, pp. 288, 290, 291, 292.

45. Ibid., p. 160; p. 296. Strapinski decides not to play, but rather to observe the Goldachers play, who confirm their baroque view of the world by willingly including him in

a *theatrum mundi*, that is, by organizing their social play so that he is assigned the only position on the baroque stage in which pure observation is possible, that of the emperor: "So saß er denn wie ein kränkelnder Fürst, vor welchem die Hofleute ein angenehmes Schauspiel aufführen und den Lauf der Welt darstellen." Ibid.

46. Ibid., p. 161; p. 297.

47. Ibid.

48. Ibid., pp. 164; p. 300.

49. For many other and only German examples, see Mieder, *Das Sprichwort in der deutschen Prosaliteratur des neunzehnten Jahrhunderts*.

50. Gregory Permyakov, "Notes on Structural Paremiology," in *From Proverb to Folk-Tale: Notes on the General Theory of Cliché*, trans. Y. N. Filippov (Moscow: Nauka, 1979), p. 141. For Permyakov, see also Peter Grzybek, "Überlegungen zur semiotischen Sprichwortforschung," *Kodikas/Code*. 7.3–4 (1984), pp. 215–49.

51. Christoph Chlosta and Peter Grzybek, "Versuch macht klug?!: Logisch-semiotische Klassifikation bekannter deutscher Sprichwörter," in Gregory Permyakov, *Die Grammatik der sprichwörtlichen Weisheit: Mit einer Analyse allgemein bekannter deutscher Sprichwörter*, ed. and trans. Peter Grzybek (Baltmannsweiler: Schneider, 2000), p. 189.

52. Erasmus, "Vestis virum facit" / "Kleider machen Leute," in *Adagiorum chiliades*, p. 546.

53. Erasmus relates it to a comment that Nausicaa makes about recognizing Odysseus only after he changed his clothes, which is quoted as well by Quintilian.

54. Wolfgang Preisendanz, *Die Spruchform in der Lyrik des alten Goethe und ihre Vorgeschichte seit Opitz* (Heidelberg: Winter, 1952), p. 134.

CHAPTER FIVE: PERCEPTION

1. For "The Emperor's New Clothes," see, for example, Albrecht Koschorke, Susanne Lüdemann, and Thomas Frank, *Des Kaisers neue Kleider: Über das Imaginäre politischer Herrschaft: Texte, Bilder, Lektüren* (Frankfurt am Main: Fischer, 2002).

2. As far as I can see, reconstructing Benjamin's *Märchenbuch* project has not been attempted before. A few studies exist, however, that concentrate on individual works by Benjamin, such as *Conversation above the Corso* (*Das Gespräch über dem Corso*) or look at the significance of text such as "The Fair-Haired Eckbert." The only extensive summary of Benjamin's relation to *Märchen*, which remains merely a documentation and falls short of recognizing the specific positioning and function of his project, is Almut-Barbara Renger,

Zwischen Märchen und Mythos: Die Abenteuer des Odysseus und andere Geschichten von Homer bis Walter Benjamin (Stuttgart: Metzler, 2006), esp. chapter 3.c, "Märchen und Mythos bei Walter Benjamin," pp. 316–84. Another general and rather unspecific short mediation is Elisabetta Mengaldo, "'Seligkeit im Kleinen' oder Schein der Rettung?: Märchen- und Volksliedstoffe in der Kurzprosa Benjamins und Adornos," *Jahrbuch der Deutschen Schiller-Gesellschaft* 56 (2012), pp. 284–306. Specifically about "The New Melusine" in the context of the Benjamin's *Gespräch über dem Corso*, see Heinz Brüggemann, *Walter Benjamin über Spiel, Farbe und Phantasie* (Würzburg: Königshausen & Neumann, 2007), especially the chapter "Unendlich Großes, unendlich Kleines / übertreibende Phantasie in den Grenzbereichen des Menschlichen (*Gespräch über dem Corso*)," pp. 116–22. A general reading of Tieck's "The Fair-Haired Eckbert" in the context of Benjamin's remarks on it has been done by Roland Borgards, "Halbpart des Vergessens: Benjamin und Tieck," in Heinz Brüggemann and Günter Oesterle, eds., *Walter Benjamin und die Romantische Moderne* (Würzburg: Königshausen & Neumann, 2009), pp. 341–54.

3. This collection partly still exists in the library of the Institut für Jugendbuchforschung, Goethe-Universität, Frankfurt am Main. For a list of Benjamin's collection, see Ingeborg Daube, *Die Kinderbuchsammlung Walter Benjamin: Eine Ausstellung des Instituts für Jugendbuchforschung der Johann Wolfgang Goethe-Universität und der Stadt- und Universitätsbibliothek Frankfurt am Main 12. März bis 25. April 1987* (Frankfurt am Main: Stadt- und Universitätsbibliothek, 1987).

4. A large corpus of work on Benjamin's work on children exists. For basic lists of Benjamin's texts on the matter and of secondary sources, see Giulio Schiavoni, "Zum Kinde," in *Benjamin-Handbuch: Leben–Werk–Wirkung*, ed. Burkhardt Lindner (Stuttgart: Metzler, 2006), pp. 373–85. Further important are works that specifically deal with the connection of childhood, writing, and media are Davide Guiriato, *Mikrographien: Zu einer Poetologie des Schreibens in Walter Benjamins Kindheitserinnerungen (1932–1939)* (Munich: Fink, 2006); Brüggemann, *Walter Benjamin über Spiel, Farbe und Phantasie*; Anja Lemke, *Gedächtnisräume des Selbst: Walter Benjamins "Berliner Kindheit um neunzehnhundert"* (Würzburg: Königshausen & Neumann, 2008).

5. Walter Benjamin to Gershom Scholem, August 21, 1925, in *Gesammelte Briefe*, ed. Christoph Gödde and Henri Lonitz, 6 vols. (Frankfurt am Main: Suhrkamp, 1995–2000), vol. 3, p. 61. Hereafter *GB*.

6. This is the list Benjamin writes to Hugo von Hofmannsthal on November 8, 1925, in *GB*, vol. 3, p. 96.

7. In an early letter, which Benjamin writes about this story to Scholem in the context

of other fairy tales, January 13, 1920, in *GB*, vol. 2, pp. 67–71. He would come back to it during the *Märchenbuch* project.

8. Benjamin to Hofmannsthal, August 2, 1925, in *GB*, vol. 3, p. 71.

9. Benjamin to Scholem, July 21, 1925, in *GB*, vol. 3, p. 62.

10. However, from the many references of *Sagen* that Benjamin makes, many of them in a recurring manner, one could quite reliably compile the likely table of contents of this book. At the time of Benjamin's contact with Weigand, the offices and archives of the Verlag Bremer Presse were located in Munich, but no former documents that Benjamin may have sent to Wiegand survive, most likely destroyed when the archives burned down completely in 1944. See Heinrich F. S. Bachmair, "Die Bremer Presse," in *Gutenberg-Jahrbuch 1950*, ed. Aloys Ruppel (Mainz: Verlag der Gutenberg-Gesellschaft, 1950), pp. 336–44.

11. Benjamin to Scholem, ca. May 25, 1925, in *GB*, vol. 3, p. 41

12. See the section "Nature of the Legend" ("Wesen der Sage") in their introduction to their *Sagen* anthology, Jacob Grimm and Wilhelm Grimm, "Foreword," in *The German Legends of the Brothers Grimm*, ed. and trans. Donald Ward, 2 vols. (Philadelphia: Institute for the Study of Human Issues, 1981), vol. 1, pp. 1–11. Especially the following: "The fairytale is more poetic, the legend is more historical; the former exists securely almost in and of itself in its innate blossoming and consummation. The legend, by contrast, is characterized by a lesser variety of colors, yet it represents something special in that it adheres always to that which we are conscious of and know well, such as a locale or a name that has been secured through history. Because of this local confinement [*ihrer Gebundenheit*], it follows that the legend cannot, like the fairytale, find its home anywhere. Instead the legend demands certain conditions without which it either cannot exist at all, or can only exist in less perfect form [*unvollkommener*]." Jacob Grimm and Wilhelm Grimm, "Vorrede," in *Deutsche Sagen herausgegeben von den Brüdern Grimm*, ed. Heinz Rölleke (Frankfurt am Main: Artemis & Winkler, 1994), pp. 11–24.

13. Walter Benjamin, "Old Forgotten Children's Books," trans. Rodney Livingstone, in *Selected Writings, Volume 1, 1913–1926*, ed. Marcus Bullock and Michael W. Jennings (Cambridge, MA: Belknap Press of Harvard University Press, 1996), p. 408. Walter Benjamin, "Alte vergessen Kinderbücher," in *Gesammelte Schriften*, ed. Rolf Tiedemann and Hermann Schweppenhäuser, 7 vols. in 14 (Frankfurt am Main: Suhrkamp, 1972–1999), vol. 3, p. 17. Hereafter *GS*.

14. Walter Benjamin, *The Correspondence of Walter Benjamin, 1910–1940*, ed. Gershom Scholem and Theodor W. Adorno, trans. Manfred R. Jacobson and Evelyn M. Jacobson (Chicago: University of Chicago Press, 1994), p. 273; Benjamin to Hofmannsthal, June 11,

1925, in *GB*, vol. 3, pp. 51–52. The alleged Grimm quotation does not appear anywhere as such in the Grimm's introduction to the *Deutsche Sagen*.

15. Benjamin to Scholem, July 21, 1925, *Correspondence*, p. 277; *GB*, vol. 3, pp. 61–62.

16. Benjamin to Hofmannsthal, June 11, 1925, *Correspondence*, p. 273; *GB*, vol. 3, p. 52.

17. Benjamin to Scholem, ca. May 25, 1925, *Correspondence*, p. 269; *GB*, vol. 3, p. 41.

18. Hans Blumenberg, "Speech Situation and Immanent Poetics," in *History, Metaphors, Fables: A Hans Blumenberg Reader*, ed. and trans. Hannes Bajohr, Florian Fuchs, and Joe Paul Kroll (Ithaca, NY: Cornell University Press, 2020), pp. 449–65.

19. Benjamin to Scholem, February 14, 1921, *Correspondence*, p. 176, translation altered; *GB*, vol. 2, pp. 137–38.

20. Peter Fenves, *The Messianic Reduction: Walter Benjamin and the Shape of Time* (Stanford, CA: Stanford University Press, 2011), pp. 227–44.

21. Walter Benjamin, "Sprache und Logik II," in *GS*, vol. 6, pp. 23–25.

22. Walter Benjamin, *Origin of the German Trauerspiel*, trans. Howard Eiland (Cambridge, MA: Harvard University Press, 2019), p. 12. "The object of knowledge, an object determined in conceptual intention, is not truth. Truth is an intentionless being formed from ideas. The comportment appropriate to truth is therefore an entering and disappearing into it, not an intending in knowing. Truth is the death of intention. Precisely this can be gathered from the fable of a veiled image at Saïs, the uncovering of which is fatal to anyone who seeks to ascertain the truth by questioning." Walter Benjamin, "Erkenntniskritische Vorrede," *Ursprung des deutschen Trauerspiels*, in *GS*, vol. 2, p. 216.

23. Walter Benjamin, "Goethe's Elective Affinities," trans. Stanley Corngold, in *Selected Writings, Volume 1, 1913–1926*, p. 333; Walter Benjamin, "Goethes *Wahlverwandtschaften*," in *GS*, vol. 2, p. 171.

24. Benjamin to Scholem, May 20–25, 1925, *Correspondence*, p. 267; *GB*, vol. 3, p. 38.

25. Walter Benjamin, "First Sketches," in *The Arcades Project*, trans. Howard Eiland and Kevin McLaughlin (Cambridge, MA: Belknap Press of Harvard University Press, 1999), p. 861; Walter Benjamin, "Pariser Passagen I," in *GS*, vol. 5, p. 1031.

26. Walter Benjamin to Theodor W. Adorno, May 7, 1940, *Correspondence*, p. 629; *GB*, vol. 6, p. 446.

27. See, for example these two parts of a schemata that place "The Fair-Haired Eckbert" at the center of an array of problems that Benjamin had worked on from the early 1920s ("Scham") through his narratology in "The Storyteller" ("Der Erzähler") ("Vergessen und die Technik des Erzählers") until the last reworkings of the *Berlin Childhood around*

1900 (*Berliner Kindheit um 1900*) in the late 1930s ("Das bucklicht Männlein").

Descended nature / Dusty human world / The primeval world and the new

The forgetting of guilt

Forgetting and animals / The Fair-Haired Eckbert

The thinking of the animals / Their fear

Forgetting as vessel of the spiritual world

Form of things in forgottenness / O d r a d e k / Disfigurement

The lowered head / T h e L i t t l e H u n c h b a c k / Attention as the natural prayer

Je n'ai rien négligé.

———

Abgesunkene Natur / Verstaubte Menschenwelt / Die Vorwelt und das Neue

Das Vergessen als Schuld

Vergessen und Tiere / Der blonde Eckbert

Das Denken der Tiere / Ihre Angst

Vergessen als Behältnis der Geisterwelt

Form der Dinge in der Vergessenheit / O d r a d e k / Entstellung

Das gesenkte Haupt / D a s b u c k l i c h t M ä n n l e i n / Aufmerksamkeit

    das natürliche Gebet

Je n'ai rien négligé. (*GS*, vol. 2, pp. 1210–11)

———

Shamelessness of the swamp world. Its power lies in its forgottenness

The reminiscence that moves eons. The district of experience encompasses.

    The swamp logic.

The forgetting and the technique of the storyteller

The rememberence of the Jews

The animals and their thinking. Why so much hinges on the interpretation

    of their attitude

The Fair-Haired Eckbert

Odradek and the form of things in forgottenness

The heavy burden. The Little Hunchback.

———

Schamlosigkeit der Sumpfwelt. Ihre Macht liegt in ihrer Vergessenheit

Die Weltalter bewegende Erinnerung. Der von ihr umfaßte Erfahrungskreis.

    Die Sumpflogik

Das Vergessen und die Technik des Erzählers

Das Eingedenken bei den Juden

Die Tiere und ihr Denken. Warum soviel von der Deutung ihres Gestus abhängt

Der Blonde Eckbert

Odradek und die Form der Dinge in der Vergessenheit

Die schwere Last. Das bucklicht Männlein. (*GS*, vol. 2, p. 1213)

28. "Franz Kafka," trans. Harry Zohn, in *Selected Writings, Volume 2, 1927–1934*, ed. Michael W. Jennings, Howard Eiland, and Gary Smith (Cambridge, MA: Belknap Press of Harvard University Press, 1996–2003), p. 810, translation modified; Walter Benjamin, "Franz Kafka," in *GS*, vol. 2, p. 430.

29. Benjamin calls it "Niobe*sage*." Walter Benjamin, "Zur Kritik der Gewalt," in *GS*, vol. 2, pp. 197–99; Walter Benjamin, "Critique of Violence," trans. Edmund Jephcott, in *Selected Writings, Volume 1, 1913–1926*, pp. 248–50.

30. Walter Benjamin, "Curriculum Vitae (III)," trans. Rodney Livingstone, in *Selected Writings, Volume 2, 1927–1934*, p. 78, translation modified; Walter Benjamin, "Lebenslauf III," in *GS*, vol. 6, p. 219.

31. "Children are able to manipulate fairy stories with the same ease and lack of inhibition that they display in playing with pieces of cloth and building blocks. They build their world out of motifs from the fairy tale, combining its various elements," Benjamin, "Old Forgotten Children's Books," p. 408; Benjamin, "Alte vergessene Kinderbücher," in *GS*, vol. 3, p. 17.

32. See the explication that the "disappearance" (*Verschwundenheit*) of the Melusine figure in Goethe's tale explains that she is not guilty in any human sense:

> "Think of giants and dwarfs. If bodily characteristics can ever symbolize spiritual ones, it happens no more meaningfully than in those two creatures of folk literature. There are two spheres of complete innocence, and they are found on the two boundaries where our normal human stature (as I would call it) passes over into the gigantic or the diminutive. Everything human is burdened with guilt. But the gigantic creatures are innocent, and the bawdiness of a Gargantua or a Pantagruel ... is just an exuberant proof of this."
>
> "And is the innocence of the tiny of the same kind?" I asked "what you have said makes me think of think of Goethe's 'Neue Melusine' — the princess in the little casket. Her seclusion, her enchanting song, and her minuscule stature always seemed to be a perfect embodiment of the realm of innocence. The realm of *childlike* innocence, I should say — which of course is different from the innocence of giants."

Walter Benjamin, "Conversation above the Corso," trans. Edmund Jephcott, in *Selected Writings, Volume 3, 1935–1938*, ed. Howard Eiland and Michael W. Jennings (Cambridge, MA: Belknap Press of Harvard University Press, 1996–2003), p. 29; Walter Benjamin, "Gespräch über dem Corso," in *GS*, vol. 4, pp. 763–71, pp. 768–79.

33. In the 1921 letter to Scholem, Benjamin already had projected that the outcome would be enigmatic: "In doing this, one is dealing with a most puzzling [*rätselhaft*] concept of time and very puzzling [*rätselhaft*] phenomena."

34. Benjamin himself uses the word in a French letter to describe his ideas about "The New Melusine," rather than the direct translation *disparition*. Walter Benjamin to Gretel Adorno, January 17, 1940, in *GB*, vol. 6, p. 385.

35. Clearly, if not explicitly, Benjamin's contact with Husserlian phenomenology and its practice of phenomenological "Reduktion" play out here in an inversed way. See Fenves, *Messianic Reduction* and Uwe Steiner, "Walter Benjamins Husserl-Lektüre im Kontext," *Internationales Jahrbuch für Hermeneutik* 9 (2010), pp. 189–258.

36. Vladimir Propp, *Morphology of the Folktale* (Austin, TX: University of Texas Press, 1968), pp. 4–5: "It is scarcely possible to doubt that phenomena and objects around us can be studied from the aspect of their composition and structure, or from the aspect of those processes and changes to which they are subject, or from the aspect of their origins."

37. Ernst Bloch, "Das Märchen geht selber in der Zeit," in *Gesamtausgabe*, 16 vols. in 17 (Frankfurt am Main: Suhrkamp, 1977), vol. 9, pp. 196–99.

38. I evoke this concept here in its recent anthropological actualization proposed by Albrecht Koschorke, *Wahrheit und Erfindung: Grundzüge einer Allgemeinen Erzähltheorie* (Frankfurt am Main: Fischer, 2012), esp. chapter 1.1.1, "Homo narrans," pp. 9–13.

39. Walter Benjamin, "The Storyteller," in *The Storyteller Essays*, ed. Samuel Titan, trans. Tess Lewis (New York: NYRB Classics, 2019), pp. 66–67; Walter Benjamin, "Der Erzähler," in *GS*, vol. 2.1, pp. 457–58.

40. Ibid., sequence numbers added, translation modified.

41. In a review of a 1930 book, *Märchen und Gegenwart: Das deutsche Volksmärchen und unsere Zeit*, Benjamin clearly warns against confusing the fairy tale setting and that of a certain historical present: "No! The night of our republic is not so deep that in it all cats would be gray and [Kaiser] Wilhelm could no longer be distinguished from King Thrushbeard [*König Drosselbart*]," Walter Benjamin, "Kolonialpädagogik," in *GS*, vol. 3, p. 274.

CHAPTER SIX: EPIPHANIES, ENACTED STORIES, AND THE PRAXEOLOGY OF SHORT FORMS

1. James Joyce, *Stephen Hero: Edited from the Manuscript in the Harvard College Library*, ed. Theodore Spencer, John J. Slocum, and Herbert Cahoon (New York: New Directions, 1955), p. 211.

2. See, for example, the culmination of the now canonical debate between Robert Scholes and Florence Walzl, "The Epiphanies of Joyce," *PMLA* 82.1 (March 1967), pp. 152–54.

3. Umberto Eco, *The Aesthetics of Chaosmos: The Middle Ages of James Joyce* (Cambridge, MA: Harvard University Press, 1989), p. 24.

4. Ibid., p. 29.

5. Ibid.

6. James Joyce, *A Portrait of the Artist as a Young Man: Epiphanies, Notes, Manuscripts and Typescripts*, ed. Michael Groden et al. (New York: Garland, 1978), p. 11.

7. Roland Barthes, *The Preparation of the Novel: Lecture Courses and Seminars at the Collège de France, 1978–79 and 1979–80*, trans. Kate Briggs (New York: Columbia University Press, 2011), p. 102.

8. James Joyce, "Epiphanies," in *The Workshop of Daedalus: James Joyce and the Raw Materials for A Portrait of the Artist as a Young Man*, ed. Robert Scholes (Evanston, IL: Northwestern University Press, 1965), p. 19.

9. Joyce, *Stephen Hero*, p. 249.

10. Morris Beja, "Epiphany and the Epiphanies," in *Companion to Joyce Studies*, eds. Zack Bowen and James Carend (Westport, CT: Greenwood, 1984), pp. 712–13. For other suggestions, see Scholes's notes to Joyce, *Epiphanies*; or, for example, David Hayman, "The Purpose and Permanence of the Joycean Epiphany," *James Joyce Quarterly* 35–36 (Summer–Fall 1998), pp. 633–55.

11. For that matter, that is, for their quality as writing and as literature, it is also secondary or even irrelevant whether Joyce actually biographically witnessed the epiphanic moment in Mullingar or not.

12. Walter Benjamin, "The Storyteller," in *The Storyteller Essays*, ed. Samuel Titan, trans. Tess Lewis (New York: NYRB Classics, 2019), pp. 66–67, translation modified; Walter Benjamin, "Der Erzähler," in *Gesammelte Schriften*, eds. Rolf Tiedemann and Hermann Schweppenhäuser, 7 vols. in 14 (Frankfurt am Main: Suhrkamp, 1972–1999), vol. 2, pp. 457–58.

13. I am using "estrangement" here as a technical term in the sense first introduced by

Viktor Shklovsky, "Art as Device," in *Theory of Prose*, trans. Benjamin Sher (Champaign, IL: Dalkey Archive Press, 1990), pp. 1–14.

14. See Hannah Arendt, "The Web of Relationships and the Enacted Story," in *The Human Condition* (Chicago: University of Chicago Press, 1998), pp. 181–88.

15. Hannah Arendt, "Socrates," in *The Promise of Politics*, ed. Jerome Kohn (New York: Schocken Books, 2005), pp. 12–13. From Arendt's perspective, the failure of this form of dialogue in the trial of Socrates pointed to the need of separation of thought, public speech, and action. In order to explain what type of speech action is necessary, Arendt returned to this scene of Socratic failure over and over for the rest of her career. Thought became contemplation, public speech became rhetoric, and action became political or legal force. In the wake of these separations, the opposition between truth and opinion (*doxa*) also came about — truth was no longer a result of public discussion, but had to be proven in its own logical or rhetorical processes. This replaced truth with persuasion, writes Arendt, which therefore became only an "unfortunate substitute for a kind of unshakeable conviction which could spring only from direct perception of truth (p. 53)." The birth of the *ars topica* and dialectics means that Aristotle intended to separate speech act from speaker because he intended that it would foster dialogues between citizens. It is exactly this "embodied effectiveness" on which Arendt's political philosophy and even more so her political anthropology in *The Human Condition* hinges. For further quotations, see Tama Weisman, "Platonic Political" in *Hannah Arendt and Karl Marx: On Totalitarianism and the Tradition of Western Political Thought* (Lanham, MD: Lexington Books, 2014); the quote above is on page 53 and is a citation from Arendt's Gauss Seminar at Princeton University in 1953 "Karl Marx and the Tradition of Western Political Thought."

16. Arendt, "The Web of Relationships and the Enacted Story," pp. 178–79.

17. Ibid., p. 181.

18. Ibid., p. 187.

19. Ibid., p. 192.

20. See Hannah Arendt, *Reflections on Literature and Culture*, ed. Susannah Young-ah Gottlieb (Stanford, CA: Stanford University Press, 2007).

21. Seyla Benhabib, "Hannah Arendt and the Redemptive Power of Narrative," *Social Research* 57.1 (1990), pp. 167–96.

22. Judith Butler, *Giving an Account of Oneself* (New York: Fordham University Press, 2005), pp. 30–40.

23. Allen Speight, "Arendt on Narrative Theory and Practice," *Collegiate Literature* 38.1

(2011), pp. 115–30.

24. Arendt, "The Web of Relationships and the Enacted Story," p. 180.

25. Ibid.

26. André Jolles, "Einleitung," in Giovanni di Boccaccio, *Das Dekameron* (Leipzig: Insel, 1921), p. lxxvii.

27. Barthes, *The Preparation of the Novel*, p. 89.

28. See the overview in Theodore Schatzki, Karin Knorr-Cetina, and Eike von Savigny, eds., *The Practice Turn in Contemporary Theory* (New York: Routledge, 2001).

29. Michel Foucault, *The Hermeneutics of the Subject: Lectures at the Collège de France 1981–82*, ed. Frédéric Gros, trans. Graham Burchell (New York: Palgrave Macmillan, 2005); Michel Foucault, "Technologies of the Self," in *Technologies of the Self: A Seminar with Michel Foucault*, eds. Martin Luther, Huck Gutman, and Patrick Hutton (London: Tavistock, 1988), pp. 16–49.

30. Andreas Reckwitz, "Kultur und Materialität," in *Kreativität und soziale Praxis: Studien zur Sozial- und Gesellschaftstheorie* (Bielefeld: Transcript Verlag, 2016), p. 95. See also Andreas Reckwitz, "Grundelemente einer Theorie sozialer Praktiken: Eine sozialtheoretische Perspektive," *Zeitschrift für Soziologie* 32.4 (August 2003), pp. 282–301.

31. Roland Barthes, *Writing Degree Zero*, trans. Annette Lavers and Colin Smith (New York: Hill and Wang, 1968).

32. See Rüdiger Campe, "Die Schreibszene," in *Paradoxien, Dissonanzen, Zusammenbrüche: Situationen offener Epistemologie*, eds. Hans Ulrich Gumbrecht and K. Ludwig Pfeiffer (Frankfurt am Main: Suhrkamp, 1991), pp. 759–72. Now translated as Rüdiger Campe, "Writing; The Scene of Writing," trans. Bryan Klausmeyer and Johannes Wankhammer, *Modern Language Notes* 136.5 (December 2021), pp. 971–83.

33. For a study of the era around 1800, see Carlos Spoerhase, *Das Format der Literatur: Praktiken materieller Textualität zwischen 1740 und 1830* (Göttingen: Wallstein, 2018). For a more sociological study of the processes of actual authors, see Carolin Amlinger, *Schreiben: Eine Soziologie literarischer Arbeit* (Frankfurt am Main: Suhrkamp, 2021).

34. Karlheinz Stierle, *Text als Handlung: Grundlegung einer systematischen Literaturwissenschaft* (Munich: Fink, 2012); Karlheinz Stierle and Carsten Dutt, "Was heißt und zu welchem Ende studiert man literaturwissenschaftliche Pragmatik," *German Quarterly* 87.1 (Winter 2014), pp. 1–16.

35. Caroline Levine, *Forms: Whole, Rhythm, Hierarchy, Network* (Princeton: Princeton University Press, 2015); Terence Cave, *Thinking with Literature: Towards a Cognitive Criticism* (Oxford: Oxford University Press, 2016).

36. Cave, *Thinking with Literature*, pp. 61–62.

37. Michael Bies, Michael Gamper, and Ingrid Kleeberg, eds., *Gattungs-Wissen: Wissenspoetologie und literarische Form* (Göttingen: Wallstein, 2013).

38. Hans-Jörg Rheinberger, *Toward a History of Epistemic Things* (Stanford, CA: Stanford University Press, 1997). For a general impact of the "return of things" in the humanities, see *Die Wiederkehr der Dinge,* eds. Friedrich Balke, Maria Muhle, and Antonia von Schöning (Berlin: Kadmos, 2011).

39. Hans Jörg Rheinberger, "Epistemic Objects / Technical Objects," in Uljana Feest, Hans-Jörg Rheinberger, and Günter Abel, eds., *Epistemic Objects* (Berlin: Max Planck Institut für Wissenschaftsgeschichte, 2008), pp. 93–98.

CODA

1. Alex Greenberger, "'Is Shakespeare Fake News?': Artist Hito Steyerl Ponders Tough Questions in an Interview about Experimental Filmmaker Harun Farocki," *ARTnews*, February 6, 2020, https://www.artnews.com/art-news/artists/hito-steyerl-harun-farocki-thaddaeus-ropac-interview-1202677179.

2. Ibid.

3. Laura Poitras, "Interview with Hito Steyerl," *Artforum* 53.9 (May 2015), p. 313.

4. Ibid., pp. 313–14.

5. Katja Kwastek, "Interview with Hito Steyerl," *Kunstforum International* 242 (September–October 2016), p. 128. "Es gibt bestimmte Regeln der Wissenschaft, die auf der einen Seite sehr hilfreich sind, aber auf der anderen Seite auch Denkbarrieren darstellen. Und die pure Spekulation oder das Fabulieren — Mittel, deren ich mich hemmungslos bediene — schlagen manchmal ungeahnte Schneisen von einem Bereich zum nächsten — zwischen verschiedenen Disziplinen oder Traditionen, aber auch sehr oft zwischen völlig voneinander getrennten geographischen Regionen. Ich glaube dass man das zusammendenken muss, was nicht zusammengehört, weil das heute die Realität ist. Und da braucht es erweiterte Verfahren."

6. Alexandra Delage, "How Not to Be Seen," in *Hito Steyerl: I Will Survive*, eds. Florian Ebner et al. (Leipzig: Spector Books, 2020), p. 77.

7. Hito Steyerl, *How Not to Be Seen: A Fucking Didactic Educational .MOV File*, 2013, video, 15:52 minutes, https://www.artforum.com/video/hito-steyerl-how-not-to-be-seen-a-fucking-didactic-educational-mov-file-2013-51651.

8. Hito Steyerl, "Ripping Reality," in *Duty Free Art: Art in the Age of Planetary Civil War* (New York: Verso, 2017), pp. 191–205.

9. Eyal Weizman, *Forensic Architecture: Violence at the Threshold of Detectability* (New York: Zone Books, 2017).

10. Sue Carter, "You Can Look at Hito Steyerl's Art, but Don't Get Comfortable," *Toronto Star*, October 28, 2019, https://www.thestar.com/entertainment/visual-arts/2019/10/28/you-can-look-at-hito-steyerls-art-but-dont-get-comfortable.html.

11. Hans Blumenberg, "Pensiveness," in *History, Metaphors, Fables: A Hans Blumenberg Reader*, ed. and trans. Hannes Bajohr, Florian Fuchs, and Joe Paul Kroll (Ithaca, NY: Cornell University Press, 2020), p. 540.

12. Rüdiger Campe, "Kleist's 'Improbable Veracities,' or, A Romantic Ending," in *The Game of Probability: Literature and Calculation from Pascal to Kleist*, trans. Ellwood Wiggins (Stanford, CA: Stanford University Press, 2012), pp. 369–89.

13. See Ludwig Fischer, *Natur im Sinn: Naturwahrnehmung und Literatur* (Berlin: Matthes & Seitz, 2019).

14. Chie Sakakibara, " 'Our Home Is Drowning': Iñupiat Storytelling and Climate Change in Point Hope, Alaska," *Geographical Review* 98.4 (2008), pp. 456–75.

15. Davi Kopenawa and Bruce Albert, *The Falling Sky: Words of a Yonamami Shaman* (Cambridge, MA: Belknap Press of Harvard University Press, 2013).

16. John Durham Peters, *The Marvelous Clouds: Toward a Philosophy of Elemental Media* (Chicago: University of Chicago Press, 2015).

17. Doc Society and Exposure Labs, eds., *The Climate Story Lab Tool Box* (Version 092020), https://climatestorylabs.org/toolbox.

18. Svetlana Alexievich, *Voices from Chernobyl: The Oral History of a Nuclear Disaster*, trans. Keith Gessen (New York: Picador, 2006).

19. Ibid., pp. 235–36.

20. Meera Subramanian, "Seeing God's Hand in the Deadly Floods, yet Wondering about Climate Change," *InsideClimateNews*, October 24, 2017, https://insideclimatenews.org/news/19102017/christianity-evangelical-climate-change-flooding-west-virginia.

21. For the connection between medieval apocryphal narrativity and current multimodal storytelling, see, for example, Hans Jürgen Scheuer, "Apokryphe Modernität: Caesarius von Heisterbach, Alexander Kluge und die Intelligenz des Mirakels," in *The Poetic Power of Theory, Alexander Kluge-Jahrbuch*, eds. Richard Langston and Leslie A. Adelson, (Göttingen: V&R unipress, 2019), vol. 6, pp. 97–114.

22. Rob Nixon, *Slow Violence and the Environmentalism of the Poor* (Cambridge, MA: Harvard University Press, 2011), p. 279.

Works Cited

Adelson, Leslie. *Cosmic Miniatures and the Future Sense*. Berlin: De Gruyter, 2017.

Adrados, Francisco Rodríguez. "Terminology of the Ancient Fable." In *History of the Graeco-Latin Fable*. Leiden: Brill 1999, pp. 3–47.

Aesop without Morals: The Famous Fables and a Life of Aesop. Trans. Lloyd W. Daly. New York: Yoseloff, 1961.

Agricola, Rudolph. *De inventione dialectica libri tres*. Ed. and trans. Lothar Mundt. Tübingen: Niemeyer, 1992.

———. Letter to Jacob Barbireau, June 7, 1484. In *Letters*. Ed. Adrie van der Laan and Fokke Akkerman. Assen: Royal van Gorcum, 2002, pp. 200–19.

Alexievich, Svetlana. *Voices from Chernobyl: The Oral History of a Nuclear Disaster*. Trans. Keith Gessen. New York: Picador, 2006.

Alféri, Pierre. *Brefs*. Paris: P.O.L., 2016.

Amlinger, Carolin. *Schreiben: Eine Soziologie literarischer Arbeit*. Frankfurt am Main: Suhrkamp, 2021.

Amossy, Ruth. *L'argumentation dans le discours*. Paris: Nathan, 2000.

——— "Publikum und Topik." In *Die neue Rhetorik: Studien zu Chaim Perelman*. Ed. Josef Kopperschmid. Munich: Fink, 2006, pp. 307–32.

Anonymous. *La comédie de proverbes: Pièce comique d'apres l'édition princeps de 1633*. Ed. Michael Kramer. Geneva: Droz, 2003.

———. "Nachschrift eines Ästhetik-Kollegs Baumgartens." In *Alexander Gottlieb Baumgarten: Seine Bedeutung und Stellung in der Leibniz-Wolffischen Philosophie und seine Beziehungen zu Kant. Nebst Veröffentlichung einer bisher unbekannten Handschrift der Ästhetik Baumgartens*. Ed. Bernhard Poppe. Leipzig: Noske, 1907, pp. 65–258.

Anscombre, J. C. "Topique or not topique: Formes topiques intrinsèques et forms topiques extrinsèques." *Journal of Pragmatics* 24.1–2 (1995), pp. 115–41.

Arendt, Hannah. *Reflections on Literature and Culture*. Ed. Susannah Young-ah Gottlieb. Stanford, CA: Stanford University Press, 2007.

———. "Socrates." In *The Promise of Politics*. Ed. Jerome Kohn. New York: Schocken Books, 2005, pp. 5–39.

———. *The Human Condition*. Chicago: University of Chicago Press, 1998.

Aristotle. *Art of Rhetoric*. Trans. J. H. Freese. Loeb Classical Library 193. Cambridge, MA: Harvard University Press, 1926.

———. *Metaphysics*. Trans. Hugh Tredennick. Loeb Classical Library 271. Cambridge, MA: Harvard University Press, 1933.

———. *Topica*. Ed. and trans. E. S. Forster. Loeb Classical Library 391. Cambridge, MA: Harvard University Press, 1960.

———. *Topics, Books I and VII with Excerpts from Related Texts*. Trans. Robin Smith. Oxford: Oxford University Press, 1997.

———. *Topik*. Trans. Tim Wagner and Christoph Rapp. Stuttgart: Reclam, 2004.

Arnauld, Antoine, and Pierre Nicole. *Logic or the Art of Thinking*. Trans. Jill Vance Buroker. Cambridge: Cambridge University Press, 1996.

Asmuth, Bernhard. "Thema." In *Historisches Wörterbuch der Rhetorik*. Ed. Gert Ueding. 12 vols. Tübingen: Niemeyer, 2009, vol. 9, pp. 528–41.

Auerbach, Erich. *Zur Technik der Frührenaissancenovelle in Italien und Frankreich*. Heidelberg: Winter, 1921.

Aumüller, Matthias. "Die russische Kompositionstheorie." In *Slawische Erzähltheorie*. Ed. Wolf Schmid. Berlin: De Gruyter, 2009, pp. 91–140.

Aust, Hugo. *Novelle*. 5th ed. Stuttgart: Metzler, 2012.

Bachmair, Heinrich F. S. "Die Bremer Presse." In *Gutenberg-Jahrbuch 1950*. Ed. Aloys Ruppel. Mainz: Verlag der Gutenberg-Gesellschaft, 1950, pp. 336–44.

Bacon, Francis. "De Augmentis Scientiarum." In *The Works of Francis Bacon*. Ed. James Spedding. 15 vols. Boston: Houghton Mifflin. 1858, vol. 2, pp. 73–498.

———. *Of the Advancement and Proficience of Learning; or, The Partitions of Sciences*. Trans. Gilbert Watts. Oxford: Lichfield, 1640.

———. *The Advancement of Learning*. Ed. Michael Kiernan. Oxford: Oxford University Press: 2000.

Badische Landesbibliothek Karlsruhe, and Bibliothèque Nationale et Universitaire de Strasbourg, eds. *Thomas Murner (1475–1537): Elsässischer Theologe und Humanist*. Karlsruhe: Badische Landesbibliothek Karlsruhe, 1987.

Baeumer, Max L., ed. *Toposforschung*. Darmstadt: Wissenschaftliche Buchgesellschaft, 1973.

Balke, Friedrich, Maria Muhle, and Antonia von Schöning, eds. *Die Wiederkehr der Dinge*. Berlin: Kadmos, 2011.

Barthes, Roland. "L'ancienne rhétorique: Aide-mémoire." *Communications* 16 (1970), pp. 172–223.

———. "The Old Rhetoric: An Aide-Mémoire" (1970). In *The Semiotic Challenge*. Trans. Richard Howard. New York: Hill and Wang, 1988, pp. 11–93.

———. *The Preparation of the Novel: Lecture Courses and Seminars at the Collège de France, 1978–79 and 1979–80*. Trans. Kate Briggs. New York: Columbia University Press, 2011.

———. *Writing Degree Zero*. Trans. Annette Lavers and Colin Smith. New York: Hill and Wang, 1968.

Baumgarten, Alexander Gottlieb. *Aesthetica*. Trans. Dagmar Mirbach. Hamburg: Meiner, 2007.

Beja, Morris. "Epiphany and the Epiphanies." In *Companion to Joyce Studies*. Eds. Zack Bowen and James Carend. Westport, CT: Greenwood, 1984, pp. 707–25.

Benhabib, Seyla. "Hannah Arendt and the Redemptive Power of Narrative." *Social Research* 57.1 (1990), pp. 167–96.

Benjamin, Walter. *The Arcades Project*. Trans. Howard Eiland and Kevin McLaughlin. Cambridge, MA: Belpnap Press of Harvard University Press, 1999.

———. *The Correspondence of Walter Benjaimin, 1910–1940*. Ed. Gershom Scholem and Theodor W. Adorno, trans. Manfred R. Jacobson and Evelyn M. Jacobson. Chicago: University of Chicago Press, 1994.

———. *Gesammelte Briefe*. Ed. Christoph Gödde and Henri Lonitz. 6 vols. Frankfurt am Main: Suhrkamp, 1995–2000.

———. *Gesammelte Schriften*. Ed. Rolf Tiedemann and Hermann Schweppenhäuser. 7 vols. in 14. Frankfurt am Main: Suhrkamp, 1972–1999.

———. *Origin of the German Trauerspiel*. Trans. Howard Eiland. Cambridge, MA: Harvard University Press, 2019.

———. *Selected Writings, Volume 1, 1913–1926*. Ed. Marcus Bullock and Michael W. Jennings. Cambridge, MA: Belknap Press of Harvard University Press, 1996–2003.

———. *Selected Writings, Volume 2, 1927–1934*. Ed. Michael W. Jennings, Howard Eiland, and Gary Smith. Cambridge, MA: Belknap Press of Harvard University Press, 1996–2003.

———. *Selected Writings, Volume 3, 1935–1938*. Ed. Howard Eiland and Michael W, Jennings. Cambridge, MA: Belknap Press of Harvard University Press, 1996–2003.

———. *The Storyteller Essays*. Ed. Samuel Titan, trans. Tess Lewis. New York: NYRB Classics, 2019, pp. 48–73.

Bennholdt-Thomsen, Anke, and Alfredo Guzzoni. "Die Träume." In *Analecta Hölderliniana III: Hesperische Verheißungen*. Würzburg: Königshausen und Neumann, 2007, pp. 141–77.

Berger, Albrecht. "Theme." In *Brill's New Pauly*. Http://dx.doi.org/10.1163/1574-9347_bnp_e1217380.

Berndt, Frauke. "Poetische Topik." In *Handbuch Literarische Rhetorik*. Ed. Rüdiger Zymner. Berlin: De Gruyter, 2015, pp. 433–60.

Bies, Michael, Michael Gamper, and Ingrid Kleeberg, eds. *Gattungs-Wissen: Wissenspoetologie und literarische Form*. Göttingen: Wallstein, 2013.

Blair, Ann M. *Too Much to Know: Managing Scholarly Information before the Modern Age*. New Haven, CT: Yale University Press, 2010.

Bloch, Ernst. "Das Märchen geht selber in der Zeit." In *Gesamtausgabe*, 16 vols. in 17. Frankfurt am Main: Suhrkamp, 1977, vol. 9, pp. 196–99.

Blumenberg, Hans. "Das Lebensweltmißverständnis." In *Lebenszeit und Weltzeit*. Frankfurt am Main: Suhrkamp, 1986, pp. 7–68.

———. "Der Sturz des Protophilosophen: Zur Komik der reinen Theorie, anhand einer Rezeptionsgeschichte der Thales-Anekdote." In *Das Komische*. Eds. Wolfgang Preisendanz and Rainer Warning. Munich: Fink, 1976, pp. 11–64.

———. *History, Metaphors, Fables: A Hans Blumenberg Reader*. Ed. and trans. Hannes Bajohr, Florian Fuchs, and Joe Paul Kroll. Ithaca, NY: Cornell University Press, 2020.

———. *Paradigms for a Metaphorology*. Trans. Robert Savage. Ithaca, NY: Cornell University Press, 2010.

———. "Theorie der Lebenswelt." In *Theorie der Lebenswelt*. Ed. Manfred Sommer. Berlin: Suhrkamp, 2010, pp. 7–108.

Boethius. *De differentiis topicis*. Trans. Eleonore Stump. Ithaca, NY: Cornell University Press, 1978.

Borgards, Roland. "Halbpart des Vergessens: Benjamin und Tieck." In *Walter Benjamin und die Romantische Moderne*. Eds. Heinz Brüggemann and Günter Oesterle. Würzburg: Königshausen & Neumann, 2009, pp. 341–54.

Bornscheuer, Lothar. *Topik: Zur Struktur der gesellschaftlichen Einbildungskraft*. Frankfurt am Main: Suhrkamp, 1976.

Breuer, Dieter, and Helmut Schanze, eds. *Topik: Beiträge zur interdisziplinären Diskussion* Munich: Fink, 1981.

Brüggemann, Heinz. *Walter Benjamin über Spiel, Farbe und Phantasie*. Würzburg: Königshausen & Neumann, 2007.

Butler, Judith. *Giving an Account of Oneself*. New York: Fordham University Press, 2005.

Campe, Rüdiger. "Die Schreibszene." In *Paradoxien, Dissonanzen, Zusammenbrüche: Situationen offener Epistemologie*. Eds. Hans Ulrich Gumbrecht and K. Ludwig Pfeiffer. Frankfurt am Main: Suhrkamp, 1991, pp. 759–72.

———. *The Game of Probability: Literature and Calculation from Pascal to Kleist*. Trans. Ellwood Wiggins. Stanford, CA: Stanford University Press, 2012.

———. "Verfahren. Kleists Allmähliche Verfertigung der Gedanken beim Reden." *Sprache und Literatur* 43.2 (2012), pp. 2–21.

———. "Writing; The Scene of Writing." Trans. Bryan Klausmeyer and Johannes Wankhammer. *Modern Language Notes* 136.5 (December 2021), pp. 971–83.

Carruthers, Mary. *The Book of Memory: A Study of Memory in Medieval Culture*. Cambridge: Cambridge University Press, 1990.

Carter, Sue. "You Can Look at Hito Steyerl's Art, but Don't Get Comfortable." *Toronto Star*, October 28, 2019. Https://www.thestar.com/entertainment/visualarts/2019/10/28/you-can-look-at-hito-steyerls-art-but-dont-get-comfortable.html.

Cave, Terence. *Thinking with Literature: Towards a Cognitive Criticism*. Oxford: Oxford University Press, 2016.

Chlosta, Christoph, and Peter Grzybek. "Versuch macht klug?!: Logisch-semiotische Klassifikation bekannter deutscher Sprichwörter." In Gergory Permyakov, *Die Grammatik der sprichwörtlichen Weisheit: Mit einer Analyse allgemein bekannter deutscher Sprichwörter*. Ed. and trans. Peter Grzybek. Baltmannsweiler: Schneider, 2000, pp. 169–98.

Cicero. *Topica*. Trans. H. M. Hubbell. Loeb Classical Library 386. Cambridge, MA: Harvard University Press, 1949.

Colie, Rosalie. "The Essayist in his Essay." In *John Locke: Problems and Perspectives*. Ed. John Yolton. Cambridge: Cambridge University Press, 1969, pp. 234–61.

Curtius, Ernst Robert. *Europäische Literatur und lateinisches Mittelalter*. Bern: Francke, 1948.

———. *European Literature and Latin Middle Ages*. Trans. Willard R. Trask. Princeton, NJ: Princeton University Press, 2013.

Dacome, Lucia. "Noting the Mind: Commonplace Books and the Pursuit of the Self in the Eighteenth Century." *Journal of the History of Ideas* 65.4 (2004), pp. 603–25.

Daube, Ingeborg. *Die Kinderbuchsammlung Walter Benjamin: Eine Ausstellung des Instituts für Jugendbuchforschung der Johann Wolfgang Goethe-Universität und der Stadt- und*

Universitätsbibliothek Frankfurt am Main 12. März bis 25. April 1987. Frankfurt am Main: Stadt- und Universitätsbibliothek, 1987.

Delage, Alexandra. "How Not to Be Seen." In *Hito Steyerl: I Will Survive.* Eds. Florian Ebner et al. Leipzig: Spector Books, 2020, p. 77.

Deleuze, Gilles, and Felix Guattari. *A Thousand Plateaus.* Trans. Brian Massumi. Minneapolis: University of Minnesota Press, 1987.

Dijk, Gert-Jan van. *Ainoi, Logoi, Mythoi: Fables in Archaic, Classical, and Hellenistic Greek Literature.* Leiden: Brill, 1997.

Doc Society and Exposure Labs, eds. *The Climate Story Lab Tool Box.* Https://climatestorylabs.org/toolbox.

Dumitrescu, Irina, and Bruce Holsinger, eds. "In Brief." Special issue, *New Literary History* 50.3 (2019).

Eco, Umberto. *The Aesthetics of Chaosmos: The Middle Ages of James Joyce.* Cambridge, MA: Harvard University Press, 1989.

Efimova, Svetlana, and Michael Gamper, eds. *Prosa: Geschichte, Poetik, Theorie.* Berlin: De Gruyter, 2021.

Eikelmann, Manfred. "Sprichwort." In *Reallexikon der deutschen Literaturwissenschaft.* Eds. Georg Braungart, et al. Berlin: De Gruyter, 2003, vol. 3, pp. 486–89.

Erasmus. *Adagiorum chiliades.* In *Ausgewählte Schriften Ausgabe in acht Bänden, Lateinisch and Deutsch.* Ed. Werner Welzig, vol. 7. Darmstadt: Wissenschaftliche Buchgesellschaft, 1972.

Farge, Arlette, and Michel Foucault, eds. *Le désordre de familles: Lettres de cachet des Archives de la Bastille au XVIIIe siècle.* Paris: Gallimard, 2014.

——. *Disorderly Families: Infamous Letters from the Bastille Archives.* Ed. Nancy Luxon, trans. Thomas Scott-Railton. Minneapolis: University of Minnesota Press, 2016.

Fenves, Peter. *The Messianic Reduction: Walter Benjamin and the Shape of Time.* Stanford, CA: Stanford University Press, 2011.

Fischer, Ludwig. *Natur im Sinn: Naturwahrnehmung und Literatur.* Berlin: Matthes & Seitz, 2019.

Flaubert, Gustave. *Dictionary of Accepted Ideas* (1850). In *Bouvard and Pécuchet.* Trans. Mark Polizzotti. Normal, IL: Dalkey Archive Press, 2005, pp. 283–326.

——. *The Letters of Gustave Flaubert.* Ed. Francis Steegmuller. 2 vols. Cambridge, MA: Belknap Press of Harvard University Press, 1980.

Fleming, Paul. "On the Edge of Non-Contingency." *Telos* 158 (Spring 2012), pp. 21–35.

Foucault, Michel. *The Hermeneutics of the Subject: Lectures at the Collège France 1981–1982.* Ed. Frédéric Gros, trans. Graham Burchell. New York: Palgrave Macmillan, 2005.

——. "Language to Infinity." Trans. Donald F. Bouchard and Sherry Simon. In *Essential*

Works of Foucault, Volume 2, Aesthetics, Method, and Epistemology. Ed. James D. Faubion. New York: New Press, 1998, pp. 89–101.

———. "Lives of Infamous Men." In *Essential Works of Foucault, 1953–1988*. Ed. Paul Rabinow. 4 vols. New York: New Press, 2000, vol. 3, pp. 157–75.

———. "Technologies of the Self." In *Technologies of the Self: A Seminar with Michel Foucault*. Eds. Martin Luther, Huck Gutman, and Patrick Hutton. London: Tavistock, 1988, pp. 16–49.

———. "La vie des hommes infâmes." In *Dits et Écrits: 1953–1988*. Ed. Daniel Defert et al. 4 vols. Paris: Gallimard, 1994, vol. 4, pp. 237–53.

Fraenkel, Eduard. "Zur Form der AINOI." *Rheinisches Museum für Philologie* 73 (1924), pp. 366–70.

Fuchsberger, Ortolf. *Ein gründlicher klarer anfang der natürlichen und rechten kunst der waaren Dialectica*. Zürich: Geßner, 1556.

Fuhrmann, Manfred. "Die zivilrechtlichen Beispiele in Ciceros Topik." In *Topik und Rhetorik*. Eds. Thomas Schirren and Gert Ueding. Tübingen: Niemeyer, 2000, pp. 51–66.

Gailus, Andreas. "Form and Chance: The German Novella." In *The Novel*. Ed. Franco Moretti. 2 vols. Princeton, NJ: Princeton University Press, 2006, vol. 2, pp. 739–76.

Geertz, Clifford. "Common Sense as a Cultural System." *Antioch Review* 33.1 (1975), pp. 5–26.

Geisenhanslüke, Achim. *Dummheit und Witz: Poetologie des Nichtwissens*. Munich: Fink, 2011.

———. *Sprachen der Infamie: Literatur und Ehrlosigkeit*. Munich: Fink, 2014.

Giesecke, Michael. *Der Buchdruck in der Frühen Neuzeit: Eine historische Fallstudie über die Durchsetzung neuer Informations- und Kommunikationstechnologien*. Frankfurt am Main: Suhrkamp, 1991.

Godzich, Wlad, and Jeffrey Kittay. *The Emergence of Prose: An Essay in Prosaics*. Minneapolis: University of Minnesota Press, 1987.

Goldmann, Stefan. "Zur Herkunft des Topos-Begriffs von Ernst Robert Curtius." *Euphorion* 90 (1996), pp. 134–49.

———, Christoph Kann, and Oliver Primavesi. "Topik; Topos." In *Historisches Wörterbuch der Philosophie*. Eds. Joachim Ritter, Karlfried Gründer, and Gottfried Gabriel. Basel: Schwabe, 1998, vol. 10, pp. 1263–88.

Gottsched, Johann Christoph. *Ausführliche Redekunst*. 1st ed. Leipzig: Breitkopf, 1736.

Goyet, Florence. *The Classic Short Story, 1870–1925: Theory of a Genre*. Cambridge: Open Book, 2014.

Graevenitz, Gerhart von. *Mythos: Zur Geschichte einer Denkgewohnheit*. Stuttgart: Metzler, 1987.

Grant, Ben. *The Aphorism and Other Short Forms*. London: Routledge, 2016.

Greenberger, Alex. "'Is Shakespeare Fake News?': Artist Hito Steyerl Ponders Tough Questions in an Interview about Experimental Filmmaker Harun Farocki." *ARTnews*, February 6, 2020. Https://www.artnews.com/art-news/artists/hito-steyerl-harun-farocki-thaddaeus-ropac-interview-1202677179.

Gretz, Nicola. "Von *hässlichen Tazzelwürmern* und *heiteren Blumenketten*: Adalbert Stifters *Abdias* und Gottfried Kellers *Ursula* im Spannungsfeld von Fallgeschichte und Novelle." In *Fall–Fallgeschichte–Fallstudie*. Eds. Susanne Düwell and Nicolas Pethes. Frankfurt am Main: Campus, 2014, pp. 274–92.

Grimm, Jacob, and Wilhelm Grimm. "Foreword." In *The German Legends of the Brothers Grimm*. Ed. and trans. Donald Ward. 2 vols. Philadelphia: Institute for the Study of Human Issues, 1981, vol. 1, pp. 1–11.

———. "Vorrede." In *Deutsche Sagen herausgegeben von den Brüdern Grimm*. Ed. Heinz Rölleke. Frankfurt am Main: Artemis & Winkler, 1994, pp. 11–24.

Grözinger, A. "Bittrede." In *Historisches Wörterbuch der Rhetorik*. Ed. Gert Ueding. 12 vols. Tübingen: Niemeyer, 1994, vol. 2, pp. 43–47.

Grubmüller, Klaus. "Zur Pragmatik der Fabel: Der Situationsbezug als Gattungsmerkmal." In *Textsorten und literarische Gattungen: Dokumentation des Germanistentages in Hamburg vom 1. bis 4. April 1979*. Ed. Vorstand der Vereinigung der deutschen Hochschulgermanisten. Berlin: Erich Schmidt, 1983, pp. 473–88.

Grzybek, Peter. "Überlegungen zur semiotischen Sprichwortforschung." *Kodikas/Code* 7.3–4 (1984), pp. 215–49.

Guiriato, Davide. *Mikrographien: Zu einer Poetologie des Schreibens in Walter Benjamins Kindheitserinnerungen (1932–1939)*. Munich: Fink, 2006.

Harsdörffer, Georg Philipp. "Das Schauspiel Teutscher Sprichwörter: Auß dem Französischen übersetzet durch den Spielenden." In *Frauenzimmer Gespraechspiel: Anderer Theil*. Nürnberg: Endres, 1642, pp. 265–356.

Haug, Walter. "Kritik der topischen Vernunft. Zugleich keine Leseanleitung zu *Geschichte als Topik* von Peter von Moos." *Beiträge zur Geschichte der deutschen Sprache und Literatur* 114.1 (1992), pp. 47–56.

Hayman, David. "The Purpose and Permanence of the Joycean Epiphany." *James Joyce Quarterly* 35–36 (Summer–Fall 1998), pp. 633–55.

Hebekus, Uwe. "Topik/Inventio." In *Einführung in die Literaturwissenschaft*. Eds. Miltos Pechlivanos, Stefan Rieger, Wolfgang Struck, and Michael Weitz. Stuttgart: Metzler, 1995, pp. 82–96.

Heckscher, William S. *"Petites perceptions*: An account of sortes *Warburgianæ."* In *Art and Literature: Studies in Relationship.* Ed. Egon Verheyen. Durham, NC: Duke University Press, 1985, pp. 435–80.

———. "The Genesis of Iconology." In *Art and Literature: Studies in Relationship.* Ed. Egon Verheyen. Durham, NC: Duke University Press, 1985, pp. 253–79.

Hegel, G. W. F. *Aesthetics: Lectures on Fine Art.* Trans. T. M. Knox. 2 vols. Oxford: Clarendon Press of Oxford University Press, 1975.

Herder, Johann Gottfried. "Von der Aesopischen Fabel." In *Zerstreute Blätter.* Gotha: Ettinger, 1787, pp. 124–73.

Herschberg-Pierrot, Anne. "Gemeinplatz." In *Arsen bis Zucker: Flaubert Wörterbuch.* Eds. Barbara Vinken and Cornelia Wild. Berlin: Merve, 2010, pp. 107–11.

Hess, Peter. "Topos." In *Reallexikon der deutschen Literaturwissenschaft.* Ed. Jan-Dirk Müller. 3 vols. Berlin: De Gruyter, 2003, vol. 3, pp. 649–52.

Hölderlin, Friedrich. *Essays and Letters.* Trans. Jeremy Adler. London: Penguin Books, 2009.

———. Letter to Casimir Ulrich Böhlendorff, November 1802. In *Selected Poems and Letters.* Trans. Christopher Middleton. Amsterdam: The Last Books, 2019, pp. 182–84.

———. *Poems and Fragments.* Trans. Michael Hamburger. 4th ed. London: Carcanet, 2004.

———. *Sämtliche Werke und Briefe.* Ed. Michael Knaupp. 3 vols. Munich: Hanser, 1992.

Homer. *Odyssey.* Trans. A. T. Murray. 2 vols. Loeb Classical Library 105. Cambridge, MA: Harvard University Press, 1919.

Hui, Andrew. *A Theory of the Aphorism: From Confucius to Twitter.* Princeton, NJ: Princeton University Press, 2019.

Huyssen, Andreas. *Miniature Metropolis: Literature in the Age of Photography and Film.* Cambridge, MA: Harvard University Press, 2015.

Ibn-Butlān, al-Muḥtār Ibn-al-Hasan. *Schachtafelen der Gesuntheyt, Vormals nye gesehen, dem Gemeynen nutz zu verstand.* Trans. Hans Weiditz and Michael Herr (1533)

Jäger, Maren, Ethel Matala de Mazza, and Joseph Vogl, eds. *Verkleinerung: Epistemologie und Literaturgeschichte kleiner Formen.* Berlin: De Gruyter. 2021.

Jehn, Peter, ed. *Toposforschung. Eine Dokumentation.* Frankfurt am Main: Athenäum, 1972.

Jeziorkowski, Klaus. *Gottfried Keller: Kleider machen Leute. Text, Materialien, Kommentar.* Munich: Hanser, 1984.

Johnson, Christopher D. *Memory, Metaphor, and Aby Warburg's Atlas of Images.* Ithaca, NY: Cornell University Press, 2012.

Jolles, André. *Einfache Formen.* Tübingen: Niemeyer, 1968.

—— "Einleitung." In Giovanni di Boccaccio, *Das Dekameron*. Leipzig: Insel, 1921, pp. vi–xcvii.

——. *Simple Forms: Legend, Saga, Myth, Riddle, Saying, Case, Memorabile, Fairy Tale, Joke.* Trans. Peter J. Schwartz. New York: Verso, 2017.

Joyce, James. *A Portrait of the Artist as a Young Man: Epiphanies, Notes, Manuscripts and Typescripts.* Eds. Michael Groden et al. New York: Garland, 1978.

——. "Epiphanies." In *The Workshop of Daedalus: James Joyce and the Raw Materials for A Portrait of the Artist as a Young Man.* Ed. Robert Scholes. Evanston, IL: Northwestern University Press, 1965, pp. 3–52.

——. *Stephen Hero: Edited from the Manuscript in the Harvard College Library.* Ed. Theodore Spencer, John J. Slocum, and Herbert Cahoon. New York: New Directions, 1955.

Kann, Christoph. "Der Ort der Argumente: Eigentliche und uneigentliche Verwendung des mittelalterlichen *locus*-Begriffs." In *Raum und Raumvorstellungen im Mittelalter.* Eds. Jan A. Aertsen and Andreas Speer. Berlin: De Gruyter, 1998, pp. 402–18.

Kant, Immanuel. *Anthropologie in pragmatischer Hinsicht.* Frankfurt am Main: Suhrkamp, 1977.

——. *Anthropology from a Pragmatic Point of View.* Trans. Robert B. Louden. In *Anthropology, History, and Education.* Eds. Günter Zöllner and Robert B. Louden. Cambridge: Cambridge University Press, 2007, pp. 227–429.

Keller, Gottfried. "Clothes Make the Man." Trans. Harry Steinhauer. In *Stories.* Ed. Frank G. Ryder. New York: Continuum, 1982, pp. 151–89.

——. *Sämtliche Werke.* Eds. Thomas Böning et. al. Frankfurt am Main: Deutscher Klassiker Verlag, 1985–1996.

Killick, Tim. *British Short Fiction in the Early Nineteenth Century: The Rise of the Tale.* London: Routledge, 2008.

Kleist, Heinrich von. "On the Gradual Production of Thoughts Whilst Speaking." In *Selected Writings.* Ed. and trans. David Constantine. London: J. M. Dent, 1997, pp. 405–409.

——. "Über die allmählige Verfertigung der Gedanken beim Reden." In *Sämtliche Werke und Briefe in vier Bänden.* Eds. Ilse-Marie Barth and Klaus Müller-Salget. 4 vols. Frankfurt am Main: Deutscher Klassiker Verlag, 1990, vol. 3, pp. 534–40.

Klinger, Florian. "Thatness in Kleist." *Deutsche Vierteljahrsschrift für Literaturwissenschaft und Geistesgeschichte* 82.4 (2013), pp. 616–36.

Kopenawa, Davi, and Bruce Albert. *The Falling Sky: Words of a Yonamami Shaman.* Cambridge, MA: Belknap Press of Harvard University Press, 2013.

Koschorke, Albrecht. *Wahrheit und Erfindung: Grundzüge einer Allgemeinen Erzähltheorie.* Frankfurt am Main: Fischer, 2012.

———, Susane Lüdemann, and Thomas Frank. *Des Kaisers neue Kleider. Über das Imaginäre politischer Herrschaft. Texte, Bilder, Lektüren*. Frankfurt am Main: Fischer, 2002.

Koselleck, Reinhart. "Historia Magistra Vitae: The Dissolution of the Topos into the Perspective of a Modernized Historical Process." In *Futures Past: On the Semantics of Historical Time*. Trans. Keith Tribe. New York: Columbia University Press. 2004, pp. 26–42.

Košenina, Alexander, and Carsten Zelle, eds. *Kleine anthropologische Prosaformen der Goethezeit (1750–1830)*. Hannover: Wehrhahn, 2011.

Kühlmann, Wilhelm, and Wilhelm Schmidt-Biggemann. "Topik." In *Reallexikon der deutschen Literaturwissenschaft*. Ed. Jan-Dirk Müller. Berlin: De Gruyter, 2003, vol. 3, pp. 646–52.

Kurke, Leslie. *Aesopic Conversations: Popular Tradition, Cultural Dialogue, and the Invention of Greek Prose*. Princeton, NJ: Princeton University Press, 2011.

Kwastek, Katja. "Interview with Hito Steyerl." *Kunstforum International*, no. 242 (September–October 2016), pp. 122–31. Https://www.kunstforum.de/artikel/hito-steyerl/.

La Fontaine, Jean de. Preface to *The Fables of La Fontaine*. London: Hachette, 1886.

Lamy, Bernard. *Entretiens sur les sciences, dans lesquels on apprend comme l'on doit étudier les sciences, et s'en servir pour se faire l'esprit juste, et le coeur droit*. Ed. François Girbal and Pierre Clair. Paris: Presses Universitaires de France, 1966.

Lancaster, H. Carrington. "Molière's Borrowings from the *Comédie Des Proverbes*." *Modern Language Notes* 33.4 (1918), pp. 208–11.

Lechner, Joan Marie. *Renaissance Concepts of the Commonplaces*. New York: Pageant Press, 1962.

Leibniz, Gottfried Wilhelm. *New Essays on Human Understanding*. Ed. and trans. Peter Remnant and Jonathan Bennet. Cambridge: University of Cambridge Press, 1996.

Lemke, Anja. *Gedächtnisräume des Selbst: Walter Benjamins "Berliner Kindheit um neunzehnhundert."* Würzburg: Königshausen & Neumann, 2008.

Lessing, Gotthold Ephraim. "Abhandlungen über die Fabel." In *Werke und Briefe in zwölf Bänden*. Vol. 4 of *Werke 1758–1759*. Ed. Gunter E. Grimm. Frankfurt am Main: Deutscher Klassiker Verlag, 1990, pp. 345–411.

Levine, Carolin. *Forms. Whole, Rhythm, Hierarchy, Network*. Princeton: Princeton University Press, 2015.

Liddell, Henry George, and Robert Scott, eds. *A Greek-English Lexicon*. Oxford: Oxford University Press, 1996.

Locher, Elmar, ed. *Die kleinen Formen in der Moderne*. Bozen: Edition Sturzflüge, 2001.

Locke, John. *An Early Draft of Locke's Essay: Together with Excerpts from His Journals*. Ed. R. I. Aaron and Jocelyn Gibb. Oxford: Clarendon Press of Oxford University Press, 1936.

———. *An Essay Concerning Human Understanding.* Ed. Roger Woolhouse. London: Penguin Books, 1997.

———. *Drafts for the Essay Concerning Human Understanding, and Other Philosophical Writings, Vol. 1, Drafts A and B.* Ed. Peter H. Nidditch and G. A. J. Rogers. Oxford: Clarendon Press of Oxford University Press, 1990.

———. "A New Method of a Common-Place-Book." In *Literary and Historical Writings.* Ed. J. R. Milton. Oxford: Oxford University Press, 2019, pp. 281–306.

———. "Of Study." In *The Educational Writing of John Locke.* Ed. James L. Axtell. Cambridge: Cambridge University Press, 1968, pp. 405–22.

Lotman, Jurij. *The Structure of the Artistic Text.* Trans. Ronald Vroon. Ann Arbor: University of Michigan Press, 1977.

Luhmann, Niklas. *Theory of Society.* Trans. Rhodes Barrett. 2 vols. Stanford, CA: Stanford University Press, 2012.

Lukács, György. "Bürgerlichkeit und l'art pour l'art: Theodor Storm" (1909). In *Die Seele und die Formen.* Neuwied: Luchterhand, 1970, pp. 82–116.

———. "The Bourgeois Way of Life and Art for Art's Sake." In *Soul and Form.* Trans. Anna Bostock. New York: Columbia University Press, 2010, pp. 73–97.

Luther, Martin. *Luthers Sprichwortsammlung.* Ed. Ernst Thiele. Weimar: Böhlau, 1900.

Mack, Peter. *Renaissance Argument: Valla and Agricola in the Traditions of Rhetoric and Dialectic.* Leiden: Brill, 1993.

Manns, Stefan. *Grenzen des Erzählens: Konzeption und Struktur des Erzählens in Georg Philipp Harsdörffers "Schauplätzen."* Berlin: De Gruyter, 2013.

Marrone, Gianfranco. "Le sottisier comme genre discursif." *Protée* 22.2 (Spring 1994), pp. 80–85.

Masanetz, Michael. "Vom Leben und Sterben des Königskindes: *Effi Briest* oder der Familienroman als analytisches Drama." *Fontane Blätter* 72 (2001), pp. 42–93.

Matala de Mazza, Ethel. "Offene Magazine für Erfahrungswissen: Sprichwörter, Fabeln, Exempel." In *Gattungs-Wissen: Wissenspoetologie und literarische Form.* Eds. Michael Bies, Michael Gamper and Ingrid Kleeberg. Göttingen: Wallstein, 2013, pp. 265–84.

Mattenklott, Gert. "Der Sehnsucht eine Form: Zum Ursprung des Romans bei Friedrich Schlegel; erläutert an der *Lucinde*." *Literaturwissenschaft und Sozialwissenschaften.* Vol. 8 of *Zur Modernität der Romantik.* Ed. Dieter Bänsch. Stuttgart: Metzler, 1977, pp. 143–66.

Matuschek, Stefan. "Epideiktische Beredsamkeit." In *Historisches Wörterbuch der Rhetorik.* Ed. Gert Ueding. Tübingen: Niemeyer, 1994, vol. 2, pp. 1258–67.

Mengaldo, Elisabetta. " 'Seligkeit im Kleinen' oder Schein der Rettung?: Märchen- und

Volksliedstoffe in der Kurzprosa Benjamins und Adornos." *Jahrbuch der Deutschen Schiller-Gesellschaft* 56 (2012), pp. 284–306.

Menninghaus, Winfried. "*Das Meretlein.* Eine Novelle im Roman. Strukturen poetischer Reflexion." In *Artistische Schrift.* Frankfurt am Main: Suhrkamp, 1982, pp. 61–90.

Meuli, Karl. "Herkunft und Wesen der Fabel." In *Gesammelte Schriften.* Ed. Thomas Gelzer. Basel: Schwabe, 1975, pp. 731–56.

Meynell, G. G. "John Locke's Method of Common-Placing as Seen in His Drafts and his Medical Notebooks, Bodleian MSS Locke d. 9, f. 21 and f. 23." *Seventeenth Century* 8.2 (1993), pp. 245–67.

Mieder, Wolfgang. "Das Sprichwort in Gottfried Kellers *Die Leute von Seldwyla.*" In *Das Sprichwort in der deutschen Prosaliteratur des neunzehnten Jahrhunderts.* Munich: Fink, 1972, pp. 152–67.

Montefusco, Lucia Calboli. "Topics." *Brill's New Pauly.* http://dx.doi.org/10.1163/1574-9347_bnp_e1217380.

Moos, Peter von. *Geschichte als Topik. Das rhetorische Exemplum von der Antike zur Neuzeit und die historiae im "Policraticus" Johanns von Salisbury.* Hildesheim: Olms, 1988.

Moss, Ann. *Commonplace-Books and the Structuring of Renaissance Thought.* Oxford: Clarendon Press of Oxford University Press, 1996.

Murner, Thomas. *Logica memorativa Chartiludiu logice, sive totius dialectice memoria; & novus Petri hyspani textus emendatus.* Strasbourg: Gruninger, 1509.

Muse, John H. *Microdramas: Crucibles for Theater and Time.* Ann Arbor: University of Michigan Press, 2017.

Nagy, Gregory. "Early Greek Views of Poetry and Prose." In *The Cambridge History of Literary Criticism, Volume 1: Classical Criticism.* Ed. George A. Kennedy. Cambridge: Cambridge University Press, 1990, pp. 1–77.

———. "Mythe et Prose en Grèce Archaïque: L'Aînos." In *Métamorphoses du Mythe en Grèce Antique.* Ed. Claude Calame. Geneva: Labor et Fides, 1988, pp. 229–42.

Neumann, Florian. "Sensus communis." In *Historisches Wörterbuch der Rhetorik.* Ed. Gert Ueding. 12 vols. Tübingen: Niemeyer, 2007, vol. 8, pp. 841–47.

Neumann, Gerhard. "Wunderliche Nachbarskinder. Zur Instanziierung von Erzählen und Wissen in Goethes *Wahlverwandtschaften.*" In *Erzählen und Wissen.* Ed. Gabriele Brandstetter. Freiburg: Rombach, 2003, pp. 15–40.

Neuschäfer, Hans Jörg. *Boccaccio und der Beginn der Novelle: Strukturen der Kurzerzählung auf der Schwelle zwischen Mittelalter und Neuzeit.* Munich: Fink, 1969.

Nixon, Rob. *Slow Violence and the Environmentalism of the Poor*. Cambridge, MA: Harvard University Press, 2011.

Oesterreicher, Peter L. "Verstehen heisst Verbindenkönnen. Die Erfindung des Selbst in der topischen Lebenswelt." In *Die Formel und das Unverwechselbare: Interdisziplinäre Beiträge zu Topik, Rhetorik und Individualität*. Ed. Iris Denneler. Frankfurt am Main: Peter Lang, 1999, pp. 15–25.

Öhlschläger, Claudia. "Poetik und Ethik der kleinen Form: Franz Kafka, Robert Musil, Heiner Müller, Michael Kohlmeier." *Zeitschrift für deutsche Philologie* 128.2 (2009), pp. 261–79.

Ong, Walter J., *Ramus: Method, and the Decay of Dialogue*. Chicago: University of Chicago Press, 2004.

"Panel and Launch Event / Clipping, Copying, and Thinking, with Ann Blair and Kenneth Goldsmith." *Cabinet Magazine*." March 18, 2011, http://www.cabinetmagazine.org/events/cp_launch.php.

Perelman, Chaïm, and Lucie Olbrechts-Tyteca. *The New Rhetoric: A Treatise on Argumentation*. Trans. John Wilkinson and Purcell Weaver. Notre Dame, IN: University of Notre Dame Press, 1969.

Permyakov, Gregory. "Notes on Structural Paremiology." In *From Proverb to Folk-Tale: Notes on the General Theory of Cliché*. Trans. Y. N. Filippov. Moscow: Nauka, 1979, pp. 130–59.

Peters, John Durham. *The Marvelous Clouds: Toward a Philosophy of Elemental Media*. Chicago: University of Chicago Press, 2015.

Pethes, Nicolas. "Epistemische Schreibweisen. Zur Konvergenz und Differenz naturwissenschaftlicher und literarischer Erzählformen in Fallberichten." In *Der ärztliche Fallbericht: Epistemische Grundlagen und textuelle Strukturen dargestellter Beobachtung*. Eds. Rudolf Behrens and Carsten Zelle. Wiesbaden: Harrassowitz, 2012, pp. 1–22.

Petrovsky, Michail A. "Composition in Maupassant." *Essays in Poetics* 12 (1987), pp. 1–21.

———. "Morphology of the Novella." *Essays in Poetics* 12 (1987), pp. 22–50.

Petrus Hispanus. "De locis." In *Language in Dispute: An English Translation of Peter of Spain's Tractatus, Called Afterwards Summulae logicales*. Ed. and trans. Francis P. Dinneen. Philadelphia: John Benjamins , 1990, pp. 49–68.

Pindar. "Fragment 43." In *Carminum poetarum novem, lyricae poeseos principum, fragmenta*. Geneva: Estienne, 1560, pp. 356–57.

———. "Fragment 43." In *Nemean Odes. Isthmian Odes. Fragments*. Ed. and trans. William H. Race. Loeb Classical Library 485. Cambridge, MA: Harvard University Press, 1997, pp. 244–45.

Poitras, Laura. "Interview with Hito Steyerl." *Artforum* 53.9 (May 2015), pp. 306–17.

Polheim, Karl Konrad, ed. *Theorie und Kritik der deutschen Novelle von Wieland bis Musil.* Tübingen: Niemeyer, 1970.

Preisendanz, Wolfgang. *Die Spruchform in der Lyrik des alten Goethe und ihre Vorgeschichte seit Opitz.* Heidelberg: Winter, 1952.

Propp, Vladimir. *Morphology of the Folktale.* Austin: University of Texas Press, 1968.

Quintilian. *The Orator's Education, Volume 2: Books 3–5.* Ed. and trans. Donald A. Russell. Loeb Classical Library 125. Cambridge, MA: Harvard University Press, 2002.

Reckwitz, Andreas. "Grundelemente einer Theorie sozialer Praktiken. Eine sozialtheoretische Perspektive." *Zeitschrift für Soziologie* 32.4 (August 2003), pp. 282–301.

———. "Kultur und Materialität." In *Kreativität und soziale Praxis: Studien zur Sozial- und Gesellschaftstheorie.* Bielefeld: Transcript Verlag, 2016, pp. 83–95.

Reformatsky, Aleksandr A. "An Essay on the Analysis of Composition of the Novella." In *Russian Formalism.* Eds. Stephen Bann and John E. Bowlt. Edinburgh: Chatto and Windus, 1973, pp. 85–101.

Reisch, Gregor. *Margarita Philosophica, totius Philosophiae Rationalis, Naturalis & Moralis principia dialogice.* Freiburg: Schott, 1503.

Renger, Almut-Barbara. *Zwischen Märchen und Mythos: Die Abenteuer des Odysseus und andere Geschichten von Homer bis Walter Benjamin.* Stuttgart: Metzler, 2006.

Rheinberger, Hans Jörg. "Epistemic Objects / Technical Objects." In *Epistemic Objects.* Eds. Uljana Feest, Hans-Jörg Rheinberger, and Günter Abel. Berlin: Max Planck Institut für Wissenschaftsgeschichte, 2008, pp. 93–98.

———. *Toward a History of Epistemic Things.* Stanford, CA: Stanford University Press, 1997.

Rocha, Leon Antonio. " 'That Dazzling, Momentary Wake' of the *lettre de cachet*: The Problem of Experience in Foucault's Practice of History." In *Foucault, Family, and Politics.* Eds. Robbie Duschinsky and Leon Antonio Rocha. New York: Palgrave Macmillan, 2012, pp. 189–219.

Ronell, Avital. *Stupidity.* Urbana: University of Illinois Press, 2002.

Rubinelli, Sara. *Ars Topica: The Classical Technique of Constructing Arguments from Aristotle to Cicero.* Dordrecht: Springer, 2009.

Sakakibara, Chie. " 'Our Home Is Drowning': Iñupiat Storytelling and Climate Change in Point Hope, Alaska." *Geographical Review* 98.4 (2008), pp. 456–75.

Schatzki, Theodore, Karin Knorr-Cetina, and Eike von Savigny, eds. *The Practice Turn in Contemporary Theory.* New York: Routledge, 2001.

Scheuer, Hans Jürgen. "Ainos." In *Historisches Wörterbuch der Rhetorik.* Ed. Gert Ueding. Tübingen: Niemeyer, 1992, vol. 1, pp. 295–98.

———. "Apokryphe Modernität. Caesarius von Heisterbach, Alexander Kluge und die Intelligenz des Mirakels." In *The Poetic Power of Theory. Alexander Kluge-Jahrbuch.* Eds. Richard Langston and Leslie A. Adelson. Göttingen: V&R unipress, 2019, vol. 6, pp. 97–114.

Schiavoni, Giulio. "Zum Kinde." In *Benjamin-Handbuch: Leben–Werk–Wirkung.* Ed. Burkhardt Lindner. Stuttgart: Metzler, 2006, pp. 373–85.

Schlaffer, Hannelore. *Poetik der Novelle.* Stuttgart: Metzler, 1993.

Schlegel, Friedrich. "Athenaeum Fragments." In *Philosophical Fragments.* Ed. Rodolphe Gasché, trans. Peter Firchow. Minneapolis: University of Minnesota Press, 1991, pp. 18–93.

———. "Critical Fragments." In *Philosophical Fragments.* Ed. Rodolphe Gasché, trans. Peter Firchow. Minneapolis: University of Minnesota Press, 1991, pp. 1–16.

———. "Dialogue on Poetry." In *Dialogue on Poetry and Literary Aphorisms.* Ed. and trans. Ernst Behler and Roman Struc. University Park: University of Pennsylvania Press, 1968, pp. 51–117.

———. *Kritische Friedrich-Schlegel-Ausgabe.* Ed. Ernst Behler et al. 26 vols. Munich: Schöningh, 1958–.

Schmidt-Biggemann, Wilhelm. *Topica Universalis: Eine Modellgeschichte humanistischer und barocker Wissenschaft.* Hamburg: Meiner, 1983.

Schoell-Glass, Charlotte, and Elizabeth Sears. *Verzetteln als Methode: Der humanistische Ikonologe William S. Heckscher (1904–1999).* Berlin: Akademie, 2008.

Scholes, Robert, and Florence Walzl. "The Epiphanies of Joyce." *PMLA.* 82.1 (March 1967), pp. 152–54.

Seeba, Hinrich C. "Ernst Robert Curtius: Zur Kulturkritik eines Klassikers in der Wissenschaftsgeschichte." *Monatshefte* 95.4 (2003), pp. 531–40.

Shklovsky, Viktor. "Art as Device." In *Theory of Prose.* Trans. Benjamin Sher. Champaign, IL: Dalkey Archive Press, 1990, pp. 1–14.

———. *Literature and Cinematography.* Trans. Irina Masinovsky. Champaign, IL: Dalkey Archive Press, 2008.

Speight, Allen. "Arendt on Narrative Theory and Practice." *Collegiate Literature* 38.1 (2011), pp. 115–30.

Spoerhase, Carlos. *Das Format der Literatur: Praktiken materieller Textualität zwischen 1740 und 1830.* Göttingen: Wallstein, 2018.

Stanitzek, Georg. *Blödigkeit: Beschreibungen des Individuums im 18. Jahrhundert.* Tübingen: Niemeyer, 1989.

Steiner, Uwe. "Walter Benjamins Husserl-Lektüre im Kontext." *Internationales Jahrbuch für Hermeneutik* 9 (2010), pp. 189–258.

Steyerl, Hito. "Ripping Reality." In *Duty Free Art: Art in the Age of Planetary Civil War*. New York: Verso, 2017, pp. 191–205.

———. *How Not to Be Seen: A Fucking Didactic Educational .MOV File*, 2013. Video, 15:52 minutes, https://www.artforum.com/video/hito-steyerl-how-not-to-be-seen-a-fucking -didactic-educational-mov-file-2013-51651.

Stierle, Karlheinz. *Text als Handlung: Grundlegung einer systematischen Literaturwissenschaft*. Munich: Fink, 2012.

———, and Carsten Dutt. "Was heißt und zu welchem Ende studiert man literaturwissenschaftliche Pragmatik." *German Quarterly* 87.1 (Winter 2014), pp. 1–16.

Stoellger, Philipp. "Geschichten zum 'Begriff': Genese der Nachdenklichkeit aus dem Zögern." In *Metapher und Lebenswelt: Hans Blumenbergs Metaphorologie als Lebensweltthermeneutik und ihr religionsphänomenologischer Horizont*. Tübingen: Mohr, 2000, pp. 334–39.

Stolberg, Michael. "John Locke's *New Method of Making Common-Place-Books*: Tradition, Innovation and Epistemic Effects." *Early Science and Medicine* 19 (2014), pp. 448–70.

Storm, Theodor. "Eine zurückgezogene Vorrede aus dem Jahre 1881." In *Theorie und Kritik der deutschen Novelle von Wieland bis Musil*. Ed. Karl Konrad Polheim. Tübingen: Niemeyer, 1970, pp. 118–19.

———. "The Rider on the White Horse." In *The Rider on the White Horse and Selected Stories*. Trans. James Wright. New York: NYRB Classics, 2009, pp. 184–284.

———. *Der Schimmelreiter: Text der Buchausgabe von 1888*. In *Der Schimmelreiter: Novelle von Theodor Storm. Historisch-kritische Edition*. Ed. Gerd Eversberg. Husum: Erich Schmidt, 2014, pp. 13–95.

Subramanian, Meera. "Seeing God's Hand in the Deadly Floods, Yet Wondering about Climate Change." *InsideClimateNews*, October 24, 2017, https://insideclimatenews.org /news/19102017/christianity-evangelical-climate-change-flooding-west-virginia.

Suleiman, Susan. *Authoritative Fictions: The Ideological Novel as a Literary Genre*. Princeton, NJ: Princeton University Press, 1993.

Tang, Chenxi. "The Transformation of the Law of Nations and the Reinvention of the Novella: Legal History and Literary Innovation from Boccaccio's *Decameron* to Goethe's *Unterhaltungen deutscher Ausgewanderten*." *Goethe-Yearbook* 19 (2012), pp. 67–92.

The Digital Locke Project, http://www.digitallockeproject.nl.

Theisen, Bianca. "Strange News: Kleist's Novellas." In *A Companion to the Works of Heinrich von Kleist*. Ed. Bernd Fischer. Rochester, NY: Camden House, 2003, pp. 81–102.

Theison, Philipp. "Gespenstisches Erzählen." In *Theodor Storm: Novellen. Interpretationen.* Ed. Christoph Deupmann. Stuttgart: Reclam, 2008, pp. 104–25.

Thys, Walter, ed. *André Jolles (1874–1946): "Gebildeter Vagant".* Amsterdam: Amsterdam University Press, 2000.

Treeck, Werner van. *Dummheit: Eine unendliche Geschichte.* Stuttgart: Reclam, 2015.

Ueding, Gert, and Thomas Schirren, eds. *Topik und Rhetorik: Ein interdisziplinäres Symposium.* Tübingen: Niemeyer, 2000.

Vico, Giambattista. *On the Study Methods of Our Time.* Trans. Elio Gianturco. Ithaca, NY: Cornell University Press, 1990.

———. *The New Science.* Trans. Thomas Goddard Bergin and Max Harold Fisch. Ithaca, NY: Cornell University Press, 1948.

Vance, Eugene. *From Topic to Tale: Logic and Narrativity in the Middle Ages.* Minneapolis: University of Minnesota Press, 1987.

Viehweg, Theodor. *Topik und Jurisprudenz.* Munich: Beck, 1969.

Wagner, Tim. "Topik." In, *Historisches Wörterbuch der Rhetorik.* Ed. Gert Ueding. 12 vols. Tübingen: Niemeyer, 2009, vol. 9, pp. 605–26.

Warburg, Aby. *Fragmente zur Ausdruckskunde.* Ed. Ulrich Pfisterer and Hans Christian Hönes. Berlin: Akademie, 2015.

Watts, Isaac. *Logick; Or, The Right Use of Reason in the Enquiry after Truth.* 2nd ed. London: Clark and Hett, 1726.

Weisman, Tama. *Hannah Arendt and Karl Marx: On Totalitarianism and the Tradition of Western Political Thought.* Lanham, MD: Lexington Books, 2014.

Weizman, Eyal. *Forensic Architecture: Violence at the Threshold of Detectability.* New York: Zone Books, 2017.

Werber, Niels. "Paullinis Gespenster. Zur Entstehung der Novelle." In *Gespenster.* Ed. Moritz Baßler. Würzburg: Königshausen & Neumann 2005, pp. 215–27.

Yates, Francis. *The Art of Memory.* London: Routledge, 1966.

Yeo, Richard. "John Locke's 'New Method' of Commonplacing: Managing Memory and Information." *Eighteenth Century Thought* 2 (2004), pp. 1–38.

———. "John Locke's 'Of Study' (1677): Interpreting an Upublished Essay." *Locke Studies* 3 (2003), pp. 147–65.

Zill, Rüdiger. "Anekdote." In *Blumenberg lesen: Ein Glossar.* Eds. Robert Buch and Daniel Weidner. Berlin: Suhrkamp, 2014, pp. 26–42.

Index

Zone Books series design by Bruce Mau
Image placement and production by Julie Fry
Typesetting by Meighan Gale
Printed and bound by Maple Press